I0095377

No Walk
in the Park

No Walk in the Park

Seeking Thrills, Eco-Wisdom, and
Legacies in the Grand Canyon

Michael Engelhard

CORAX
BOOKS

CORAX BOOKS

Published in Fairbanks, Alaska, May 2024.

Copyright © 2024 by Michael Engelhard
All rights reserved. No part of this publication may be reproduced, stored in a retrieval system or transmitted, in any form or by any means, electronic, mechanical, audio, photocopying, recording, or otherwise (except for copying permitted by Sections 107 and 108 of the U.S. Copyright Law and except for book reviews for the public press), without the prior written permission of the publisher.

For permissions or review copies, contact michaelengelhard.com

Printed in the United States of America

Editor: Doreen Martens
Design and Layout: Nadine Ludd
Front Cover Photos: *Havasu Creek*, Erin Whittaker (NPS),
Emery Kolb at Havasu Creek (NAU Cline Library Special Collections and Archives)
Maze Petroglyph: Michael Engelhard
Author Photo (*Couch Potato*) and Frontispiece (*Esplanade*): Melissa Guy

Library of Congress Control Number (LCCN): 2024902240
ISBN (paperback): 979-8-9899202-0-4
ISBN (e-book: 979-8-9899202-1-1

To Melissa Guy, my soul mate and best friend even though life with this curmudgeon isn't always a walk in the park.

Author's Note

Many of these essays were written in Moab and Flagstaff, within sight of ranges now known as the La Sal Mountains and the San Francisco Peaks. They, the foothills, nearby mesas, and canyons are the rightful home of Indigenous peoples. Diné or "Navajo" raiders approached Dzil Ashdlá'ii, "Five Mountains," the main La Sal peaks. The Seuvarits regional band of the Núuchi-u or "Utes," stalking elk on the slopes of that sierra, singled out boldly ridged Tukuhnikivats—"Where the Light Lingers Longest." No fewer than thirteen tribes hold sacred the blown-top volcano above Flagstaff, a place, for the Yavapai-Apache Vincent Randall, "where the Earth brushes up against the unseen world." It's a pilgrim destination, seasonal home of Hopi rain-bearing deities, one of four pillars that prop up Diné homelands and the cosmos. Sadly, the Diné name, Dook'oosłííd, "Its Summit Never Melts," no longer fits. We'll never learn in which tongue ancestors newly arrived from Beringia—or emerged locally, old stories claim—addressed these mountains and rivers. But I feel honored, grateful to the original caretakers, to have dwelled there.

I hereby also grant that this planet's plundering enables my lifestyle and standard of living, that I am a privileged dirtbag. Short of leaving the grid, it seems, there remain few places where one might live sustainably.

The following pages owe much to the fact that nature, culture, and history have shaped each other ever since humans stepped into the scene. Ethnicity and economies merely provide varied conduits through which such energies flow.

"Finding out everything you can about the people whose land you live on and allying yourself with its rightful owners is vital, but there's something even deeper," the radical thinker Derrick Jensen reminds us. In the canyon country, it's the ringtails and mountain lions, the rock wrens and bighorn sheep, the junipers and the humpback chubs, to whom the land first belonged.

I have met with but one or two persons in the course of my life who understood the art of Walking, that is, of taking walks—who had a genius, so to speak, for sauntering.

—HENRY DAVID THOREAU, "The Wild," 1851
(the year he became head surveyor of lands sold to loggers)

It takes a particular kind of knowledge to go with the river, whatever its mood. It is about there being no difference between you and the movement of water as it seasonally shifts its tracks...

—ALEXIS WRIGHT, *Carpentaria*, 2006
(the year Grand Canyon National Park limited rafting, as beaches eroded downstream of the dam)

What does not kill me makes me stronger.

—FRIEDRICH NIETZSCHE, *Twilight of the Idols,* 1888
(the year of his mental collapse)

Whatever doesn't kill you simply makes you stranger.

—THE JOKER, *The Dark Knight*, 2008
(the year of financial collapse)

Contents

Prologue: The Best of Beyond

To be fully human is to fully experience the spectacular formations of the planet: particular mountains, particular rivers, certain rock structures.

—THOMAS BERRY, cultural historian

IN 1959, THE YEAR I WAS BORN, tunnels blasted through Glen Canyon's cliffs opened to divert the Colorado River and allow dam construction to begin, which doomed that canyon and dozens of tributaries to flooding. In 2022, with Lake Powell down to a fourth of its storage capacity, Grand Canyon guides having seen their livelihoods threatened by a pandemic, and with the Cathedral in the Desert reemerged, freed by decades of drought, the Glen Canyon Institute announced that federal officials were considering overhauling that dam. Proposals to decommission it, to drain the reservoir to increase the amount of water stored in Lake Mead near Las Vegas and to designate Glen Canyon a national park are being batted about. Due to outdated management and a climate running amok, the Colorado currently heads the list of the nation's most endangered waterways, according to the conservation organization American Rivers. Still, it is a survivor, hemmed in but not broken.

My ongoing fascination with Glen Canyon and the Grand Canyon, and by extension the Colorado Plateau, owes much to the dynamics these locales represent: the conflict between hubris and awe, between greed and restraint, between myopia and conservationist vision. "Fascination," I must quickly add, is such a lazy catch-all for a driving force rooted much deeper. You can choose your region but not your character, a fan of the desert once wrote. But for some people, character *dictates* the choice of a homeland, which in turn keeps rewriting their personality.

I firmly believe there are landscapes that speak to certain individuals more than others do, even to the extent where only one ever makes a perfect match for such a person. A first exposure to this "soulscape" resembles a homecoming. I found my match in 1982, when I first traveled the Colorado Plateau as so many do, as a tourist.

The region concentrates the greatest number of national parks and monuments in the US, but its wealth lies as much in its human heritage as in its natural splendor. It has always drawn fringe dwellers. Slavers, mountain men, desperadoes, explorers, immigrants, missionaries, and miners thirsted for bounties, pelts, other folks' livestock, unfettered country, religious freedom, souls, or yellowcake to blow up the planet. But when colonial powers claimed this "wilderness," a veneer of traditions already layered the land. It had long been cultivated.

"Place is security, space is freedom: we are attached to the one and long for the other," the footloose cultural geographer Yi-Fu Tuan asserts in *At Home in the World*. And, as the Diné short story writer Stacie Shannon Denetsosi elaborates, "There is beauty in remaining in motion." Today still, while I no longer live there, the Southwest sets my heartstrings to humming. The dry, luminous air deceives about distances, accenting details and truths like the veins in dragonfly wings. Nowhere else have I seen stars in such numbers and that seem within reach. Encounters with bighorn sheep, rattlesnakes, cougars, or tarantulas left me breathless, riveted to that terrain. Sounds and scents somehow carry farther there than they do elsewhere or perhaps just stand out more against the sere background. Temperatures rocketing seventy degrees over a single day or peaking at 110 tested my heart and mettle; and that was before things got off-kilter. The Plateau's climate and topography may rank among the harshest, most exacting, in North America, but what this desert asks of you and what it offers in return sometimes balances finely.

Compared to other American "badlands," the Plateau shocks

the senses with mercurial seasons, due in part to its elevation. While Indian summer often lingers into November, frost can settle in for 180 days of the year. Spring's rioting, with foliage shining as if it were lacquered, succumbs to summer's yellow brittleness, punctuated by downpours of biblical force that briefly cleanse an atmosphere gloving you with an oven mitt. Heralding the monsoon months, flash floods rampage through blond expanses. Soon, wildflower starbursts yield to the autumnal russet of scrub oaks, the gold of box elders and cottonwoods. Before you've had your fill of color or scent, temperatures plunge below freezing, frosting cacti and rocks. Claret cup blossoms wear caps of confectionary sugar. Pothole ice cracks under your steps, transparent fine china. All the drama and spectacle mix in a paradoxical, at times treacherous, cocktail that can hit the uninitiated ill-prepared and leave them reeling.

There's something carnal about this desert, a sculptural muscularity absent from the Mojave, Sonoran, Chihuahuan, and the Great Basin. The same ingredient colors its flaming rock and our blood, all vertebrate blood: hematite, "bloodstone," an iron oxide mixed into paint to stripe faces and inscribe lithic flanks. In an origin myth of Utah's Goshute, who survived in alkali deserts south of the Great Salt Lake, the founding members of different tribes—Utes, Paiutes, Shoshoni, and others—dispersed after busting out of a basketry jug. The last to emerge from this rough and tumble was the Goshute, the toughest of people, "all covered with dust" and therefore bulletproof. One great saga cycle starring the animate and inanimate is thus inked in identical pigment.

In canyon country, this red, often windborne or waterborne (too thick to breathe or drink; too thin to chew), is ubiquitous, from dirt roads to Wingate sandstone, cracked hardpan to turbid rivers. It clings to your notebooks, food, and hair. It clogs zippers, camp stoves, and nostrils. You wear it as makeup or camouflage. It tints creeks and bushes, your vision, your very soul. It dyes dust devils and deepens the color of sunsets. The petrichor of rain dimpling brick-red soil—wet wool with hints of sage and juniper, scent equivalent of the canyon wren's burbling cadences—uniquely signifies place.

Between bloated cow carcasses and the shell horizons of tiny marine organisms that fused into limestone, this landscape does not conceal death. Reminders of our own mortality are everywhere. The shard from a pot that hands long since withered smoothed and painted or coiled and indented for a corrugation effect. The red stop sign on a widow spider's jet-black abdomen eerily shaped like an hourglass. The fossilized segments of extinct conifers, chunks of a broken rainbow. Seedpods of fallen yucca stalks, rattling skeletally when you kick them. Some people take comfort from these tokens, and joy at the sheer fact of being alive in this eternal moment.

Canyon landscapes can afford, and demand, patience. Absences, too, define them. Mountains diminish visibly; erosion scoops out gulches, gorges, and arroyos—inverted ridges, negative space. The Grand Canyon is Vermont's Green Mountains, a 280-mile range, washed into the gulf. But don't call it "The Big Ditch"; that is plain disrespectful and not doing it justice. Noise seldom intrudes in the stony depths, or at least, seldom used to. (You know it is quiet when you can hear your empty stomach complaining.) Stripped of the extraneous, these lands lie bared to all senses. With few exceptions, the wildlife is secretive, seasonally scarce, often nocturnal, most often revealed only in evidence of its passing. Unruffled by lush plant life or built structures, the mind can latch on to geology, which, far from static, betrays entropy at a pace and scale that elude the imagination. You weigh your lifespan against the eons. Not long now till I'll donate my own teeth to archaeology. The topographic breakdown, in tandem with aforementioned tokens of transience, highlights the curve of our own existence more vividly, providing unexpected relief.

Colorado Plateau landscapes have a built quality that touches of the ever-changing light glorify and accentuate. There were cathedrals already in this desert, landmarks that showcased "humanity's relationship to the eternal," in the words of Ron Fricke, the lens wizard of the time-lapse film *Koyaanisqatsi*. For millennia, indigenous peoples had cultivated narratives of their own as a means to position themselves in all this. Tread lightly on this storied pavement.

Working as an outdoor instructor and wilderness guide for twenty-five years, I based many life decisions on scenery and concomitant open space, which career-wise did not always pan out. Still, I was granted that one gift nature writers dream of, a setting to forever captivate me at the micro as well as the macro level. It's a rich juncture of history and natural history. In all roles, I was of two minds about this: wanting to share that which thrilled me, yet wanting to keep it a secret, fearing its profanation.

Rabbit holes riddle the desert, in the Four Corners perhaps more densely than elsewhere. An observation or tale of one of its features leads to other tales or to personal memories, which in turn may be linked like burrows inside a warren—this could be due to a lack of distractions. The lines of these essays braid, overlap, coming at topics repeatedly, from varying angles. In this, they mimic rivers in beds with a low gradient, or trail networks.

I love places in which history flows deep though not obviously, overwhelmingly, except when it's Earth's history. On the Colorado Plateau, that stares you straight in the eye. Between Canyon de Chelly's brindled flanks and Bryce Canyon's peekaboo world, numerous lesser known natural artworks await connoisseurs willing to risk dehydration and getting lost on labyrinthine dirt roads. I love places with accounts of river runners gone missing on their honeymoon through the abyss and of a nonstop run on a flood that nearly took out that dam, places where conversely one stone bowl full of rain can make a life-or-death difference. I love places where scorpions, snakes, bats, ants, and centipedes or black bears invade our space because, actually, it still is theirs. I cannot love places that are easy, easy to access, easy on the eye—green, bucolic, well-watered, veiled obscenely in thick vegetation—easy to forget, easy to comprehend. What the Alaskan essayist John Messick ventured about religious faith holds true for writing: maybe, it "isn't so much about truth as about paying attention." The canyons first instilled such focus in me when, twenty-five years ago, I explored more than a hundred within a year, to grasp the magnitude of loss incurred when Glen Canyon was dammed. Attention is a small price to pay for insights that channeled not just a career. It's its own reward, you might say. With attention comes first care and then responsibility.

In Marcel Proust's opinion, "The voyage of discovery is not in seeking new landscapes but in having new eyes." Craving novelty as a younger man, I wished to climb a thousand different mountains. Today, in late midlife, in a mindset akin to prayer, I'd rather climb the same mountain a thousand times to learn all I can; how it looks in different seasons and angles of light; how it sounds and smells; the creatures and plants it hosts; how it and I fit in with the rest. Except that my mountain is arctic Alaska's Brooks Range, or the Grand Canyon, or the Colorado River that I descend. I'm with Wolfgang Laib on this. The German artist, for weeks on end, collects wild pollen in meadows by painstakingly flicking flower after flower with a finger, catching the fallout in a cup. His credo is "introspection and spirituality through repetition." For his "Five Un-climbable Mountains" installation, Laib sifted hazelnut pollen into conical piles. Navajo healers creating dry-painting mandalas and Hopis leaving corn pollen offerings would understand his practice.

For a spun-out magical time, the muddy Y of the Colorado and Green River confluence had me enthralled. My email handle, nedludinmoab, perfectly situated and suited me, though going online smacked, a bit, of surrender. I *was* a Luddite in redrock nirvana. One of my literary heroes, Cormac McCarthy—"The Camel," to one of his sons, because he rarely if ever drank water—ran his car over a cellphone that his son had given him, McCarthy père having owned it for only one day. And then there's the iconic photo of Edward Abbey leaning on the stock of his shotgun next to a slug-pierced TV. I'm a sucker for the theatrical gesture, be it drama or farce. I had not driven since the Army made me, did not wear a watch, or have a phone; the most complex gadget I owned was a backpacking stove. I lived by the words of John Mead Gould, though I hadn't yet read them. In his 1877 manual *How to Camp Out*, this Civil War veteran cautioned against outdoor gear fads. "Every year," he wrote, "there is put upon the market some patent knapsack, folding stove, cooking-utensil, or camp trunk and cot combined," advising readers to "leave them all alone." I later moved to Flagstaff, where my wife enrolled in school, and we both thrived on the Grand Canyon's doorstep, embracing, as they say there, "poverty with a view."

Regrettably, progress, or what commonly passes for progress, has a way of leaving places I've come to love compromised. I try in vain to outrun development. Why do I sometimes return? Memory is a doddering fool, and mine keeps romancing the past and the spatially faraway. I should, years ago, have heeded Aldo Leopold's advice to never revisit old haunts. Moving on, or back, I often discover that recollection has not gilded his lily of wilderness. Its glow has been tarnished, traded for trinkets or craven cash. At present, runaway heating is wilting it. It pains me to say (and I forget who said it first) that while I could live without writing, I could never live without the places and subjects about which I write. "Let your life be a counter-friction to stop the machine," Thoreau wrote with regard to the Trojan horse of civilization. Hopefully, this book can be a fistful of sand thrown into its gears, for myself and for others.

All those tourist attractions notwithstanding, too many people still see the desert Southwest as terra incognita, a grim, alien void like the sea, fit only for dumping bodies, junk, cars, and toxic waste, or for selling it piecemeal, or siphoning off nature's resources, or, nowadays, for farming sunshine and wind. But in more than just literal ways, if you can love it beyond its Instagram views—and if we'll manage to save some of it—it will widen your horizons. It does retain some of the best America has to offer: room for us and other beings to breathe, and space to disappear in, temporarily, of your own volition, though that has become harder.

Frank Hamilton Cushing, a controversial, eccentric ethnographer, lived five years with New Mexico's Zunis and dressed the part. Critics accused him of having "gone native." As an initiation requirement, he may have taken the scalp of an enemy of this pueblo, likely an Apache's. Even starchy John Wesley Powell, director of the Smithsonian's Bureau of Ethnology, wore fringed buckskin head-to-toe, posing for a photo on one occasion. Anthropologists have been accused of discontent with their own culture since their discipline's infancy. As a tribe, almost by requirement, they value the underdog. Obsessed with semantics and the names of things, I have always rooted for Manuelito over Kit Carson, coyotes over Chihuahuas, Trickster over the trinity, black widows over Black Diamond, and stream water over Evian. To me, that gulf, that frisson of conceptual contrasts and their visibility, not select locations, is the essence of these incomparable lands.

The Snows of Yesteryear

"LOCATION, LOCATION, LOCATION," the mantra of realtors and vacation brochures goes. I say timing is equally crucial when looking at scenic lands. I knew the timing was right, because during a recent snowfall, the crew that's supposed to clear our Flagstaff driveway got stuck and their truck had to be winched out by another. I'd checked the South Rim's Yavapai Point webcam obsessively when that low-pressure system rolled in, and the canyon had vanished most days, shrouded by gray nothingness. The Park Service shut down Desert View Drive and the Hermit Road, as they do if conditions warrant it. The Southwest's aridity notwithstanding, heating unchecked now vaporizes more ocean water, which travels and precipitates, dumped at certain times and places counter-intuitively while others lie dry. I, for one, was not about to let such wealth go untapped.

Hoping for information from the entrance booth ranger about a good place on the rim to snowshoe or cross-country ski, my wife and I were disappointed. The Chinese family in the car ahead of us would have known just as much.

Having surveyed the areas accessible because they had already been cleared, we parked at Yaki Point, where buses disgorged sightseers psyched to gaze at this picture-book wonderland. Snowplows had mounded high berms that attracted kid-mountaineers. Black holes on hooves, the mules in their corral absorbed sunshine and the ground's glare. Hikers at the South Kaibab trailhead had been strapping on cleats for their descent to Phantom Ranch, the trail's upper switchbacks having become a bobsled chute.

At Yaki Point, eager to skedaddle, my wife, Melissa, stepped into her ski bindings and I into my snowshoes', and we both set out for Shoshone Point. The maze of knee-deep trenches to nearby overlooks that shoes had compacted soon thinned. We followed a major fork, rusty from lack of practice, trying to get our groove back. At least two feet of snow had fallen overnight, alighting on an older stratum and, this early, remaining feathery. We knew that as the day grew balmy, the splendor wouldn't last.

Cloudless sky spanned the canyon, a blue so dark it contained traces of outer space. Even the tree shadows were blackish cobalt. From the first break in the pines, we witnessed a scene few of the park's six million annual visitors are fortunate to see. The tiered cliffs plunged staggeringly, a geological cake with intricate icing. They brought to mind William Henry Holmes' *Panorama from Point Sublime*, from Clarence E. Dutton's famous 1882 atlas, but with the lithograph's filigree ink-lines chalked. The contrast between red stone and white accents was delicious, like autumn leaves' veins or spider silk glinting at dawn. As low as the Bright Angel shale, below the Redwall, slopes lay under gauze fanning toward the Tonto bench.

Historically, this spate of winter is nothing special. "Spring does not come until June," wrote Theodore Roosevelt, who hunted cougars on the North Rim's Buckskin Mountain, where "the snow lies deep for seven months." In December 1967, a storm system that sat for eight days dumped eighty-six inches on Flagstaff, record amounts for Arizona. Aircraft dropped food for people and livestock on the Navajo Nation. Unlike the Inuit, for obvious reasons, Navajos have a paltry two words for snow, one for the falling kind and one for it on the ground. Cultures split verbally and most finely things most important to them, be that car brands or corn varieties. Yet Diné elders describe times when snow reached the chest of their horses. They say that snow bathing makes young people strong, cleansing and preparing them for hard times. An infant would be taken outside and rolled in the snow in its first winter. Older kids were encouraged to run barefoot and wash their face with it, and some adults still dive into one of the season's first drifts, in a hardier form of snow angels.

This self-discipline and acquired hardiness mattered during "The Fearing Time," when Navajos fleeing from Kit Carson's bluecoats hid near Navajo Mountain and Utah's Bears Ears and in the Grand Canyon. More than 8,000 captives weathered winter at Bosque Redondo, in New Mexico, marched there through blizzards and then languished without firewood, in pits covered with blankets.

Recent years have been erratic, to say the least. The North Rim, 1,000 feet higher, always receives more snow, and the road from Jacobs Lake therefore stays closed between December 1 and May 15. On a multi-day ski trip around the Walhalla Plateau in 2007, I'd stuck to the blacktop's yellow centerline, stripping my skis' bottoms on many thawed stretches, but a polar front plastering exposed DeMotte Park nearly had us snowbound on the way out. Formerly, this headland could see over 200 inches of snow a year. With winters neutered, tourism officials have been requesting to keep the Jacobs Lake road and North Rim lodge open longer.

Grand Canyon hibernations of the past have been gnarly. Park employees at the Yavapai Observation Station in the 1950s routinely shoveled snow off the porch, flinging it over the canyon's lip, and hauled oil for their stove up from a tank in the parking lot. His second winter at the South Rim, where he'd settled in 1884, flabbergasted the squirrel-hunting Tennessean John Hance. This was Arizona—the desert, after all. Still, he was "mighty nigh swimmin'" in snow. "It was plum to my neck on the level, an' I was mighty short on provisions," Hance told a journalist. Trying to hightail it to Flagstaff on snowshoes, he tumbled between boulders and was laid up at his camp with a disjointed kneecap. The legendary tour guide would also accost guests on the El Tovar Hotel's terrace, snowshoes slung over his shoulder, and announce that the fog appeared thick enough to pass over on. He'd then saunter to the rim and stick out a leg to test it before announcing that he'd rather go to Yaki Point for the nine-mile crossing to Cape Royal. He *did* mount his favorite mule in the fall and drive cattle 6,000 feet down the trail that bears his name, to reach "perpetual summer," a dude literato he wrangled wrote, while on the high plateau "far above him the harsh winds howl and the whirling snow falls foot by foot."

Gaping so far outside the pale of mundane experiences, the canyon has spawned tales of outlandishness galore, some of which ring just about true. Rumor, the Internet of Powell's day, had the whole river dropping from sight in one place, filling a series of caverns, or roaring over ledges mightier than Niagara's— and Grand Falls, on the Little Colorado, is massive and higher indeed. The gorge also hid an elusive nugget hoard behind seasonal falls that drove a searcher to suicide. An underground citadel for 50,000 people, complete with mummies, gold urns, hieroglyphic tablets, and a 700-foot mess hall, was said to be the foothold of an Egyptian civilization, which the Park Service and Smithsonian for decades sought to cover up. Had emissaries of Ramses sailed all this way and tunneled the warren for access to snow? Closer to the present, during Christmas, the bearded visage of Fred Harvey greets guests at El Tovar on a hotel-room TV screen, the Ghost of Mass Tourism Past.

In the winter of 1899-1900, William Wallace Bass, another miner turned host-entrepreneur, moved his family from the rim to a more sheltered camp, a tent at Shinumo Creek, above the river's north bank. His music-teacher wife, Ada, tended the site, which was sunny enough for an orchard and garden. The Ancestral Puebloan irrigation ditches he repaired proved that it had been a balmier refuge for millennia. The summer months yielded figs, peaches, apricots, corn, grapes, tomatoes, and melons. When the Basses relocated to the rim in late March, they found blizzards had ruined their kitchen roof. Trappers, however, considered those months to be the best for tracking mountain lions; their pugmarks were easier to read, and hounds didn't overheat. On that ski trip on the North Rim, I came across a lion's marks. At the fringe of the Walhalla Glades, I stood over his print as snow, grainy as cottage cheese, filled in the paw's outline and lightning flickered, followed by thunderclaps.

The Navajos believe that inside-out weather patterns announce the world's pending doom: winter thunder and summer snow show that their Holy Beings are upset.

As we beeline between trees from peep to promising peep on this so much more radiant day, a breeze whiffs diamond-powder from random branches. The quiet is absolute, as softness muffles all noises. On this cool day, I cannot smell any terpenes, the piney and citrusy compounds in the conifers' resin that shield them against bark beetles and fungal pathogens. I've tasted the limonene in jelly made from tender, pea-green spruce tips. Released in greater amounts in warm weather as aerosols, these chemicals may play a role in cloud seeding. The forest, our backyard piñon-juniper Amazon, could be producing its own shade and precipitation. Science is investigating the hydrocarbons that also bestow medicinal benefits upon us as an alternative energy source. As a further defense mechanism, pine needle wax wards off ultraviolet radiation and, together with the leaves' small surface, reduces water loss to the dry high-plateau air.

A few imprints betray nonhumans passing through—too few, I think, for a national park. Angel-wings stamp a hillock where a raven landed to dig up a morsel. The zipper spoors of squirrels end at pines. These tracks are from Abert's, the tassel-eared, gray-and-white gnomes separated from their North Kaibab kin by the canyon, having evolved separately. The same rascals each year bite dozens of South Rim visitors who ignore the rangers' warnings against feeding them. They've become so emboldened they crawl into backpacks, trying to nab anything edible—they'll gnaw holes into fabric to get to it. And their fleas carry the plague. (A wildlife biologist died after performing an autopsy on a plague-riddled Grand Canyon mountain lion.) But they're essential to the cycles of healthy forests. The vocal little dynamos dig up and nibble on truffles, the fruiting bodies of fungi that cling to ponderosa pine rootlets. Passing through the squirrel's digestive tract, fungal spores are spread throughout the forest with bonus parcels of fertilizer. The fungi in turn assist ponderosas with absorbing water and nutrients from the soil. In the summer, the squirrels shed their distinctive brush-tip ear hair and thick winter coat. Severe, snowy winters cut short lives by starving the animals.

By now, Melissa and I have figured out that the rut we're in is the work of equine trailblazers. Sure enough, a string of mules announced by chiming voices approaches through the trees. A young woman wrangler in Carhartts and an earflap hat leads the cavalcade. Dudes strung out behind her grin like partiers at a punchbowl, red-cheeked and puffy in colorful down. Several mounts, true to their reputation, are wearing a cribbing muzzle, a Hannibal Lecter-style nosebag that prevents the mule in front or a rider being nipped. A second wranglerette, tailing the procession, speaks on a crackling radio to her dispatcher, letting him know they are inbound.

The mule trail is perfect for Melissa, on skis, though a little too narrow for my bear-paw snowshoes, which frequently catch on each other. Mine are not the elongate, webbed kind and, being shorter, require solid fabric to increase their floatation. So, with each step, sinking inches, you lift some of this fluff like sand on a shovel. Don't get me wrong. I am not complaining. Even in powder, breaking trail is good exercise, as I'm reminded each time I detour to the edge for a view. The fat-incinerating activity burns more calories than skiing or running at the same pace. Which is badly needed in the wake of a drawn-out sedentary season.

Uprooting *their* settled existence in their twenties, in 1902, Ellsworth and Emery Kolb, from Pittsburgh, fell into the business of photographing tourists on mules at the South Rim. Nine years later, the brothers embarked in two custom-built boats, *Defiance* and *Edith*, on a hardcore trip from Wyoming to the Gulf of California and took the first-ever footage of the Grand Canyon's rapids. It was a rerun of a youthful adventure during the Johnstown

Flood, when the Allegheny River almost claimed them and the raft they'd cobbled together from scrap lumber. Emery had lain across the disintegrating raft, bracketing it with his fingers and toes, while Ellsworth rowed hell-bent for shore.

The brothers reached their Colorado River camp number fifty-one, near Bright Angel Creek, in October, two months and eight days after their Green River launch, "Ragged and weary, but happy; a little lean and over-trained." There they interrupted their journey for a month, to develop and review what they had filmed. Having stashed the decked wooden boats and gear, they climbed eleven miles on a trail, which has since been rerouted and shortened, to their studio on the plateau.

By November, two nights before their planned departure, a foot of snow cloaked the rim. The thermometer had dropped to zero. Drifts obliterated the trails for a distance below the rim. "The walls were white with snow down to the [Tonto] plateau, 3,200 feet below," which Ellsworth thought "something unusual, as it seldom descends as snow lower than two thousand feet, but turns to rain." A week of cold, cloudy weather and hard winds had pushed all warmth from the canyon, letting this snow descend lower than usual. The inner canyon's cold, not impressive in numerical terms, is more penetrating because of the dampness. The Kolbs found consolation knowing that "it was some warmer at the bottom than it was on top."

They returned to their boats six days before Christmas and found that ice lidded pools near the river. The motion picture documenting their feat, shown twice daily on the rim from 1915 to 1976 and narrated in person by Emery until 1932, holds the record for the longest continually running film in US history. Theirs had been the eighth successful journey though the canyon. John Wesley Powell, on neither of his two Colorado River explorations, went all the way to the sea, into Mexico, though two crewmembers did. The brothers took part in the search for the honeymooners Glen and Bessie Hyde, who had vanished running the canyon in the winter of 1928. Water buckets at camp froze solid that December, eddies iced over, and upstream near Moab, floes, whispering as they brushed against each other and shore, finally jammed the river.

Winter boating in the Grand Canyon is for hardy souls, clearly. You spend many hours at camp, grouped around a fire. I recall it snowing on us during my first float there in March, when we assembled our rafts on the Lees Ferry boat ramp. Our delight today was that distant day's worry.

After a quick snack, we traverse a burn area possibly torched by 2013's Halfway Fire. Skeletal trees stand at the great seam, crooked, ivory limbs encrusted with alligator-skin charcoal patches. The stark silhouettes tell the story of piñon-juniper forest adapted to dryness, fire, and low temperatures. Two-needle piñon largely depends on snow, banked as soil moisture. A waxy cuticle sheathes the reduced leaves, shedding snowflakes and slowing transpiration. But the wax is highly flammable, and needles brown from drought are ready tinder.

A fellow canyon guide told me about a flash flood shortly after the North Rim's 2006 Warm Fire. Ashen slurry had rushed through a tentacled canyon, a geological squid spewing ink into the river. Veteran Grand Canyon river guides and Park Service river rangers can tell which upstream side canyon is being rained on and flushed by the shade of color the chameleon Colorado assumes.

Trees and their understory on the rims anchor topsoil, a sponge whose water trickles downward to feed weeping walls speckled with maidenhair fern and nodding columbines, or to pulse from Coconino and Supai sandstone or from Muav and Redwall limestone, thousands of feet below.

Perhaps the Hopi goddess Nuvak'chin Mana—in charge of cold weather and the white gift saturating the earth for next year's crops—has been offended. Tramping toward Shoshone Point, roughly two miles from Yaki Point as the cumulus sails,

I glimpse the San Francisco Peaks, Nuvatukya'ovi, the "Place of the High Snows," her home and that of fellow katsina elemental spirits.

The San Francisco Peaks are the heart of winter in Arizona, "an island of snow surrounded by desert," in the words of one backcountry skier who has cut powder turns there. Perched on the margins of the Colorado Plateau, the range can be seen for nearly one hundred miles from any direction, and from the top, both rims of the Grand Canyon stand out against the western horizon. Six summits crowd around Mt. Humphreys (12,633 feet), the highest point in the state, clad with its only stretch of true tundra. The peak is a stratovolcano, like Japan's Mount Fuji, steeper than shield volcanoes and estimated to have once reached nearly 16,000 feet. After winter storms, avalanches scour gullies and ravines. An underdressed runner died from exposure one May, with temperatures dipping to twenty-two degrees and winds of up to forty-five miles per hour. Summer is equally risky. Lightning killed a teenage hiker near the summit in an area struck over a hundred times in an hour. Within minutes, rain can corn into hail, bouncing off rocks crusted with lichens. It is no surprise that weather gods are thought to dwell on these heights.

Squirrel—Laqan—was one of them, visiting the mesas for the winter dances. These days, wastewater snow for a Flagstaff ski resort defiles the mountains' hallowed flanks. Many Hopis condemn snowmaking itself as sacrilegious, since it interferes with the natural water cycle. The musician and painter Okhuwa P'ing (Ed Kabotie), a grandson of Fred Kabotie, who painted some of the Desert View Watchtower's murals, sees such meddling as "shaking your fist at God." Perhaps he was being more considerate of other people's beliefs than they were of his. Snowmaking from the dregs of households and businesses to me seems more like flipping off God. Even more appropriately, other Hopis have compared it to "urinating on the altar at the Vatican," and anthropologists liken it to baptizing babies with dishwater. The effluent of the affluent includes runoff from mortuaries and hospitals, associated with death, disease, and spiritual contamination. The Grand Canyon's Hualapai fear that it will seep into the ground and from there into a sacred spring below the Snowbowl.

Indigenous Mountain Protectors praying and protesting at the resort have been insulted, attacked by snowboarders, and arrested. For these tableland dwellers, springs and their source are linked to the health of the world and all things living in it. Like certain shrines, ruins, trail cairns, and petroglyphs, ceremonial springs are "footprints" that Hopi ancestors left behind on their wanderings to the center place. Spring water is "wild water," in which benevolent water serpents dwell.

A katsina song that Emory Sekaquaptewa, the "Noah Webster of the Hopi nation," recalled offers a mesa perspective:

They are preparing themselves,
Over there at the snow-capped mountains.
The clouds,
From there, they are putting on their endowments,
To come here.

Hopi women, children, and men, after death, become clouds.

Skiers as well, and backpackers and river runners, should understand the katsinas' cargo, those blessings from the departed, as a divine endowment.

Members of the tribe continue to make pilgrimages to shrines nestled on those distant slopes, to pray and pay their respects and collect conifer boughs for the katsinas' costumes, as well as healing herbs and ceremonial eaglets. They gather Douglas fir branches for plaza rituals; a frostlike, silver-gray coating on the needles augurs moisture, especially rain, whereas dull green portends drought.

The peaks and Paayu, the Little Colorado River, from whose

depths the wandering clans first proceeded, are a sublime dyad of water and land, pivotal poles to which traditional Hopis orient themselves. Desertification like that which currently rakes the Southwest has not been seen since their ancestors settled in this canyon 1200 years ago. Between 1930 and 2010 alone, snowfall across this sparsely peopled quarter lessened by two-thirds. Yet people, through songs, "Remember when the rains moved along from down below, drizzling all night long," and "Everything on the sand altar would become bright with flowers." The "sand altar"—need I say it—is the earth now being pissed on.

Spring types in the Grand Canyon are as varied as the water's voices. Among over 225 perennial seeps and gushers are cave springs, cliff springs, fault springs, perched springs, hillside springs, fracture springs, stream-bed springs, travertine springs, and, perhaps most spectacular, cave spring waterfalls. You plan below-the-rim treks by connecting these dots, prayer beads on the string of your route. More than precipices or the heat, they're the crucial limiting factor.

The *environmental* impact of sewage snow with bacteria resistant to antibiotics pales in comparison to groundwater pollution from uranium, large deposits of which rest in the Hermit Shale. Mines have reopened north of the canyon (in the Kanab area) and south of it (in the Kaibab National Forest, near the gateway town of Tusayan). One, close to the most sacred Havasupai sites, was grandfathered into the new Baaj Nwaavjo I'tah Kukveni National Monument. Drilling there, Energy Fuel pierced shallow aquifers from which tainted water then gushed. When their evaporation pond threatened to overflow, grunts hosed the Devil brew into the surrounding forest. Defunct hell pits like the ominously named Orphan Mine, a Superfund site in the park's Horn Creek drainage, already leak dangerous levels of dissolved uranium. At least fifteen springs have been affected, and the Park Service warns hikers not to drink from them.

In an essay that sketched his conversion from wolf killer to conservationist, Aldo Leopold espoused a long-term inclusive perspective or "Thinking Like a Mountain." We could gain as much from thinking like a watershed. Yet few politicians and urbanites know where their water comes from, beyond the turn of a spigot.

Towering on average a thousand feet above the South Rim, the North Rim receives not only more lightning strikes but also more snow, and throughout the year it remains about ten degrees cooler. Consequently, the larger, more reliable springs burst from north-side cliffs, with the most prominent ones born from the Redwall Limestone formation. An angelic share from Roaring Springs, on the North Kaibab Trail, which discharges about 160 gallons per second, supplies the South Rim village via a pipeline that crosses the river on one of two spans near Phantom Ranch. (To guides abhorring a mouthful unless it is beer or chow, it's the "Silver Bridge," in contrast to the older "Black Bridge" upstream, the start of the South Kaibab Trail.)

Half a mile from our destination, we come upon a clearing trampled in a circus-ring way. This is clearly the mule train's turnaround spot. I'm surprised they did not try for Shoshone Point, with its excellent upstream vistas. Maybe the dudes got shivery, or the mules hungry, or the wranglers have an after-noon ride booked. Melissa chooses to stay behind, since skinny cross-country skis perform worse than snowshoes off-trail.

I move on, post-holing by myself.

There's a quiet thrill in marring the untracked expanse. It provides me with a sense of discovery, as fresh snow draping a landscape gives it tranquil novelty, even a place as busy and familiar as the South Rim. For a few seconds, I can believe I'm the first here, the only person for miles and miles around. "Snow provokes responses that reach right back to childhood," says the land artist Andrew Goldsworthy, who sculpts the stuff into abstract ephemera. For me, it elicits romantic cravings, a desire to live and survive in northern climes. Too much Jack London at a susceptible age, you could say.

One man's paradise can be another's purgatory. Robert Brewster Stanton, scouting the canyon by boat in January 1890 for a railroad at river level, felt trapped by these forbidding walls. With "the whole upper country covered with its winter mantle of inhospitable snow" and it "hanging down hundreds of feet over the rim and in the side gorges," he knew that if mishap struck, his only escape was downstream, through dozens of explosive rapids.

My face already is slightly burned. I take off my sunglasses to de-fog them, and my eyes instantly water. The blinding quilt is a trifle heavier, wetter than when we started—the day is warming. When I briefly sight a river bend, it runs milk-coffee brown. Snow higher up in the Colorado's watershed must be melting, or it rained there. Or perhaps the Paria is pumping. Rowing tourists through the canyon with no ranges visible, I often forget that much of the bounty that buoys, excites, and sometimes scares us witless is the previous winter's currency, water from north-central Colorado's Never Summer Mountains and subsequent ranges detained by Glen Canyon Dam. The link becomes obvious at Vaseys Paradise or Dutton Springs, North Rim snow-fed oases, popular river trip stops. I was shocked, last June, to find Vasey's cascade a mere trickle and Dutton's barren, earlier in the year than any of the other guides could remember. We'd stoked our clients' anticipation for the "Throne Room," an auditorium-size alcove with stone-slab seating that hikers built adjacent to Dutton, which the vaporized plashing normally cools. It's like a concert hall where the setting is the orchestra. A trail from the box elders wends up to an undercut behind the falls, where you can sit pleasantly misted behind its blurred crystal curtain. We instead dealt with cases of heat exhaustion on that mid-morning climb. Something that was never fully ours alone had been snatched away.

That bottom world feels remote right now, a memory from some other life. Much closer Shoshone Point gleams, at the end of a scalloped bay in the rim. I rest repeatedly, panting or knocking back water that gives me an ice cream headache before resuming my march. Luckily, retracing my steps will be less of a workout. At last, I pop out of the woods near white-capped benches and picnic tables, glad to have this viewpoint to myself—not at all a given on a bluebird, weekend day. Weary of cornice trapdoors into the abyss, I down-climb to the cape that sprouts a menhir-shaped, monumental boulder. The canyon's wound, splayed wide open, poked by the finger of the Walhalla Plateau, appears to pivot around its tip. I recognize Palisades of the Desert upstream and Vishnu Temple's pyramidal bulk across. Wotan's Throne, a block off the old North Rim, truly looks Nordic in its sparkly garb. Warm, rising air evaporates fallout from the frost giants' pillow fight and starts to jell into clouds below the far brink.

Contemplation comes easily here, where meteorological quirks meet the seemingly eternal chasm. Like yesterday's snows, or yesteryear's, we shall be gone soon, as individuals and as a species. To every thing there's a season—let's celebrate each as if it were the last. For you or me or a wilderness, it may well be.

By the time Melissa and I return to Yaki Point, the parking lot is slag heaps and slush. Along the trail, icicles dripped from pine trees; angelic fleece had compacted into lumpy cement. Soil darkly edged the mules' hoof prints.

The naturalist and Sierra Club founder John Muir, in mid-January of 1902, took the train to Bright Angel Hotel but found the setting dry and bare, which, he learned, was unusual for that month. The good snow might arrive at any time, he was told, in a riff on promises hoteliers have been making since the industry's dawn. Later, from the lee of a rim ledge, Muir watched as "The first flakes and crystals began to fly...sweeping straight up the middle of the canyon, and swirling in magnificent eddies along the sides." Another canyon visitor, one Edwin O. Standard Jr., on May 3, 1898, scribbled a quick comment into John Hance's guestbook: "Would do it again in similar weather, if necessary. Better in a snow-storm than not at all."

Or better yet, right after a snowstorm.

On Little Lake Powell

"IF THERE IS MAGIC ON THIS PLANET, it is contained in water," the philosopher-anthropologist Loren Eiseley wrote. The sentiment rings even more true in the desert, millions of Lake Powell visitors agree. Surprisingly few recreationists know a much smaller, no less beguiling destination five miles southeast of Winslow, that northeastern Arizona town of 10,000 made modestly famous by an Eagles song and consecutively, two bronze statues at that corner. They're indeed a fine sight to see.

Melissa and I arrived at the put-in for our half-day East Clear Creek Reservoir jaunt at 7 a.m. McHood Park that early in late October lay abandoned. The concrete picnic benches and tables, shade ramadas, restroom facilities, and boat ramp appeared defunct, with the park—a far cry and 6.5 car hours from Powell's Hite Marina—seemingly suffering from the Southwest's lingering drought. But a 1930s dam coffers plenty of water, at least for the roughly three miles between the launch ramp and the place up-canyon where the runoff from a Payson reservoir, briefly resurrected as East Clear Creek, again yields to stagnation. Unlike Lake Powell's blue-green amoeba, the flagellate beyond the tips of our sandals would at noon look like milky jade. Listed among Arizona's best swimming holes, pinched by fifty- to hundred-foot cliffs, it offers a lot more than bathing or barbecuing.

We unloaded packrafts already inflated—boats as small as boats get. If you've never seen these vehicles, imagine gaudy six-foot oblong Hypalon donuts with a bottom. Birds in the reeds clucked as if commenting on the proceedings. Mist trailed off the water, and the wide gorge wrapped itself in shadows. Fall hung in the air, cast iron on bare skin. Prompted by the temperature, I donned neoprene booties, knowing there would be wet landings.

East Clear Creek Reservoir, like its larger counterpart outside

Page, pleases divergent tastes: water-skiers, cliff-jumpers, picnickers, paddleboarders, climbers, and anglers cherish it—Game and Fish stocked it with carp, sunfish, largemouth bass, channel cats. The beneficiaries sometimes also belong to the boom box–toting crowd. This park had a reputation for being overrun, yet we saw only one kayak flotilla, halfway back to the boat ramp, plus a few souls bracing to shove off when we lunched there afterward. The day's chill had kept rowdy revelers at home.

Climbers are the most recent addition. They engage in "deep water soloing," boat-based bouldering, without ropes and serious consequences. The reservoir's padding, up to twenty-five vertical feet, absorbs any tumbles. The trick is picking a route with a clean fall line. Rocks or sand bars rather than sharks lurk below, and impact zones must be carefully scouted, because water levels and the bottom's topography change with the seasons. On hundred-degree days, you'll go from broiling to blue-lipped in a jiffy, testing your strength, agility, and fear threshold on contortionist classics like "Yeah Buddy," "Full Value," "Wrath of Kong," or, poignantly, "Last Day of Summer."

As we slipped underneath the Highway 99 bridge, a sign reminded us of the five-mile speed limit. It wasn't for us, this admonition, but for motor-heads whose amplified wakes in that desert gully could flip kayaks and canoes.

The highway and attendant power line quickly receded. Slotting up, the cross-bedded, cream-and-rust Coconino Sandstone—dunes laid down and wandering 275 million years ago—also grew higher. Where breaches in the cliffs allowed access by dirt road, the Permian matrix crawled with idiot-graphs, territorial markers not unlike the lampposts that dogs love. When had this kind of urban claim staking started to infest the backcountry? Superhero graffiti were in fashion on those walls. We marveled at Batman, Superman, "Spidey," and Captain America logos. A ledge by the batwings was a popular jumping point. Did bathers wear capes and masks when reenacting their idols' aerial stunts? And why don't we have superheroes fighting environmental crime?

The Green Thumb. Recyclops. Dam Buster and Dodo Boy. Monkey Wrench Woman.

The spray-painted doodles petered out within three-quarters of a mile, which made it easier to imagine this engineered lake as wilderness. Vacant, honeycombed swallow nests clung inside overhangs, with some crumbling adobe bird condos less than two feet from the waterline. Grebes with snake necks and ruby eyes dove after gauging our proximity, popping up again, corklike, in unpredictable spots. Choosing a different escape tactic, sooty duck-y coots, churning water like Roadrunner does dirt, streaked into reed thickets on shore with wing sounds of a riverbank sloughing. A piece of slate skipped off the still surface, rippling it into rings—a kingfisher snatching up fingerlings.

Despite the low sun that blinded us at alternate bends, I glimpsed the day's first ancient rock art site. The glyphs, crisply pecked into mineral varnish, exposed a lighter substrate, though the contrast was slight, and it took effort to detect them. My cramped neck and tearing eyes proved it. Luckily, the ancients' works had been spared the *Kilroy Was Here*–type treatment. A series of panels starting at reservoir level signaled an exit, a slanted slab-stairway to lion-skinned country. Or rather, an entry, as East Clear Creek centuries earlier had been an important water source, one not navigable. I raced to land among boulders while Melissa stayed afloat. There was hardly enough space for one packraft in that cove, and I was the one with a rock-art obsession.

Designating these expressions of bygone lives "art" really misconstrues their true nature. It's a bit like using that term for orthodox icons, a Gothic cathedral, or Gregorian chant. There was no art for art's sake in the ancient world. These stick-figure shapes announced human presence and title to the land more subtly than the comic-book badges down-canyon; the difference, besides the labor and care invested in carving them, was that their makers had dwelled here full-time, dusty yet fully immersed.

They'd sanctified animate, shade-giving stone like the stream it embraced, instead of treating it as a Water World climbing gym.

Currently robbed of its vigor, the canyon that links wooded highlands and riven plains—the Mogollon Rim and Little Colorado hamlets—once sheltered travelers from the desert's glare. I wondered if, tracing the Colorado too, those invented any watercraft. Neither remains nor depictions of one have been found. Their marks brought to mind the Glen Canyon Linear style—think striped sheep and stretched humanoids—and San Juan River Basketmaker rock art, both created by fellow flowing-water fans and dated to the Late Archaic era, which made them at least 2,000 years old. In conversations about Europe's art and historical monuments, Americans enthralled with those sometimes decry the lack of depth and diversity of comparable landmarks in their own country. A farmhouse in which George Washington slept while campaigning, they may quip, makes it into the National Register of Historic Places. This is a serious blind spot. If only they knew what timeworn eloquence blazes rocks in their own outback backyard.

Looking for rock art in these twisting corridors resembles beachcombing, in which, in the words of the essayist Lara Messersmith-Glavin, "from the noise of complex visual static, a new image emerges suddenly, visible and plain where nothing was moments before." Except that many a figure that electrified you upon your approach turns into an oxidation stain or a natural set of grooves. It's a case of the mind sometimes seeing what it wants to see, like shapes in the clouds or political progress or your position in unknown country compared to what you plotted on the map. We are compelled to perceive wholeness, coherence, meaning or intent, so badly that we bend realities, presuming correlations where none exist.

That particular East Clear Creek wall featured not a trick of the eye but petroglyphs, mostly of humanoids: skinny triangular torsos with wave lines or grids, "X-rays" of abstracted ribs, spines, guts, and lungs, or else, body ornaments. Horned headgear and dangly earrings adorned those fancy lads. I was guessing their sex, of course. The intermingling of a few sheep with those figures led me to believe the two-legged ones were men—big game hunts had been and largely remained a male preoccupation.

I savored the view from the lip of the galleried exit. The sun strafed a single bundle of yucca spearheads near the rim, while the reservoir's bulk below still lay muted with shade. On the water, though, fifteen minutes later, sky interlaced with the earth, blue steel riffling with gold on the surface.

A second petroglyph site, to my knowledge, was the only one in those parts that you could admire seated in your boat, even without binoculars. It was better than most of Lake Powell's rock art. A horned serpent squirmed under the hooves of over thirty deer and bighorn sheep in various poses, led by a two-headed elk or deer from whose back sprouted a person. The ratio of animals to humans was the opposite of the first site. Perhaps the two long ago formed a set of shrines pilgrims visited.

We next faced a piece of modern hydro-architecture far less intrusive than Glen Canyon Dam. About two miles in, close to the East Clear Creek reservoir's end, sandstone blocks flush with the cliff foundations suggested an Ancestral Puebloan fort—one reinforced with railroad-rail ceiling beams, not piñon or ponderosa trunks. It was the pump house part of an old Santa Fe Railroad station. Built in 1898, the plant had been coal-fired. At low water, you could see intake pipes that lifted coolant to the rail yard and drinking water to Winslow. From our boats, we also spied the berm of a storage- or settling-basin on top. A postcard from the early 1900s shows a thousand-step staircase plunging from the rim to the creek. I'd picked up an amber-glass medicine bottle at the sheep-petroglyph panel, one manufactured in those days. The millennia bridging the stone glyphs and these waterworks signified progress, a passage from nature worship to gargantuan plumbing.

It was almost lunchtime, but brush hedging silted-in coves along the cliffs kept us from landing. So, we pushed on. Stroking past vines tinged with fall's yellows and reds, we suddenly moved against sluggish current. The vibrant colors bled into it, stirred by our blades. Rays ricocheting off the water wove dancing silver webs onto alcove roofs. The rich, funky odor of plant decay filled the canyon, which began to rival the famous Zion Narrows, but at a smaller scale. Tree roots lay submerged, mangrove-style. Farther on, maidenhair fern of an unreal shamrock-green burst from a cleft, veiling one gurgling spring whose moss pillowed lushly.

Success! Peace, like a river. Civilization had shrunk to a lone airplane buzzing up high. The instant it was gone, we heard our double-blades drip as they rested on the tubes.

Hormone-fueled risk-taking and a craving for "suffer fests" have melted away as I've aged. In my twenties, I never could not thread a rapid, or pass a waterfall without stepping under it, or an ice-choked lake without playing seal, hauled out on a floe, barking, butt-naked. Colorado Outward Bound considered the Utah canyon program for which I worked too laid back, "too cowboy," though I'm sure ranch hands would beg to differ—or probably, punch to differ. In our lifestyle, manners, and preferences, we rather refracted Lake Powell's aquatic subculture. We carried bocce balls, horseshoes—for throwing—and bags with costumes for beach parties (sans alcohol, since we were with students). A Grand Canyon guide I knew wore a cardboard hat shaped and painted in the bright stripes of his dory and at other times donned a knitted rasta tam with nylon dreadlocks. Another, nicknamed "Dirtbag" or "Dirt" for short, lit the path to the portable toilet with glow sticks and pranked people by putting clothespins on them unnoticed. A Moab guide greeted clients with a broad smile that revealed fake Billy-Bob dentures. For myself, I preferred wearing flashy sarongs around camp—airy leisure wear with a tropical feel. Mind you, these were all middle-aged men, not pubescent teens. (And men they exclusively were; female guides had too much dignity, or perhaps it was because they got to dress up every day back home.)

Desert rivers will do that to you. They are boundaries as much as they're liminal spaces. They strip away pretense, just as rapids do unsecured gear. Unlike strenuous, snowy alps, they invite contemplation, long periods of rest and relaxation with spikes of frantic excitement when they flip a raft or suck or catapult somebody out of one. Their pace and demeanor rub off. With rivers, there is no striving, no high ground to conquer. Saying that river runners go with the flow is almost clichéd. (We don't always. We can be recalcitrant and make lateral and upstream moves, too.)

These days, I'm content to sit on a boulder in shorts, soaking my bones in the sun, watching the world spin. Now, whenever it's late and the summit tauntingly distant, or a wind kicks up mad whitecaps, I can head back or hunker on shore, glad to have made it that far.

The beauty of midlife: nothing to prove, not even to myself.

I by no means took the calm or creature comforts for granted. My mind strayed to a packraft outing preceding East Clear Creek, a Lake Powell overnight trip the summer before. We'd just set up camp on a dome in the cove of a slickrock island and were sipping merlot at the tip of that former butte, watching storm clouds roll in, when a squall like a fist punched up spray and then sand. It flattened our tent and broke a pole, whose sharp ends shredded the fly while I—having nimbly descended—held on to the nylon corpse, struggling to keep our home from blowing away. Who says reservoirs can't turn mean in an instant? Bereft of cover, we aborted our sojourn there. Wet and shivering, we dug deep into the teeth of the gusts, barely able to regain the beach, meeting the baffled gazes of oiled, glistening sunbathers now being breaded by sand and chasing down towels.

East Clear Creek demanded attention for the first time where it shifted from riffles to pools and vice versa, an antsy customer jockeying, sluicing through funnels of boulders that low branches framed. Repeatedly scratching the bottom (and my neck), I had to duck and work harder, pushing upstream. Melissa paddled ahead, her silhouette seesawing toward glowing backgrounds. Our transitions from shade into sun—palpable as massages at that time of year and day—evoked the Northumbrian saint who once likened the human lifespan to the wing beats of a sparrow flitting across a lit mead hall: brief luminescence, a beacon's beam bookended by winter's dark void. That sparrow could have had a second go, unless the hall had been barred. We get but one run on this glorious earth.

Autumn thoughts, these, and in the autumn of a life.

Where the flow shallowed further, I stepped out of the packraft before parking it to explore on foot. Had this been Lake Powell, we would have seen sediment cutbanks and crackled, newly bared flats mantled with willows and tamarisks. Melissa stayed behind in a clearing, basking in late-season warmth. In the honeyed, stained-glass glow seeping through box elder canopies, I was drawn to a mint-and-burgundy-colored sprig inside a rock niche. Leaves with three lobes and jagged edges gave it away. Poison ivy. "Leaves of three, let it be," the saying goes. "Leaves of three, turn and flee," I say. Had I brushed against any on my way in? Touched my eyes? Lips? The plant's oil, transferred to clothing, can trigger rashes years later. Herbalists who have handled century-old specimens still contracted the plant's sting. When burnt, specks of its ashes inflame your lungs. Bruised or crushed, leaves of this member of the cashew family secrete urushiol, a sticky, easily transferred compound that troubles some people but not others. Itchiness, skin inflammation, and eventually clear blisters are the price the allergic pay. *Those* fall colors I did not need. On the upside, urushiol can be used to treat paralysis, arthritis, and—strangely enough—as a sedative and cure for certain skin disorders. Once, years ago, looking for a flat, sandy campsite on the Dolores, we were checking the shade of an overhang. Due to the low water levels of past springs, that camp had not been used in a while. Brush had hindered our progress to the stream bench. My redheaded, freckled river-running companion, who had bush-whacked ahead, suddenly shouted out. "Oh, no! Not again!" Then he'd rushed past me back to the river's edge, where he frantically rinsed and rubbed his pale arms and legs. With one of our party cursing under his breath, we untied and launched our rafts again, looking for more hospitable beaches downstream.

I sometimes wonder if, toward the end of a richly lived out-door life, any other thing you encounter kicks loose old anecdotes and recollections—if the land can become so familiar that you feel you are walking through your own past. This is the memoryscape, a perfect fusion of self and the world. It does not mean that you no longer see the thing itself. It's like wearing bifocals.

Melissa and I could have continued up Clear Creek, though several bottlenecks with wall-to-wall water would have required a portage or swim. Bedrock tanks and prime fishing for browns, rainbows, and brook trout reward hardy souls that proceed far-ther. But while packrafts are meant to be carried, I hadn't brought a pack big enough to carry ours. And it would have been a bad place to get caught by a monsoon drencher that within minutes could swell mini-cascades into monsters.

Regretting all the sights left unseen, I rejoined my mate for a snack and the second half of our journey, the return enveloped in mounting midday heat. I was hoping no headwind would hamper our tandem flight through the light.

Gone Glyphing

WEDGED INTO A VERTICAL CREVICE, I reach up with my camera, trying not to back-flop twelve feet onto the canyon's bedrock floor. It's the only way I can get a better picture—and up-close view—of the enigmatic figure gracing the wall. Commenting on the rock art, my companions patiently wait for their turn.

Charles "Chuck" LaRue, who insisted I should check out this particular stretch near Holbrook, and with whom I rode over from Flagstaff, is an ornithologist who advises museum collections, identifying species ancient Southwesterners, or Anasazi, used in arrow fletching and in feather blankets that shrouded their dead. Typical of the aficionados from various backgrounds that get sucked in by this obsession, Chuck sometimes carries a curved "rabbit stick," a one-way boomerang for bludgeoning bunnies, which he fashioned after depictions in the region's rock art. It once double-functioned as a defensive weapon for deflecting atlatl projectiles. Chuck considerately leaves any rabbit meat as coyote dinners. Today, pharaoh-like, he wields a replica crook-neck staff, a sort of trekking pole with a hook for dislodging chuckwallas or pinecones loaded with piñon nuts and for tearing apart cactus-fortified packrat nests, all of which used to promise great protein snacks to ancient foragers. "As handy as a pocket on a shirt," it's also useful for removing rattlers from camp. Then there is Mike, a Bureau of Land Management archaeologist who wrote his dissertation on "waterglyphs"—runic incisions on Arizona Strip scarps—and his dog Baxter, a skinny, golden-haired reservation mutt he adopted and that's forever underfoot. A couple whom Chuck hasn't seen in thirty years completes our party: he, the former Chief of Interpretation at Chaco Culture National Historical Park, she his counterpart at Aztec Ruins National Monument. Trained as a cultural anthropologist, I myself, soon after graduation, found the customs of the dead to be as thrilling as those of the living. A yen for graphic puzzle pieces on backcountry jaunts connects our motley bunch. Such treasure hunts yield mostly insights and the occasional good yarn.

Chuck and I still wax mirthful about getting locked out of his truck on the brink of Cedar Mesa, where his mind was already at "an amazing track site" he wanted me to see, a single-file bird spoor that stops at a boulder's edge in the two-footed stance of a raven taking off from there. Upon our return, Chuck tried in vain to smash one of the truck's vent windows with a rock. Subliminally reluctant to damage his property, I guess. I, having no such qualms, succeeded right away.

Like the Colorado Plateau's layer-cake strata (always in your face), its prehistoric artifacts (ubiquitous, though often hidden) tickle your curiosity over time. Who were these people? What were their routines, their beliefs? How did they survive in these tight-fisted lands? Rock art—a ceremonial stocktaking, not merely "art"—offers more profound clues to their myths and visions than any ruins, bones, or projectile points, or potsherds scattered about. For true, hot-blooded glyphers, crumbling Anasazi condos are simply a bonus; architectural appetizers. For the record: most glyphers also are graphers. They value painted pictograph designs just as much as the pecked petroglyphs. I hold the former more precious, because they are less permanent, more fragile still.

My mentor in becoming an amateur sleuth, or "recreational archaeologist," as professionals label us, was a one-armed retiree who'd lost a limb in a farming accident and then chose Hanksville, at the foot of southern Utah's Henry Mountains, as his home base, because it abuts Barrier Canyon pictograph country; this two-thousand-year-old painting style was named for its signature panel in Horseshoe Canyon, the ghostly "Great Gallery." A sprightly septuagenarian with closely cropped, silvery hair, mustache and twinkly blue eyes, Morris Wolf started sharing his insights and favorite finds after giving me a lift when I was hitchhiking. This kindred spirit paints pictograph tees he decorates from photographic memory, reconstructing details lost to erosion, and sells his work at the local steakhouse. Not bothering with rags, he wipes his brushes on what my wife calls his "Jackson Pollock sweatshirt." He drives rutted dirt roads and single-handedly pitches his tent, and once, reenacting a John Wesley Powell pickle, I hauled him out of a gulch with my fleece jacket, instead of a rope or the long-johns that saved the one-armed major's bacon the time he got stuck on a ledge.

"The term *cult* often refers to the veneration of or devotion to a person, ideal, or thing by a group...sharing a sacred ideology with associated rites and symbols," the Chaco expert Gwinn Vivian wrote. We certainly qualify. We're driven as much as those who go "herping," looking for reptiles and amphibians, or those into scarabs or monarchs, birds, minerals, mushrooms, or geocaching. And fond, like them, of minting swell words. Because of the potential for human impact—oils and etching sweat from your fingertips, food bits luring critters, campfire soot—sleeping near the art or making direct contact with it are taboo. So is the outlining of figures in chalk, a method earlier researchers used to improve photographic contrast. In fact, I hereby motion that Mussentuchit, the flats in the San Rafael Swell that hold an intricate petroglyph panel, be renamed "Mustn't touch it," to spread that commandment.

You may understand why information sharing is not a given among adherents of our sect. I don't welcome those who trade it the way people trade baseball cards. Nor embrace guidebook authors. I swear even friends to secrecy, asking them not to pass on directions, before I reveal extraordinary or especially vulnerable sites. Audience members at a lecture on Barrier Canyon rock art tried to milk the presenter for details about the location of one particular pictograph. "It's closer to Moab than to Paris," the ranger responded, with a Cheshire-cat smile.

Like many cliques, we have associations, newsletters, and formal get-togethers, desert symposia during which glyphers listen, quaff, quibble, hook up, scratch backs, exchange notes, workshop, pick brains, and tour nearby sites. For a couple of days, laypeople mingle with scientists there. Some rogues consider these gatherings nothing but clubby academic blather. URARA may sound like a raucous rallying cry, but the acronym hides the mundane realities of the Utah Rock Art Research Association.

We expect the unexpected. Once, looking for pictographs deep in Canyonlands National Park, I chanced upon a case of dynamite sticks in an alcove, rodent-ravaged, melting into the dirt. I neither touched it nor called out to Melissa, irrationally nervous about nitroglycerin that might have become unstable. And a ranger with whom I discussed pictographs at a site near Sedona told me that he'd once walked in on a nude woman in the alcove who had held a lit candle in each hand. (The driver of a car in Sedona that time rolled down his window and asked me what those "vortexes" are and how he might find them—clearly an out-of-towner. Vortexes, in case you haven't heard about them, are quantum-energy ports. They facilitate healing and communication with angelic spirits and serve as charging stations for flying saucers and portals into the hollow earth, where aliens live.)

One of my life's highlights—do not shake your head in pity—has been my discovery of an Archaic pictograph panel nobody had ever mentioned. Research at home afterward yielded no clues, no photos online, no descriptions or sketches in books or articles, no knowing nods from acquaintances. Zip. Zilch. Nada. I'd stumbled across it in a Utah monocline, on my way to another spectacular site, forced to detour by a pour-off, looking for an alternative route. Red splotches framed by juniper lattices caught my eye as I trudged up a wash. Up close, the work looked so crisp on the white, sandpapery background, the details so sharp, seemingly painted yesterday, that I considered that the panel might be a fake. If so, it was the work of a master who'd deeply studied this subject. Melissa, who was with me, had the same initial response. Rock-art forgery is not unheard of. Near Moab, Pleistocene profiles from the Chauvet Cave in France accent a slickrock wall with artfully rendered megafauna. Mud handprints that Scouts leave near authentic ones are far more annoying.

The surprise panel solely featured the burnt sienna of hematite. Others are polychromatic, drawing their colors from the land, though time has muted their brilliance. For thousands of years, artist-seers on the Colorado Plateau refined the purest kind of dirt into matter for rock paintings: orange ocher, white kaolinite, yellow limonite, blue and green copper oxides, and black charcoal, often combined to Miró-like effect. You can find grinding slicks—up to dozens—on boulders right at the foot of a panel, divots sometimes complete with a stone loaf for hand-milling pigments. I favor pictographs even over petroglyphs, because of their transience, the slim odds of their survival.

The images I stared at open-mouthed, which precisely matched a local type resembling that of the Horseshoe Canyon dwellers, seemed to cohere in a narrative, which is extremely rare. I wondered if they were telling a nightmare or myth. In the main grouping, a faceless Giacometti figure holds a horned serpent with two tails by the neck. The other hand, raised up high, cradles a bird (?) or insect (?), spirit beings that sometimes helped and empowered shamans. Another snake, this one drawn hairline thin, crowns the head of this priest or deity. A similar snake handler stands vis-à-vis. And between them, drawing the eye, perhaps meant to be the focus: a person (?) ripped apart at the waist, with one severed hand flying in a different direction, its fingers clawing agonizingly. Carmine from dissolved pigment blown through a reed tube spatters the position of his injury, the violation of him—a Tarantino slow-motion special effect. There is more. A humanoid off to the side holds another horned serpent with tiny forelegs overhead. A second snake twists around his (?)

torso like a boa constrictor. A chimera partly abraded by time—half wolf, half iguana—rushes pugnaciously (?) in, next to another spatter, a sanguine mist. The dynamism of the whole is exquisite.

Snakes and figures handling snakes show up consistently in Barrier Canyon pictographs. In a rock shelter on a butte not too far away, several supplicants kneel with raised hands, facing a snake. Reptilian skin-shedding hints at transformation, and snakes are thought to have been shamanistic spirit helpers, bestowing their powers upon religious specialists involved in augury, healing, and trance travel to other realms. I always walk more carefully, more aware, reminded of ground-level danger, near rock art with snakes. Few desert animals will stop you as cold in your tracks as the "buzzworms" do. Coming upon one without warning literally gives me goose bumps, though in general, they seem shy and leave the scene if given that option. I've stepped over some that did not rattle, informed of their presence only afterward by Melissa. On another occasion, clearing a campsite of cow patties, I picked up one to find a sluggish midget faded *Crotalus*, a boldly flecked spiral, underneath—and I jumped as if I *had* been bitten.

Throughout the indigenous Southwest, snakes are associated with springs, rivers, thunderstorms, and fertility. Their whole body is in contact with the earth's benign powers. "They really are incredible creatures," the English biologist author of a book about predators writes, "superbly adapted for a form of movement that is mesmerising." And it would be astounding if rattlesnakes, with their forked-tongue flick, elongate zigzag shape, and a strike faster than the blink of an eye, were *not* thought of as lightning incarnate. Even the sizzle of their rattling carries a charge of something electric, a mix of wires short-circuiting and the humming of power lines. Still, I did not dare speculate about the meaning of the drama on that unnamed gulch's wall. It had played out there for millennia, between eight and one-and-a-half, between the Fertile Crescent's rise and the Vandals' sacking of Rome, depending on which expert's guesswork you accept. As part of a cycle, it always ended the same way. The Hopis, removed in space and time from this graphic artist's hunting culture, dance with rattlesnakes in their plazas before releasing them in the four directions, pleading for rain. For traditional Navajos, thunder and lightning bring dead snakes back to life. A Moab panel that *does* share close stylistic roots with "Broken Man," as I brazenly dubbed my find, shows a snake and humanoid below an element that has been interpreted as a cloudburst—a plea to a rain spirit, perhaps. Lastly, snakes worldwide slither through myths and art that addresses fecundity, in traditions that far predate Freudian psychology. An obsession with seasonal, unpredictable water aligns all desert creatures.

It is hard to convey how alien these images appear to the modern viewer. Yet through them shines a shared humanity, the difference one of surfaces only. Whether our fears involve nightmare demons or spiking global temperatures, we wrestle with them by telling stories. In part, the unceasing force these ancient panels exert stems from how they stimulate the imagination, offering seeds for our own fabulating.

When I sent photos of the new pictograph to a friend for his opinion, I did not scrub their GPS data from the digital files. He overlooked that as well and passed them on to a friend, who promptly went to the site. Thus do hype and stampedes and site deterioration begin. I felt like a colossal fool, a damn rock-art rookie.

There are those who say, rightly, that with GPS, Instagram, and the internet, archaeological Kohinoors can no longer remain hidden. The only way to protect them, they aver, is by educating people about their importance. While I agree in principle, this assumes people will do the right thing once they learn what it is. There's a numbers problem, too. It takes just one dimwit among hundreds of well-behaved visitors to seriously damage a rock-art panel.

"Leave No Trace" for us therefore means "Leave No Tracks,"

as footpaths betray dear locations. (Leave no truck nearby either; parked by a trailhead, it might attract rock-art vultures.) Discovery of an unknown panel is its own reward, and the discoverer often names it, largely for reference. Due to the clandestine nature of the enterprise, various names can coexist, confusing lay researchers. Territoriality and competitiveness and the wish to protect sites plagues many tight-lipped rock-art buffs. Trampled cryptogamic soil, GPS coordinates on the Internet, and spray-painted doodles, or "idiotglyphs" are all too common these days. The curious will notice that splendid volumes about the region's rock art do not contain specific location information, but people have managed to position sites through clues from the setting, geology, skyline, or landmarks. Drawing more attention to a place generally can be detrimental.

Sprawling graffiti and other outrages committed against public monuments have leaked beyond the subways and concrete of cities. Despite Park Service admonitions and threats, each year, thousands of self-proclaimed fans of the Southwest scratch their names into boulders and cliffs rather than trail registers. The signatures and initialed hearts, plus bullets the locals fire for target practice, damage records created by missionaries, traders, scientists, Native Americans, and pioneers that can contribute to our knowledge about the past. Perhaps more importantly for Max King, the chief of interpretation at Glen Canyon National Recreation Area, such artifacts provide "a tangible, inspiring connection to the determined spirit of the early explorers of this land."

Volunteers with Lake Powell's Graffiti Removal Intervention Team (GRIT) clean up rock surfaces near the reservoir with hammers, squirt bottles, wire brushes, and much elbow grease. They live for a week at a time on a donated houseboat, *True GRIT*. In a typical year, they log 1,400 hours and scrub 17,280 square feet of sandstone tagged mostly by recreational boaters, removing manifestos of ignorance or contempt.

In 2007, at Padre Bay, near an ancient ford across the

Colorado River later named "The Crossing of the Fathers" (and now inundated), one such team discovered a faint phrase beneath a scrim of modern graffiti: *paso por Aqui Año 1776*. The phrase "passed by here" is typical of 17th-century Spanish inscriptions, like those in New Mexico's El Morro National Monument, a busy noticeboard of immigrants and explorers. James Page, the GRIT-houseboat pilot and president of the Armijo Chapter of the Old Spanish Trail Association, almost immediately thought of the Dominguez-Escalante expedition, whose journal he had studied. "I knew we had a winner," he said, recalling the thrill of discovery. "There was never any doubt in my mind that it was authentic."

The Franciscan friars had attempted to find a route between Santa Fe, New Mexico, and Monterey, California, where they hoped to establish new missions. They'd already been forced to eat some of their horses when a fierce storm trapped the party. "Stopped for a long time by a strong blizzard and tempest consisting of rain and thick hailstones amid horrendous thunder claps and lightning flashes," their terse journal entry of that day reads. As they carved into the soft Entrada sandstone, they may have thought they were writing their own epitaph.

The newly discovered inscription would have been the only known physical mark the expedition left anywhere. But first, it would have to undergo a battery of sophisticated tests to prove its authenticity.

It was too late to keep it safe through secrecy. Already, Rob or Kathi had eternalized the couple's communing right across that of the friars. My guess is it was Rob wielding the tool.

"What's the difference between some old Spaniard's scrib-bling and ours?" people like them may ask. The answer is simple, transcending mere age: Theirs are the testimonies of bold, singular feats, of journeys earned with blood and sweat; yours just the whirring of a locust swarm. Or, as one rock-art researcher puts it in a more level-headed way, "Fifty years of antiquity elevates certain inscriptions to historic status in terms of their significance

...simply because our records of human travel and interaction become increasingly sparse as we move back in time." Midden heaps of tin cans from Cold War beans-and-bacon dinners thrown out from alcoves are now protected artifacts.

There's a large Grand Canyon petroglyph panel on the South Rim inaccessible by car, to which a culprit had to have carried white paint and a brush for a mile to tag it *ACE*. Plain stone is not exempt, either. Hand outlines on the slickrock at popular overlooks bear the names and dates of the hands' owners. The anthropologist in me wonders what such Johnny-come-lately pronouncements signify. Are they seeking to stave off a still young society's fear of insignificance in the face of petrified eons? Are they to grant individuality in a world groaning under the weight of almost eight billion of us? "Essential loneliness and the thought that one's life is inconsequential, both of which are hallmarks of modern civilizations," Barry Lopez surmised, "seemed to me to be derived in part from our abandoning the therapeutic dimensions of a relationship with place."

"I too lived. I mattered," the words seem to shout. They are protesting time's fleetingness. Rob and Kathi's chicken scratches share one motivation with the glyphs Dominguez or Escalante incised, as perhaps they do with all writing: "We passed by here," they inform later readers. "We saw this." The first signature spawns consecutive ones, as if an idea had been planted, permission granted, a barrier of scruple breached. Abbey, while he rangered at Arches, put up a sign at the Balanced Rock campground, a futile attempt to deflect attention away from the iconic formation. *If You Must Carve Your Initials Please Do It Here*, it pleaded. It's not just the rash of graffiti, however. In the Moab area alone, several pictographs have been scoured into oblivion.

Though you can see tribal members engaged in graphic acts of fertilization also, it takes only one present-day dick to break a millennium's spell of continuity. Some desecrations broadcast ironclad values. *WHITE POWER, EAT ASS*, and a crude phallus to drive home the point scarred a pageant of birth and creation near Moab; *THIS IS PRIVATE PROPERTY NO TRESSPASSING* [sic] mars a red elk pictograph in Nine Mile Canyon, clearly directed at glyphers who visit what has been called "The World's Longest Art Gallery." Would that command have stopped the pilgrims at Plymouth Harbor? The black letters—blocky, all caps, as seems to be the preferred register for this type of messaging—look stenciled. They sketch a worldview unlike the underlying images, one in which race drives a yearning for law and order, the protection of capitalism's golden calf.

By contrast, to mark a rock is to replace the rock's desire with a human desire, many Paiute people believe, and therefore ought to be weighed carefully.

Do wanton tagging or the defacement of religious symbols on stone shock me? When *T-34*—the name of a Soviet tank—has been seen sprayed in black on the bulk of a Siberian polar bear, compromising its camouflage and survival?

The placement of the Glen Canyon inscription's Spanish phrase yielded a first clue about its primacy: chest-high, in the panel's center, it fills exactly the place a person would choose if given a clean slate. A laser scan helped map and document the find and made it more visible while adding information about its reflectivity, which contrasts with that of modern rock etchings.

Paleographers identified the script as eighteenth-century New World Spanish Cursive. Comparing the inscription with samples from El Morro, they saw striking similarities, like flourished descenders, strokes below a word's baseline, on the letters p and the upper case A. Hook or "serif" flourishes evident at both sites, and a slight elevation of the date's last numeral, were consistent with usage on period maps.

An investigation of the rock varnish showed varying levels of thickness and lead contamination. The patina from mineral oxidation on modern graffiti was thinner, thus newer, with higher lead concentrations indicative of industrial air pollution. The metallic coating on *paso por Aqui Año 1776* was thicker, and its deeper layers contained no lead residue; it likely predated the 20th century by several centuries. Slow-growing lichen led one ecologist to estimate that the underlying inscription was at least a hundred years old.

Additional support for the inscription's antiquity came from the friars' journal. Though they did not mention carving one, its location matched the diary entry for November 6. A nearby alcove could well have been the one that sheltered the stormbound padres and waits to be excavated for proof.

Based on the available evidence, Glen Canyon officials declared the inscription genuine. King compared the discovery to "finding a lost speech of Lincoln." The site's exact location was kept secret to protect it, while further archaeological work was to be conducted. Alas, secrecy proved insufficient to veil this graphic treasure, and the Park Service put a steel cage around it.

The battle to safeguard Southwestern cultural resources is far from over. Since 1998, the Park Service has funded archaeological preservation and restoration projects in forty-five parks between Texas and California, as part of its Vanishing Treasures program. Land managers, whose budgets are stretched to the maximum, bank on legal deterrents. Violating stone surfaces in national parks and monuments can result in a $6,000 fine and misdemeanor charge, and federal law covers all inscriptions fifty years and older. Many experts consider educating the public the more effective part of a two-pronged strategy of prevention. Novel approaches to enlighten visitors include hands-on programs that incorporate archaeology and scientific methods used in digs. "All of us recognize that we need to maintain this public connection," King offered. "Without that, we will gradually lose our support as a park."

The vigilance, not just manual labor, of volunteers—often rock-art buffs like myself—is crucial. Prevention beats remediation. In January 2015, a preservationist patrolling near the town of Bluff in southeastern Utah revisited a rock-art panel of a humanlike figure at least five times older than the Liberty Bell and found it marred by a similar crack. A thief had tried to cut the petroglyph from the cliff with a rock saw, to keep or sell to a collector. The botched result was an irreversibly disfigured piece of the First Peoples' history and an argument for including the area in Bears Ears National Monument.

As a writer, given my interests, I have to tread extra carefully. Once, soon after I'd emailed a photographer about an article I was working on, a Park Service archaeologist contacted me, asking that I not mention sensitive rock-art sites or include photos of them. I had not planned to do either. The way word got around was a bit too Big Brother, though I welcomed their concern.

Ironically, I myself have been a suspect of archaeological transgression. Returning from a day of poking around in the far corners of the Painted Desert, looking for glyphs, my companion, the Moab rock-art guide and cowboy-poet Rory Tyler, alerted me to a Park Service ranger waiting by his truck, watching us through binoculars. After questioning us about where we'd been and why, the ranger gave us a choice: we could either turn our pockets inside out voluntarily; or he could detain us and get an official search warrant. On our hike, we had seen two perfect arrowheads and of course left them after close inspection, and our pants produced only a cigarette lighter, small change, and lint. Approaching the blacktop and The Law, Rory, stopping smartly and pretending to tie a shoe, had slipped his baggie of weed under a rock, to retrieve it later.

Rory is a Basketmaker man; his main focus lies on the pre-ceramic culture that inhabited the Colorado Plateau's core region, the larger Four Corners, between 1500 BCE and 750 CE. Within the vast canon of ornate Basketmaker rock art, depictions of bighorn sheep drives and archaeo-astronomical sites have become Rory's singular obsessions. He has studied Moab area panels so often, spending so much time scrutinizing them at different times of the day and year, that he noticed relations between glyphs and celestial events, convergences he thinks led to the images' specific placement. Such astronomical markers are well documented in the literature. The most famous case is Fajada Butte, a possible sun shrine in New Mexico's Chaco Canyon. There, funneled light bolts—the famous "sun daggers"—slice spiral petroglyphs at both winter and summer solstices and fall and spring equinoxes. Near solstices, the sun's horizontal drift slows, and it rises in practically the same place for a week. For historic pueblo dwellers, the winter standstill must have been a time of existential dread; they might have feared that, like life, time itself would grind to a halt, seized by unending cold. Elaborate festivals nudged the sun on its way again.

In a Moab sea of sandstone fins, a wonderland plainly known as Behind the Rocks that Rory frequently visits, summer solstice light knifes through a keyhole slit and onto Entrada Sandstone like molten, radiant steel. Within seconds, the beam mutates into an arrowhead—razor-edged, side-notched, tapered like a perfect triangle—that aims downward, at the head of a petroglyph snake. Its skillfully rendered body flexes across more than thirty feet on the cliff face. The six dips and seven crests of the 900-year-old undulating reptile's curves add up to the total of new moons in a year. The lightshow lasts about thirty seconds while the sun hurries on; it has other appointments to keep.

Outsider archaeologists like Rory Tyler, and Morris Wolf, who has guided academic researchers that furthered their careers through their guide's knowledge, may feel inferior, even slighted by the mainstream, despite their meticulous documentation and expertise. Without degrees or peer-reviewed publications, they remain amateurs in the best sense of the word: their heart is invested in the redrock setting and hunt. They combine traits of the sage and naïf, the oracle and the bard, Alexander von Humboldt and Stephen Hawking.

Rory disagrees with me about keeping rupestrian secrets,

because no artist he's ever met has said, "Please don't show any-body my work," or "Don't tell them where to see it." This, to me, conflates modern and ancient perspectives. On a laptop he carries in his car, wherever you happen to meet, he pulls up YouTube vid-eos, slide shows, and unpublished manuscripts he's put together. In his slight lisp, with salt-and-pepper bristles framing his nut-brown face, and an Indiana Jones hat and khaki or plaid shirts as his uniform, he'll point out arcane "entanglements" till your head spins. He's discovered a Hidden Valley observatory, and in the boulders of Arches a goose laying a silver dawn egg, part of a story that unfolds as our brightest star rolls through the sky bowl. Near a Barrier Canyon-style pictograph dubbed the "Comet Thrower," a rock tower with an erosional peephole caught his attention. From a certain perspective, it becomes "a Spirit Sheep whose eye is made of the Sun, looking directly at you on the first day of Spring and first day of Fall...a plausible metaphor, metaphysical and poetic." He convinced a rock-climber friend to belay him on a ledge arcing above the mouth of the pictograph's alcove so that he could photograph shallow steps the ancients had chiseled all the way to the top, where a shadow play he had scoped from the ground is projected onto a wall.

Last I heard from Rory, he was pushing seventy, "Hobbling along, slowing up, breaking down, falling apart...right on sched-ule." They've broken the mold from which such men were cast. I would rather spend a day in their company than with a celebrity—Dian Fossey even, or T.C. Boyle or Tom Waits.

Luckily, no signs of self-centeredness in the form of plein-air graphomania defile the not-to-be-named Holbrook canyon I am walking with Chuck LaRue—yet. *Oohing* and *aahing* at almost every bend, we stroll down the quiet aisle. Morning sun in our faces makes it hard to read patterns pecked into the blue-black rock varnish. The group unravels as pairs linger over choice petroglyphs, discussing them, snapping photos, or climbing up benches or into nooks. Our voices ring faintly in this natural echo chamber. To our delight, recent, much-needed October rains did not glut the canyon with mud pits.

This is as easy as our off-trail exploring ever gets. It may involve creek wading, snake or cow-pie dodging, gunk holing, fence vaulting, heat stroking, or free soloing. Scarred shins tell the story of our exploits, as do our scribbled-on maps. Pulling myself into a bandshell alcove, I once lacerated my palms on a mop head of razorblade beargrass and had to be careful not to sully the pictographs as I pointed out details to Melissa. She's an enabler, not a full-fledged rock-art addict. Says my pace and posture change when I'm chasing a fix, like a beagle on a scent. The cryptic scrawls really are habit-forming. We may get cliffed out but never ever glyphed out. Acquaintances have morphed from day-hikers into backpackers only to access remote niches that hold America's oldest images.

In the farthest reaches, rock art can cost you your life. In 2012, Bill Ott vanished on a three-week solo hike through hinterlands on the Hualapai reservation. Ott, a former river guide, was the first person to stitch together the North Rim traverse route, which took seventy-eight days. He probably could have gone faster but didn't want to. "Please let there not be an end to this," he scribbled into a journal during that record-setting attempt, which he afterward stated had been "a fine walk." A desire to locate pictographs of a style only known from the North Rim on the river's south side precipitated his last adventure. The Hualapais had curbed hiking on tribal lands, so Ott went in furtively, which made land and air searches for him harder. His body was never found and, except for two boot prints, there were no traces that could explain the sixty-eight-year-old's disappearance.

Grand Canyon search and rescue teams log more missions than those in any other US national park. It is good to know such country still exists. We need places that test us, that continue to brim with mystery and are wild enough to swallow us.

A friend had asked Ott to bring an emergency locator beacon with him, which the old desert rat declined. He believed in hiking without satellite crutches, as some of us still do.

Our craving not only has scarred me but also marked me otherwise. Tattooed on my right upper arm is "Mosquito Man," one of Morris Wolf's designs, copied from a pictograph in the San Rafael Swell. And on my left thigh, the ink of a stylized bear paw, a common petroglyph, like a subcutaneous memory fades and blurs with the years.

Art on the rocks outlines homelands, as it can on the skin. With rare exceptions, indigenous groups have been evicted from national parks. Hot spots of civilization once peppered "wilderness," webbing it with similar nodes. Graphics by people uprooted—by drought, civil strife, increasingly alkaline soils, and tree cutting for hearth fires and construction—remind us of the need for long-term perspectives, best practices. As benchmarks, those graphics can consolidate increasingly fragmented landscapes through the protection of "viewsheds," archaeological bookends to watersheds. Hooliganism is not the only threat. Decay from frost, roots and lichen, wildfire, sunlight, and river erosion and rain amplifies damage sustained through development such as road and dam building or seismic testing in oil and gas exploration. Acoustic properties—wind effects, birdsong, echoes, or running water—may have driven the selection of some sites, but anthropogenic noise now degrades soundscapes in which they lie embedded.

For Christopher Cokinos, who joined meteorite hunters in his research for a book, "We're all treasure hunters of a kind." There are foragers in Armani suits with nuts stashed in hedge funds, their mammoth ambushes making a killing. Like the precursors who painted and engraved this canyon, we glyphers hunt and gather, the latter only mentally or by camera. You'll recognize us from our handprint car decals and *I Break for Rock Art* bumper sticker. With Melissa driving on canyon bottom roads or along cliffs, I wish for a convertible, twisting and squirming in the shotgun seat until my neck cramps, conducting windshield surveys. Tailgaters should stay alert. We quickly develop an intuition for likely sites, reading the landscape, as did sandaled travelers long ago. Embracing modern technology where it does not interfere with backcountry bliss, we bring ultraviolet-light, rechargeable water purifiers, fancy cameras, emergency locator beacons for hardcore outings, and foldable solar panels you can strap to a pack top while hiking. We scope out talus slopes with binoculars, and, twitching over Google Earth, decode topographic features. Searches on foot can be just as exhaustive; people who suffer from ADD or weak calves don't make good glyph-hounds.

A pour-over near the draw's junction with a deeper gorge concludes today's outing. Thrashing through greenery that hides some foul red runoff pools prompts us to exit even sooner. Glyphs petered out anyway in the last quarter-mile.

Migrant sandhill cranes bugle off-key, pterodactyls rattling from beyond piñon and juniper screens, while we walk the canyon's jagged lip back to our trucks. I spot two petroglyphs invisible from the bottom, on a table-like surface tilted away from it. A few more, including a giant bear, emblazon a boulder top right in the wash. What else, I fret, might I have missed?

Let There Be Night

WE HIT THE TRAIL near the Kolb Studio. As always, the transition between the South Rim's busyness and the canyon's tranquility is gradual, though no less affecting. It is past 7 p.m., and most lodgers are still digesting their dinner, downing cocktails, watching nightfall at one of the viewpoints, or have retired, worn out from the day's activities. The only walkers we meet are a returning Polish family, whose father asks me to snap a picture of them. There's barely enough light left for that. While Melissa soon switches her headlamp on, I hold off, relishing twilight, the brief window in which Earth's upper atmosphere reflects scattered, residual sunbeams into the lower atmosphere. As a sort of personal dare, I try using my night vision—like a muscle in training—as long as possible, the kind of opportunity not many of us have very often in these electrified times.

To most members of industrial societies, night remains a foreign country. "We have created a blurred barrier of light, like an impenetrable dome covering our world, and only in the most remote places can we see beyond the lights," the bat researcher and activist Johan Eklöf writes in *The Darkness Manifesto*. Already, more than a third of humanity can no longer look up and ponder the Milky Way, Shakespeare's canvas "painted with unnumber'd sparks," and in twenty years, most major constellations will have faded into illegibility. Birds migrating through the night get sidetracked as the glare of our cities absorbs their star beacons. Insects, too, alter their flight paths, and night-active prey is exposed to predators.

Lately, even in canyon country, Starlink satellites launched as pods weird the deep well above. Like familiarly-shaped rock formations, my river clients point out, once you see them, you cannot unsee them. Several nights, at the same time, on the way to their orbit, fifteen or twenty rise bumper-to-bumper, strung out in crude cosmic traffic. After a couple of minutes, the ghostly procession enters Earth's shadow, which extinguishes it. The magnitude and ominous linearity of this train—a squashed constellation; symmetry unmatched in the firmament—offend sky gods and nyctophiles like myself.

I admit, to my embarrassment, that, too preoccupied with the delights underfoot and at eye level throughout my outdoor and guiding life, I myself have neglected to study in depth what the Flagstaff historian and astronomy devotee Don Lago hails as "nature's largest dimension"—Gaia's canopy, cloudless above these parts for 160 nights each year. It was the forest I could not see for the one tree under my feet, opulence shunned since it remains unreachable, my blindness the offshoot of Ptolemaic and biocentric biases. It was a bit like the "blue" of fair-weather skies that desert dwellers take for granted and whose nuances we seldom register. I should have heeded Lowell Observatory astronomer A.E. Douglass, who developed the method of tree-ring dating. Or Alfred Wegener, the geophysicist and meteorologist who intuited continental drift and, by conducting impact experiments with gypsum powder, concluded that moon craters were not volcanic in origin but the result of meteorite strikes. I failed to acknowledge that our bodies are composed of dust from old supernovas. While the occult maxim "as above, so below" served as the footing for astrology, it hints at a truth: the universality of physical processes in terrestrial *and* stellar environments.

Our hometown, Flagstaff, was the first city to gain Dark Sky City status in 2001, but it already had banned advertising spotlights over four decades earlier. Astronomers at the nearby Lowell Observatory, established in 1894 to prove the existence of Mars canals and which discovered Pluto and the first evidence that the universe is expanding, had pushed for this, the world's first light regulation. Public lands managers followed suit, declaring certified International Dark Sky Parks throughout the Southwest, including Grand Canyon. There, tourists catch literal glimpses of the basement of time.

We have reasons to start our July excursion this late in the day. During mild fall and spring, the Grand Canyon's prime backpacking seasons, it's hard to get short-term reservations for Bright Angel Campground or Phantom Ranch cabins, and the trails are too crowded for those who love solitude. You can avoid this by going in the off-season, though winter days are short and often cold. Conversely, July, August, and early September can be lethal at worst and unpleasant at best; heat on this trail has claimed at least fourteen human lives. Night hiking is one way to reap all the advantages, preferably timed to a full moon. Less water and clothing are needed, so backpacks are lighter. And, equally suffering from the heat, wildlife is more active. As yet another bonus, moonlight makes the familiar unfamiliar, even on oft-trodden paths.

The Park Service put up signs at South Rim trailheads that warn hikers of overexerting themselves in the heat. They show a fit, blond, clean-cut guy, sort of an outdoorsy Ken doll, above the line *Over 250 people are rescued from the depths of Grand Canyon each year...*followed by: *Most look like him.* In a picture Melissa took and Photoshopped, she grafted my mug, crowned by a straw hat two sizes too small, onto that beefcake body. But the Frankenstein montage didn't look quite right—it appeared that I could swivel my head like an owl, past my shoulder, or that I'd already broken my neck falling off the rim—and we've yet to plaster her mockup onto the Park Service signs.

Nighttime exploring without the help of an artificial light source requires an attitude adjustment. Hiking becomes walking with darkness instead of racing to beat it. This switch in perspective holds countless rewards. Vision diminished by darkness heightens other senses. You notice how the day's jug band of cicadas differs from the cricket night shift in rhythm and pitch. As color drains from slopes and dunes, yucca, primrose, and sand verbena mouths open, having avoided water loss during the furnace hours. Evening primrose, yawning white at dusk and folding after the sun balloons at dawn, wanes in that day's heat. So does datura, whose wads of wet paper tissue droop amidst gray-green foliage all too soon. Blooming cliff rose or willows at Indian Garden—that Shangri-La five miles down the Bright Angel Trail—take on an exalted dimension, their perfume fit for bottling, so rich as to be almost tangible. Bits of luminescent matter along the path glow like spider eyes, though I'm unable to determine their nature.

Mystery still inhabits the endangered dark. And that's before you meet ringtails or *Fledermäuse*, "flutter mice," bats.

In my proudest feat as an outdoorsman, I recognized a campsite once by its scent alone. We were floating as an Outward Bound group through Cataract Canyon, and the night was moonless, a cave. Worn out from the rapids and heat, we wanted to stop at Dark Canyon, a tributary near Hite Marina, for a few hours of sleep. I had backpacked there before and remembered "moonflower," hyacinth-white sacred datura, pillowing near its mouth. Before long, narcotic tendrils ensnared our fleet of rafts. The trumpet blossoms broadcast their availability to their moth pollinators— and the canyon's location to me. Sultry, with a hint of vanilla, the plant's come-on can be almost too much. But it evoked a daytime image of the confluence. Seduced by the promise of bedding down, we stepped ashore, home if just for one night.

On the program's Cataract courses, having run through the final rapid, we'd often raft up, strapping the boats together for a night float to "Planet of the Apes," a slickrock dome camp on Lake Powell, near the takeout, where scenes from the original film had been shot. Students on watch shifts took the oars, now pulling on starboard, now pushing on larboard, riding the main current to keep our barge from beaching. We'd hear sloughing cutbanks go *plunk*, beaver tails whacking the water, whirlpools lapping, critters rustling in brush—all through the scrim of chorusing crickets. The canyon's silhouette glided past in a deeper shade than the sky. The dark, with faces invisible, brought forth confessions. Students talked about hang-ups, worries, family, and ambitions, or about hobbies, or foods they were craving. They'd review the past week and their lives while their peers lay about in a massive slumber party.

Excitement could spring on you like a cougar. The Colorado, returning to life as reservoir levels were dropping, trenched lake sediment near the inflow, sometimes carving a step in the course of headwater channel erosion. It built rapids where none had existed. The unmistakable noise roused instructors on one night drift. The cones of their headlamps caught lucent foam; students scrambled from mummy bags while the river geysered from the rollercoaster rafts, slapping hulls, soaking gear, and eliciting shrieks.

Even Lake Mead, the river runner's flatwater nemesis, wraps itself in nocturnal magic on occasion. At another trip's end, we guides had become wind-bound near Scorpion Island for three days in one of Lake Mead's barren bays. The county sheriff had extricated our clients by motorboat; they had planes to catch, jobs to go back to, after all. Sometime past midnight, when the blow had exhausted itself, the trip leader woke me. "Michael! Time to go." In my sluggish raft, I'd soon lost sight of the dories and steered in the direction in which they had disappeared—toward the Pearce Ferry boat ramp, I hoped. I was not the least bit concerned about losing my way, though; longing, rather, to postpone landfall. The night gleamed, a crystal ball with myriad floating stars my only company. Handfuls danced like glowworms in the vortexes from my strokes. No sound but the soft splashing of oars. I could not discern the horizon ahead, as the still lake doubled the glitter. I was weightless, sculling in interstellar space.

Night's appeal, like that of the canyon, extends beyond the

merely aesthetic or philosophical. Our need to perceive order in a universe baffling in its complexity and unpredictability led us to become diligent stargazers. Ancient civilizations personified heavenly bodies, elevating them to the status of deities whose pacing governs human lives, giving rise to astrology. On the Colorado Plateau, too, indigenous peoples heeded the circling of seasons, the orbits of planets and stars. Their observations fixed dates for rituals, feasts, or pilgrimages, and schedules for planting, harvesting, hunting. They plucked medicinal herbs when the plants' curative powers were most potent. They tied the four directions to cosmic processes. And they closely observed lunar cycles, which provided a measure of days. Moon halos allowed the forecasting of weather, and lunar phases that of childbirths. Each new moon reflected momentous Earth phenomena, parceling out a year's months. The Moon of Fledgling Raptors. The Moon of Big Wind. The Moon of Boiling Ice. The Moon of Parting Seasons. Eclipses or comets broke the routine, spelling crisis or doom. Cosmic symbols expressed profound, lasting truths.

Shadow and light are an existential duality. One generates and requires the other.

The Navajo Shoe Game, a ceremonial contest over a wound yucca-root ball hidden inside one of four boots, commemorates a match between the day animals and the night animals, who could not agree on the sun and moon cycles. The two groups wanted it to be either light or dark all the time; the match ended in a tie. Today's reenactments, restricted to the winter months, can last all night, ending only when dawn bloodies the eastern sky.

Forever changing, forever moving, forever ruling the lives of women and men and a universe perfused with life, the moon, planets, and stars easily became vested with personalities. Celestial katsinas enliven the annual round of Hopi mystery plays: Sohu, whose three horizontal stars match Orion's belt. Tawa, the Sun Katsina, with its spray of eagle feathers. And Mastop, a winter solstice katsina dressed in a torn woman's kilt, cheeks flecked with the Big Dipper and Pleiades, who beats village dogs he encounters with a short black-and-white staff and simulates copulation with women spectators young and old.

Formerly less sedentary peoples, like the Navajos, also took advantage of stars and natural light displays. In late September, the Pleiades ("Pinlike Sparkles") resurface in the northeastern morning sky. People ceased planting then, because frost would soon settle in. When the constellation Corvus (Raven) tilts up in the east, winter is near, and the Diné got ready for deer hunting. They still distinguish each night in the twenty-nine-day lunar cycle with a special name, honoring changes in the restless shell disc that many of us would be hard pressed to detect. The Colorado astronomer Chris Wetherill sees the Diné as "more night-sky oriented, perhaps, than any other native people of North America." Don Lago elaborates on that thought, maintaining that the Southwest's desert inhabitants formulated worldviews with a greater number and more apt metaphors of humility for a cosmos "in which life is a tiny and fragile thing amid vast emptiness."

Unlike the solid, errant shooting stars, comets impress us as clockwork galactic snowballs, fists of frozen dust, rocks, and gases that punch above their weight, aesthetically speaking. Halley's, on its solar orbit, can be admired from Earth, which passes through its tail roughly every seventy-five years. It is famous for its back flare, a streamer millions of miles long, visible to the naked eye; at its peak, it sweeps across almost a quarter of the sky. Petroglyphs in New Mexico's Galisteo Basin may commemorate Halley's appearance in the fall of 1301 CE. One shows a four-pointed star with a tail like an eagle's. Others personify a star by giving it a face and anthropomorphic body, arms wielding arrows, or bedecked with an eagle's talons and tail. The merging of sky symbols, bird and star, also characterizes the Hopi Nangasohu (Chasing Star or Meteor) katsina, whose helmet-mask bears an outlined star but no facial features and is hemmed with a feather ruff. Elsewhere, the theme has been reduced with quirky minimalism in the petroglyph of a star with two cartoon stick legs that seems to be in a hurry. The Navajo term for comet, *so' náádiilwo'*, translates as "star that repeatedly runs."

For all its revelations, night hiking also poses challenges. Melissa and I should have waited two hours after the moon rose, so it could have cleared the rim and climbed high enough to illuminate the gorge. With only traces of nautical dusk (when both the horizon and brighter stars are visible) and scant depth perception, thanks to the build of our eyes, the trail's steps need to be taken with soft knees, slightly bent legs that provide buffering should the drop be higher or lower than expected. Sturdy poles, third and fourth legs, are a must for probing in front of you. Headlamps of ill-mannered trailblazers will blind you momentarily, crippling the vision you've cultivated and which takes half an hour to fully regain.

Melissa is therefore hiking far ahead of me—and promptly runs into wildlife. When I catch up, she tells me how she called out to me at one of the hairpin turns, addressing a black shape by the trailside, only to find, before it pogoed away, that "me" was a stately mule-deer buck.

Fifteen minutes later, she surprises a coyote trotting toward Indian Garden. Such a sighting would never occur in broad daylight, not here. Mesmerized by her headlamp, the trickster's eyes shone neon-green in the gloaming, due to light-gathering ocular tissue, the tapetum lucidum, or "bright tapestry," which we humans lack.

It has been said that theories about the origin of the universe reflect the predominant society's fixations more than they do scientific reality. Thus, the Victorian era's seven-day creationism gave way to the Big Bang theory favored by our noisy nuclear age.

Perhaps unsurprisingly, a culture with a sense of mischievous humor, a love for the underdog, and an eye for nature's fickleness, has ascribed sidereal beginnings to a prankster. Coyote, who himself is the product of Earth and Sky's brief contact, is held responsible for randomness in the Navajo night sky.

Long ago, when humans still slept as unformed clay, Black God hung the stars on the firmament. He began with Dilyéhé (the Pleiades), crystals he wore on his ankle. Each time he stamped his foot they skittered up his body, until they settled on his dark brow, where they still can be seen—speckling the mask of Haskéshjini, the Navajo personification of this deity. He built more constellations, or "Star People," from gems smoldering on a buckskin blanket at his feet: Central Fire (Polaris), Man With Spread Feet (Corvus), and Rabbit Tracks (the tail of Scorpio). First Slender One (Orion) protected Dilyéhé, imagined as children who trail him on his nightly excursion. Black God set Revolving Male (Ursa Major, the Big Dipper) and Revolving Female (Cassiopeia) to circle opposite each other around Central Fire, the homestead's hearth, as a model for couples in their hogans. Coyote, who loitered nearby and eyed the proceedings, felt left out. When Black God rested, he asked to plant a star of his own. He was allowed to and put it in the south (possibly Antares). Impulsive as always, Coyote then grabbed the blanket and, flinging the remaining glitter upward, dusted the velvet vault. That is why chaos and order mix in the universe, a combination many people find reassuring.

The Big Dipper and northern direction are bound to the ritual color black (łizhin, also: "darkness"), symbolizing the end of the day and spiritual knowledge. Various healing rituals, chantways, are performed accordingly between sunset and sunrise, often over several consecutive nights, ending in an all-night "sing."

No discussion of the Navajo relationship with the dark can claim to be balanced, however, without touching upon the delicate subject of witchcraft. "Skinwalkers" or "Navajo wolves," mainly active at night, go about as were-animals. Donning the hide of a wolf, they transform into one, able to practice their evil with greater freedom and speed. Ghosts can take many forms, including those of nocturnal creatures, owls and coyotes. Whistling after dark attracts ghosts, and older Navajos remain loath to leave their homes unaccompanied at that time.

From the top of the Redwall formation we see the Kolb Studio lights at our back (and those of campers at Indian Garden below), low-pressure sodium beacons that keep us on course and light pollution to a minimum. At the second set of switchbacks, four beam-slinging, river-bound runners pass us, briefly ruining my cherished new skill. All of a sudden, in comparison, our outing does not seem quite so crazy.

Moonrise finds us among transplanted cottonwoods at Indian Garden, recently renamed Havasupai Gardens in acknowledgement of those who gardened here before this became a park. The quicksilver still hovers at 100 degrees. While Melissa fills up her empty bottle with tepid water from a spigot the Park Service installed, I crunch chunks of ice from lemonade I froze solid before our hike.

The full moon can sneak up on you in this country. *A car just pulled up*, I sometimes think when it first peeps over a canyon's rim, mistaking its brilliance for headlights. Tonight it announced itself by silvering clouds and cliffs.

The moon's overwhelming presence spoils our chances of seeing shooting stars. But I can't complain, since we picked this date specifically so that Earth's pale offspring would light the way. The Perseids should be active, though they peak later, by mid-August, with up to sixty sparklers per hour. They're a dust shower in the wake of the comet Swift-Tuttle, the cloudy, drifting tail from its 133-year orbit. The best hours for watching the year's greatest meteor show fall between 2 a.m. and pre-dawn, when it's darkest and Perseus the monster slayer—the "radiant" or constellation from which these tracers seem to zip—stands high in the vault instead of crouching on the horizon.

Slivers off the teeming sky roaring down to Earth, some of which contain iron, have been retrieved from ancient dwellings in Central Arizona. Fragments at a total of ten sites came from Meteor Crater, a 50,000-year-old, privately owned strike zone between Flagstaff and Winslow billed as the "best-preserved meteorite crater on Earth." The 60,000-ton, 160-foot Canyon Diablo Meteorite, regally called "the impactor," arrived in a swarm that peppered the ground nine miles around its main handiwork. Four thousand feet wide and 550 feet deep, the divot this near-collision gouged into the Painted Desert's pink crust became a NASA moon-buggy training arena. Over a quarter-century, mining investors sunk half a million pre-Depression dollars into drilling toward the hidden giant, a hoped-for nickel-platinum bonanza whose size they overestimated, only to learn that it had detonated in midair. Thus Meteor Crater is properly named. Any shrapnel pellet from a meteoroid, comet, or asteroid that survives its passage through the atmosphere and then impacts is a *meteorite*. Fireballs that flame out to vaporize in airy friction are *meteors*. The former qualify as the only real aliens to ever land on this planet.

We cannot know if this local apocalypse played out in darkness or daylight. Mammoths, bison, camels, horses, and large ground sloths may have burned to a crisp or been killed or maimed by the shock wave and rock missiles. Piñons and junipers would have been uprooted in a ten-mile radius. Eyewitnesses to a 2013 bolide above Russia's Ural Mountains described a bright flash visible through windows, "a huge line of smoke, like you get from a plane but many times bigger," or how "something that looked like the sun fell."

Extraterrestrial debris has cropped up in unexpected locations throughout the Four Corners. As in Antarctica, such fallout is easily spotted in the desert. In 1921, Navajos led investigators to one specimen buried at the base of a cliff. The split, pitted lump weighed as much as a white rhino. It appeared to have manmade markings—a stick figure, with rays emanating from its head—that had been there when Navajos first found it in about 1600 CE. According to their oral history, "prehistoric pottery makers" had incised those. An eight-pounder in Mesa Verde, Colorado, sat in the rubble of the Sun Shrine House ruin, placed there during construction in 1275 CE. Wear on an edge near perfectly placed grip depressions showed that another, strawberry-sized one from Deadman Mesa, had been used as a scraper. Charcoal smudges on yet another matched the dates for a Sinagua-culture building that had burned down and from which a kid on a hike had taken it.

In a Verde Valley ruin south of the Plateau's rim, a pothunter unearthed a stone-lined cyst in a room on the east side of a sunrise plaza, which cradled a meteorite wrapped into a turkey-feather blanket. It echoed Paquimé, in northern Mexico, where members of the Mogollon culture built an adobe chamber around a meteorite too heavy to move, swathed it in coarse linen or "mummy cloth," and interred some of their dead with it. Perhaps magnesium streaks in the night sky outlined paths the souls of the departed took, or their previous life. Another symbolic meteorite burial occurred near Winona, north of the Interstate linking Flagstaff and Albuquerque.

Notations in old records state that Native Americans hand-carried Canyon Diablo fragments to new destinations. Were they exchanged in transactions comparable to the trade in medieval relics, like pebbles from Holy Land sanctums, nails from the true cross, or St. Cuthbert's gallstone? Some clearly had been treated as sacred objects from the heavens, embers from the eternal fire.

Kenneth Zoll, a retired director of the Verde Valley Archaeology Center, has a different, more prosaic take. The distribution of sites aligns with the bearing of the meteorite's flight close to its touchdown, its elliptical "strewn field," suggesting to Zoll chance collecting by the ancients, not barter.

A poet, not a scientist, amazingly answered the question of why the night sky, with uncountable suns and reflecting planets and moons in every direction, is mostly black. Edgar Allan Poe, master of Gothic Noir, surmised that while the number of light sources and their spread in outer space may be infinite, not enough time has passed for photons from the beginning of the universe to reach our home, the marbled blue bead. Too few stars spatter the observable part of the cosmos to turn night skies white. Also, we now know, with entropy ruling, the universe will run out of nuclear fuel to form new luminosity.

Enigmatic star patterns looking like swarms of plus signs dapple the ceilings of rock shelters in the Four Corners, mainly near Canyon de Chelly, the historical heartland of Navajo resistance. Little is known about their purpose or meaning. Some of these polychrome pictographs, which cultural geographers dubbed "star charts" or "planetaria," soar well out of reach above the dirt floors; most likely, they were shot onto the ceiling with pigment-tipped, blunt-headed arrows or stamped after climbing a pole or ladder. Though it could have been a pastime of teenagers, sacred rites may have framed the activity. The Diné attribute beneficial influence to the stars and to juniper berries, which, having dropped, blue the ground near a trunk as stars packed together at their highest concentrations do the heavens; the Milky Way is a path of corn pollen, a substance sprinkled in prayer and for protection. Stars could have kept those ceilings from caving in, just as they rivet the sky into place. Stars also decorate rattles shaken in curing ceremonies and perhaps drew healing powers to the overhangs.

A version of Cat's Cradle—one of humanity's oldest and most widespread games—helps Navajo children in traditional households to learn constellations, together with the related stories and beliefs. Taught originally by Spider Woman, the string game reminds the Diné of connections. Changing a part affects the entire configuration. Stylized stellar designs like the square diamond of Big Star or the Milky Way's chain of lozenges not only appear as string game figures, but also in curative drypaintings (or "sandpaintings") and on wool rugs. The diamond abounding in Navajo weaving comes from designs used in the Little Star and Great Star Chantways. The first credits the unnamed sidereal plentitude while curing symptoms from incorrect stargazing or night illness; the second, calling upon named stars, ranks among the tribe's most important religious healing ceremonies. Stargazing in this context describes a traditional form of divination in which a stargazer called to a patient's hogan prays and sings to the star spirit, asking for the source of the illness to be revealed. The star answers with a ray whose hue predicts the treatment's outcome.

Navajo ritual, like Black God's star launching, weaving, and the string game's "dancing of hands" spin intriguing correspondences—healthy harmony—from randomly tangled skeins.

Having watered up, we follow Bright Angel Creek down-canyon. Before long, it entrenches, its voice a magnified babbling of almost-comprehensible tongues. Near the Tonto Platform's edge, where it plunges into abyssal schist, Melissa, who again forged ahead, comes rushing back up the trail.

"I think I saw a mountain lion," she half-whispers, excited, out of breath.

Her headlamp's cone caught the rounded head, its large eyes ablaze, tawny fur, the telltale gait, a buff incarnation of power and grace. The adage "All cats are gray in the dark," dismissing physical appearance as unimportant, is untrue and, in this case, dangerously misleading.

The hairs rise on my neck. The night no longer feels safe. When did I learn to dread the dark? Or have we always dreaded it, huddling inside caves against the threat of eradication? I'd feared snakes hunting with infrared heat-sensing nasal pits or coiled up on the still-warm trail, but not this. The lion may have come here for a drink, or to stalk deer in the lush vegetation.

Mountain lions cannot see in complete darkness but do single out details in low light six times better than we, due to a greater number of colorblind rods in their retinas. Their visual field spans almost 300 degrees, with a binocular overlap of 130 (compared to 200/120 in humans); their depth perception focuses best fifty to eighty feet in front of them, the perfect strike range for a stalking and ambush predator. Whiskers on their muzzle and eyebrows further aid them, picking up slightest airflow changes as prey moves—that is why mule deer and bighorn sheep in the presence of a cougar may freeze. A wildlife biologist told Barry Lopez that the paws of a lion are so receptive that, instantly feeling the direction in which hair grows, it grapples for its victim's head for that deadly bite between vertebrae, even sightless.

An alcove on Cedar Mesa gave up a unique Basketmaker sandal 1,900 years old. It had been cut from the foot and lower leg of a mountain lion. The skin's hair side had become the sandal sole, the opposite of what common sense would dictate. A human's foot fit right on top of the lion's, toes touching his leathery footpad in intimate contact. The symbolism is clear: one hunter wanted to share in the power of another. Electricity must have surged from the sandal terminal up his legs, into his heart. Hair on the underside would have made any stalking on slickrock soundless. The Basketmaker may have worn a lion-skin skullcap too, to borrow the animal's vision, its stealth—Navajos raiding enemies for their horses did so. Or he slipped into the sinew toe loop only in rituals, a nimble, assertive dancer.

The eye of a lion can be its weakness. When a lion pounced on a Coloradoan near Denver in 1998, the man pushed his thumb through the attacker's eyelid "all the way to the muscle at the back of the eye." The victim escaped after also fighting back with a small knife, but he had to undergo six hours of surgery, which entailed seventy staples for his head wounds alone. In a rare coda, the same lion—missing one eye and with a telltale scar—was caught almost a year later in a garden nearby. Given the choice, her one-time victim, who had made major life changes because of the attack, told the park rangers to let the lioness go.

You may not see a mountain lion in the wild in a lifetime. But they are out there, watching from the cover of boulders and pines. When prey is abundant, they stick to isolated mesas, areas we once seldom visited. Unfortunately attracting homebuilders and developers now, these rugged lands have been engulfed by suburban sprawl and recreational influx. As an ironic twist, in the words of conservation biologist Adam Hart, "a large predator, even unseen, enhances the sense of wilderness and may be a factor in drawing people to stay"—at least those of a more adventurous stripe.

My sole mountain lion encounter, though less traumatic than the eye-gouger's, was no less impressive. A fellow Outward Bound instructor and I were bivouacked by a water pocket in a slickrock bowl outside of the Canyonlands Needles district. The students lay scattered in the vicinity, each under his or her tarp, for a three-day solo experience, an exercise in ascetic introspection.

Dawn had barely grazed the horizon and color leaked back into the world, when my co-instructor roused me.

"Michael!"

"What?"

"Lion!" Nancy said it under her breath but with urgency. She motioned for me to come to where she'd bedded down on banded stone.

"Where?" I whispered, out of my bag, crouching, unaware that I was clad only in underpants. But she had lost sight of the cat the Diné call "one who walks stealthily behind rocks." When it heard us it must have paused, standing stock-still. It blended in with the sandstone, a superb example of predator camouflage.

The lion finally moved again, rippling over rock benches like a brook. The long tail squirmed nervously. At the rim, she stopped briefly. Her profile against the desert sky stays forever etched in my memory, in the company of a backyard Alaska lynx.

After she'd dropped off the skyline, we heard caterwauling for a while. I felt bad that our camping had kept her away from her water source. When we debriefed the students later that morning, none had reported anything extraordinary.

That apparition was crepuscular, technically neither nocturnal nor diurnal, a straddler of worlds like myself.

Melissa and I are relieved, having escaped becoming a midnight snack, when the trail winds through a final breach in the plateau and zigzags down ramparts to the river. While Luna's bald stare has washed out most stars, the inner gorge lies drowned in ink. The terrain appears simplified, strangely flattened, like the rough draft of a novel or a half-finished wood carving.

As clouds gauze the moon's face, its light dims, a visual chill. Shadows weaken or intensify, and ours escort us, whispering lines by the Tang dynasty poet Li Bo:

> I raise my cup to toast the moon on high.
> That's two of us; my shadow makes it three.

Our mobile shadows, I realize, are minute eclipses, with the moon as our sun. Light itself is invisible. What we are seeing are *effects* it causes by falling on surfaces or passing through things— in the case of our eyes, both; it does not exist in the way it appears.

Like too much wine or that orbiting visage that space rocks scarred, ancient light on ancient geological strata staggers the mind. We take in the flickering luster of stars long extinct, and compared to them and the galaxies pushing outward, even the canyon's oldest layers strike one as young.

Built a mere blink of an eye ago, a pueblo near two stone spires on a mesa top at the southern edge of Colorado's San Juan Mountains may have functioned as an observatory. Every 18.6 years, at the time of the Northern Major Lunar Standstill, the moon, seen from the remaining, waist-high walls, rises in the notch the twin towers form. The pueblo's foundation, as well as two construction bursts ascertained by tree-ring dates, coincided with eleventh-century lunar standstills. This astronomical gun-sight arrangement, Chimney Rock, is an outlier of Chaco Canyon's Great Houses, where solstice observations took place.

A modern temple dedicated to the waxing and waning of light that clocks the passage of days, seasons, and years, hides in the bunchgrass-and-brush plains northeast of Flagstaff, not far from Grand Falls and Wupatki. It hides inside Roden Crater, one of the easternmost cinder cones in the San Francisco Volcanic Field, a fifty-mile belt of more than 600 former hot spots. The inactive volcano's low, weathered profile looks nearly symmetrical and certainly sensual. Kissed by sun, it blushes at dawn. The owner, the land artist James Turrell, has compared Roden Crater to Man Ray's celebrated canvas of scarlet lips in the sky. For more than five decades, Turrell, loosely affiliated with California's light-and-space school, has been crafting his masterpiece, a theater of and for the ages, the architectural equivalent of the Great American Novel. His hallways and hollows house the cosmos: celestial rhythms and "old time." His blueprints outline nine underground chambers, four above-ground chambers (oriented to the cardinal directions), one large outdoors arena (the volcano's throat), and walkways and tunnels connecting these focal points. The integrated, largely subterranean structure's spaces stage sky events in a sculptural manner. This Lighthenge is a shrine in the mold of megalithic tombs and circles in Ireland and Scotland, Iron Age hill forts in England, Egyptian pyramids, and, yes, Southwestern archaeo-astronomical sites.

Turrell grew up with a Quaker grandmother who urged him to sit quietly and "greet the light inside." The physics of photons bewitched him early on, as an independent child with scientific leanings. He once pricked holes into an old World War II blackout curtain in his room that, when daylight fell through them, struck him like night sky constellations. When he cut an opening into the roof of a studio he leased in a ramshackle Los Angeles hotel—for his first interior "skyspace"—his landlord made him fix the damage.

Roden Crater's Sun and Moon Space, one of the rooms already completed, could be the most remarkable feature. It works like a pinhole camera. At its center stands the largest single marble piece ever quarried in the United States, a thirteen by fifteen-and-a-half-foot counterpart of 2001's metaphorical slab. A keyhole-shaped tunnel slopes upward from the chamber for almost nine hundred feet. Facing southwest, this shaft channels light downward during the moon's southernmost apogee. Once every 18.6 years, when the full moon pauses at its lowest in the southern sky, it projects an eight-foot image of itself on the central monolith, an image so clearly defined that lunar surface details stand out. "The sky is no longer out there," this druid in cowboy duds told a journalist. He has brought it "down into our territory."

The South Space at night will allow astronomical sightings aided by stainless steel maps set into the black floor. This "chart room" will also yield dates for eclipses during the Earth-and-moon minuet around the sun.

At the head of the east tunnel, a skylight has been cut into the ceiling of a large, elliptical room. A basin below this East Portal will hold white sand, which, saturated with rainwater, reflects starlight. According to Turrell, the glow of Venus alone will be enough to see your shadow by. A second aperture will frame Polaris—or whichever star marks the celestial pole in a future that may or may not contain us. The oculus will keep the star centered while the observatory apparently rotates on its shine like a wheel on an axle. This defies our expectation of stars arcing across the firmament, but, because only planets wander (all stars are fixed), it's exactly what happens. Celebrants in the East Portal's cosmic kiva can slip off Earth's tethers, questioning their position relative to the thing observed.

For the full Monty, bulldozers moved more than a million cubic yards of soil and rocks, landscaping the cone's rim into an elegant, even-leveled oval, an almost-perfect parabola. Four tilted limestone platforms arranged like compass points at the bowl's center invite viewers to lie on their backs and, engulfed by humming silence, lose themselves in a dome made of sky. *Am I looking up or down?* they may ask. *Am I going to fall or levitate into space?* This sleight-of-the-eye, "celestial vaulting" is more pronounced from a position far above the ground.

A man-moth drawn toward our planet's largest natural light source, Turrell does not limit himself to optical phenomena. The music of the spheres will caress you in a light-catching cistern near the crest of the fumarole, a secondary vent like smaller outgrowth born from the crater's flank. Light sucked into a quartz ring around a pool will be redirected to lid the water with a radiant layer. A parabolic dish under the pool will collect echoes of the Big Bang, electromagnetic waves from quasars (ginormous black holes) and other massive entities—stars, comets, and galaxies—and transmit them into the water, where floaters can hear and feel them. Turrell, who was convicted as a conscientious objector and spent time in solitary confinement, is a child of the '60s. He collaborated with a physiological psychologist, experimenting with soundproof sensory deprivation chambers in the style of John Lilly and Timothy Leary. Both experiences may have influenced his spare architectural style, perhaps even his fortress-like excavating, and reinforced his choice of subject matter. Unlike any deprivation tank, though, Turrell's pool will immerse the fortunate few, chosen by lottery, in the pulsing, birthing, unbounded universe.

"Desire" is a bud from the Latin *desiderare*: to "long for, wish for," even "demand, expect." The original sense may have been "await what the stars will bring." The word is based on the phrase *de sidere*, "from the stars." Its nucleus, "star," cannot be reduced beyond its Proto-Indo-European root *ster-, with any further meanings lost in time's bottomless pool.

If your head spins at Turrell's vision, so does mine, simply from reading about the planned fireworks. I won't describe his equally dazzling solar revelations here. Unfortunately, with the exception of a few journalists and possible donors, no visitors are admitted to Roden Crater until the project's completion, which has been delayed repeatedly. Some critics say that, like Antonio Gaudí's trippy Sagrada Familia cathedral, the naked-eye observatory meant to outlast our moment will never be finished in the artist's lifetime. For all we know, it will become Turrell's burial mound.

To preserve his artwork's integrity and that of its setting, the eighty-year-old demiurge-trickster with the Santa beard has vowed to safeguard Roden Crater's viewshed. The lands he owns and some that he leases and on which he runs cattle act as a buffer around the crater, preventing any form of development. In 1997, he also persuaded Coconino County authorities to pass a "dark sky ordinance," which eliminates unwanted brightness from upward-directed commercial and domestic lights within a thirty-five-mile radius of the site.

Age-old night sky traditions elsewhere too imbricate with the modern like Earth strata, revitalizing each other in the cross-fertilization of ideas. Dense with meaning, celestial bodies exert gravitational pull on young minds also. On one current trajectory, the Indigenous Education Institute in Bluff, Utah, developed teaching tools based on Navajo star lore. They include a book of comparative astronomy, a CD of star stories, and a poster of the Diné universe. The poster depicts the night sky as you would see it throughout the year from the Navajo Nation, with the thirteen primary constellations. The institute helped devise the Starlab, a portable planetarium, and arranged for John Herrington, the Chickasaw astronaut, to speak at reservation schools.

Imagine the setting, if you will. Next to a Hubble Telescope photo of the Horsehead Nebula—swirling close to Orion's hip—hangs a chart of that constellation. Beside it on the blackboard, the Navajo poster. Some bright, button-eyed fifth-grader will notice that Orion carries a bow, just like its cultural double, First Slender One. Perhaps she will even notice that the Greek hunter's three-star belt matches the guardian's low-slung quiver. Enthralled by the luminous galactic swirling, she might intuit that time does not arrow straight but wheels about, like a bullroarer on a string.

Some river runners are camped at Pipe Creek's pocket beach, their headlamps an enclave of dancing terrestrial lights. Wave caps phosphoresce against the obsidian current, while another segment of river resembles aluminum foil. Farther upstream, the lower bridge straddles the Colorado with gunmetal swagger.

Moonlit nights offer up exquisite grayscales as opposed to the days' richer palettes. I will discover only upon our return home that none of the photos I took turned out well. Despite the small tripod I brought, they're all underexposed, blurred and murky. I may have the artist's thirst, but my technical skills leave much to be desired.

A long time ago, a Kern River Paiute tale informs us, Coyote wanted to go to the sun. He asked Pokoh, Old Man, to show him the trail. Coyote went straight out on this trail, and he traveled it all day. But Sun went round so that Coyote came back at night to the place from which he started in the morning. We are like Coyote: forever chasing the light.

In his wager, the astrologer Faust (like his creator, the polymath-poet Goethe, a spirit forever wandering) pledged that he'd forfeit his soul if the Devil could lure him with any one earthly pleasure into standing still and imploring a fleeting moment to "Linger a while [verbatim: an "eye-gaze"]." One wonders if the Moab snake on a solstice day would have tempted him. At the end, with his life force flickering, Goethe may have called for "More light," but these final words are contested. The photographers clustering at the site, "writing with light" in the literal sense, *do* arrest that moment. They are kin of a sort to Turrell and the petroglyph makers and even yours truly, the onetime ethnographer. The words for all three persuasions have their roots in proto-Indo-European *gerbh-, "to scratch" or "to carve." All three sculpt reality with varying means.

The art of photography sprang from our quest to understand the gears that keep shifting the universe: the science of astronomy. It's yesterday's news that a camera functions much like the human eye, or that of a lion. But who knew that the mathematician and astronomer Johannes Kepler employed a primitive one in 1604, in the form of a tent? The German and his fellow stargazers called it *camera obscura*—the "darkened chamber." The process is simple: light from an outdoors scene passes through a single pinhole, striking a surface inside a dark box, and reproduces itself there, upside-down and smaller but with color and perspective intact. Turrell's moon replication on the stone stele operates that way. The smaller the pinhole, the sharper the image, though it dims as the amount of light is reduced. Ground-glass lenses, comparable to the Plateau's dry air, elevation, and remoteness from urban light pollution, later sharpened such pictures while admitting additional photons. Mirrors, added in still later models, flipped the likenesses right side up. The light, alas, never lasted. Until centuries later, when treated glass plates and silver chloride-coated paper trapped its fickleness on a plane.

Simple applications of the principle already were known two thousand years before Kepler's time. The Chinese philosopher Master Mo and his disciples deduced from them that light travels in straight lines, which we moderns consider obvious. About the same time, Aristotle is said to have watched a partly eclipsed sun by looking at the ground, where gaps between the leaves of a tree painted the crescent. He reproduced the effect with wickerwork and even with interlaced hands. But the great Leonardo da Vinci perhaps was the first to use a pinhole camera for artistic endeavors, retracing on paper the shrunk projection for a facsimile after nature.

Sweaty zombies, we reach the campground long after midnight and don't even set up our tarp, as all cloud shreds have melted away. The creek is too warm to chill our two beer cans, which we enjoy regardless.

The next day, having aborted a trip to Ribbon Falls, halfway up the North Kaibab Trail, we laze under tamarisks on the boat beach and sip iced lemonade sold at the swamp-cooled Phantom Ranch lodge. The heat weighs on us, oppressive, a smothering phantom itself. Thermometers read 109 in the shade and 145 near baking stonewalls. Cicadas *chirrrp* deafeningly, in salvos, or it may be the blood in our ears. Some hikers cross the bridge, bound for the rim, where it should be balmy, in the 80s, when they arrive, *if* they arrive. We shake our heads in disbelief. I silently wish them Godspeed, hoping I won't read about them later.

We set our alarm to 4 a.m. the day we leave. When I awake, other campers already are packing, with faces rouged by their headlamps' red cast. Anybody with any sense gets an "alpine start" this time of year. Strings of lights bob toward the river long before dawn, like glowworm processions or rope teams on summit day. Despite the South Kaibab's barrenness and the need for a shuttle ride back to our car, we choose this way out. It's much shorter, and the ridge route promises refreshing breezes.

Astrophysicists have noted that we, and our entire world, are made of stardust, not just of the same chemical elements but, in fact, of recycled debris from exploded stars. In an effort to share the skies and perhaps to remind us of this inheritance, the Astronomical Society of the Pacific (ASP) links astronomers with local educators and students. Its NASA-funded outreach program brings cutting-edge science to Hopi and Navajo youths. On their visits to reservation schools, ASP members provide teacher training, supply educational materials and help conduct experiments or demonstrations. Hands-on activities and group projects like building a comet from paper—complete with tail and a cotton ball nucleus—account for differences in culture and learning styles. Elders often visit the classroom, telling traditional stories about "that which is placed in the sky" (the Diné phrase for astronomy). Parents, family, and community members also participate in nighttime star parties, sometimes hosted by the Lowell Observatory on Anderson Mesa, far enough from Flagstaff's competing sparkle. Especially when elders are present, taboos are a great concern. Navajos only can tell traditional stories between first frost and first thunder, but modern star parties are acceptable anytime. There are taboos against looking at the moon and other astronomical objects. One should never observe an eclipse, especially if the viewer is pregnant. Never speak ill of, or curse, clouds or the moon. With advance warning, however, numinous payback can be blunted or avoided by rituals before a star party.

In the powder-blue dawn, we switch off our headlamps and steel ourselves for heat's onslaught. By the time we top out on the laminate sandstone of the Tapeats, sunlight caresses the South Rim with rosy fingers. It falls on us at the foot of the Redwall's forty switchbacks, its fingers curled all too soon into a merciless iron fist.

Custodian of the Past

AT EIGHTY-TWO, BRANTLEY BAIRD is one of the nation's oldest ranching vaqueros, though he swapped daylong horseback rides for driving after one hammerhead recently bucked him off. "When you get to be my age, you don't bounce so easy," he says. "I now throw my saddle in the back of that Honda—I'm a drugstore cowboy." The lanky gent in the paint-spattered, dusty Stetson and camouflage vest, however, is anything but a phony. He's roamed the five-thousand-acre Rock Art Ranch near Winslow since 1945, when his parents leased it. Three years later, at the age of eleven, he found his first ancient pot on that range, the one prominent in a photo in the ranch's museum, tall as his knees, black-and-white, with complex geometric designs.

My wife and I meet Baird there, at his operation's headquarters, after making our reservation by phone the day before. For almost twenty years, the grizzled stockman with the lithe, rolling gait of someone much younger, someone who's spent twelve presidencies in the saddle, has been showing visitors his property, an open-air museum of pioneer history and prime glypher destination. Stylish wire-rim glasses braced by a bulbous nose add a scholarly note to Baird's demeanor. While he's waiting for more sightseers, we explore the premises. A steel-framed barn, crammed and eclectic in the way of Renaissance cabinets of curiosity, shields from decay relics of a livelihood wrested from Painted Desert sand: a stuffed elk; a spread-eagling, tub-size tom turkey; a badger baring its teeth, perched on a shopping cart; a straight razor collection on pink velvet; a sampler of classic barbed-wire types on a Texas-shaped board; arcane ranching implements; a squad's arsenal of rusty guns; folksy sayings and cowpoke cartoons; Brantley's portrait, flanked by rowel spurs, encircled by a lariat. Under the same battered hat, he looks younger and his weathered face fuller. He's become a celebrity lately, though he'd chuckle at that designation. *National Geographic* has visited, and the *New York Times*. He hosts NASA cookouts and Arizona Game and Fish meetings, and last week hired a mariachi band to entertain "old fogies" from the region's rest homes here. The ranch also offers horseback outings, retracing the Mormon Honeymoon Trail and other pioneer roads. One of Baird's four "kids," or twelve grandkids these days, leads cavalcades, yet in bigger decisions all defer to their elder, the Wrangler-clad lord of this estate.

The barn's heart, "the pot room," is a dimly lit cave overflowing with artifacts unearthed on the ranch, objects that would make college museums proud. Fanned-out, mounted arrowheads, spear points, and atlatl or throwing-dart tips crowd around massive Clovis lance heads that Paleo-Indian mammoth and bison hunters deftly flaked, and then lost, in this leonine scrubland, 4,500 years before Spaniards invaded it. Shelves and glass cases hold gray urn-size vessels, smooth or "corrugated," made by coiling clay. Zebra-colored mugs, pitchers, and water ladles, with zigzag, stair-step, and circle outlines filled in by hairline hachure, in Baird's words, are Anasazi "tea cups, coffee pots, ice-cream scoops." I wonder if they drank corn beer from steins.

"No two designs are alike," Baird insists. Youngsters in tow, Hopi tribal council members from the mesas to the north drop by each year to study their clans' roots and décor, almost unchanged since Europe's crusades.

More guests have trickled in, and the pot room only accommodates ten at a time. One of Baird's granddaughters corrals half the group in the barn while the patriarch has the rest riveted. A shorthaired border collie, constantly underfoot, has replaced Brandy, a longtime spaniel-poodle companion that died the year his wife did. Brantley points out several ollas formerly buried with a day's march in-between, big-bellied greyware serving as water caches along routes through roughshod country. Interment prevented breakage and evaporation and kept contents cool. The Anasazi sealed each with a flagstone, leaving a ladle on top to assist thirsty travelers. The cowboy, as a rule mounted, fifteen hundred years later spotted the lifesavers that winds or rare rains exposed in the dunes and arroyos that line his family's spread— sprung from damp soil, under the sun, these containers easily cracked. Others, girded with sinew or yucca fiber, could be hung from junipers, safeguarding emergency rations of wild seed or corn from tunneling rodents. "We only get the four-legged rats," Baird elaborates. He had made a quip about lawyers earlier, chin pointing at a straw dummy.

Outside, there is plenty more to see: A covered chuck wagon with kitchen utensils—a butter churn, Dutch oven, washbasin, pails—the wheeled equivalent of an Anasazi camp. Cross-sections of petrified wood picket groomed paths to the ranch's attractions. Planted in the center of one agatized rainbow slab, a hedgehog cactus provides the perfect metaphor for the homestead endeavor. The rickety, furnished bunkhouse from 1900, hauled here from the banks of the Little Colorado River, once belonged to the Joseph City headquarters of the Aztec Land & Cattle Company. It is that cattle empire's last standing building. From 1884 to 1901, the famous, some would say notorious, Hashknife Outfit managed two million unfenced acres, grazing sixty thousand head on a ninety-by-forty-mile strip between Holbrook and Flagstaff. It was the biggest such enterprise in Arizona, North America's third largest. A hash knife, I'm told, was not a specialized tool but rather a run-of-the mill blade trail cooks used for chopping spuds. The Bairds' own hot-iron glyph augments the *H* brand on a matted steer hide draped over a fence. Inside the Hashknife hands' domicile, a two-level bunk with rope webbing instead of mattress springs illuminates the adage "Sleep tight..." Wedges outside the bedframe allowed for tautening the ropes when they were sagging. Sound sleep after twelve hours on horseback was never a given but rather a luxury. As an ex–trail guide, I remember this well. Even my back end, now accustomed to cushy, kitchen-box raft benches, does.

Playing follow the leader in our cars, all twenty of us caravan to the next of Baird's dirt-road destinations. He fenced the site in, barring his cloven-hoofed beauties from trampling it. While he waits for human stragglers, our guide ticks off distant landmarks, vaguely waving at each with a sinewy, age-spotted hand. Lightning once torched a juniper in the vicinity with him within spitting distance, belying the truth he had learned as a child that trees promise safety besides shade. His phone jingles frequently, a florid tune, not the expected country bit. Callers make reservations or ask again for directions, having lost their way after exiting Interstate 40. To us, Baird summarizes the current drought, which browned many trees. "We only had one two-inch rain this summer"—he pauses for the punch line—"with drops two inches apart." Cattle had to be fed expensive hay, as so often before. Baird used to own thirty "buffaloes" but sold them, though not for a lack of native forage. The bison simply were too pesky, knocking down fences, goring and killing a cow, hooking and flipping ranch vehicles.

Baird unlocks the gate, and we troop up a roped-off path. *Please don't pick up potsherds*, a sign says. "There's not much else to do for fun on a ranch," he remarks, overly modest about his passion for poking around. Fragments of many tones and sizes litter the plot like shattered skulls, mixed with chipped flint—bowl rims, pots' bottoms, mug handles.... The treasure suggests some archaic rite, like Polterabend, the German pre-nuptial smashing of china for good luck (sublimating future domestic strife?), or a Fallstaffian banquet. It's in fact the debris of daily existence, flawed crockery dumped on the trash heap together with ashes, animal bones, cornhusks, and on occasion, eggshells or turkey dung. Early Puebloans pushed from their homelands by famine or war stored household goods they hoped to retrieve in better times. Most never returned. Erosion of their pits caused much damage. Looting, which can account for such wreckage, never affected this ridge, thanks to Baird acting as caretaker.

A sheet metal shed roofs a three-room pueblito from circa 1500 CE. Excavated by Northern Arizona University archaeologists, the knee-high stacked-stone foundations mark the home of several families, owners of the puzzle-piece pots outside. Bones of a two- to three-year-old girl, a relative perhaps, surfaced in nearby Bell Cow Canyon. The researchers reburied them after examination, and volunteers poured a concrete gravestone.

"Ky-otes," according to Baird, dig up human remains; calcium-starved livestock then chews on those.

Back in our trucks, after a peek at an Anasazi map carved into a wash's bedrock, we bump-jostle to the next stop on Baird's curatorial merry-go-round. That's Irene Esky's former camp, upgraded into a heritage park. Before the Hashknife broke up and was sold by the parcel, this malpais sustained other lives, if barely. Prior to 1876, Hopis and Navajos grazed sheep here; a Basque successor did the same. Of the fenced-in structures only the Hopi natural-stone house and parts of the woman's rotund, mud and beam-roofed hogan are original. The stonewall sheep pen, a shade ramada of cut branches, a men's hogan—a juniper-scented combination of adobe tipi and log chapel-workshop for post-puberty males—and a sweat lodge with fire pit ringed by basalt chunks carted in from Flagstaff were built to Irene's specifications. Her family maintains these dwellings, blessing and re-mudding them every year. We do not meet the Navajo matriarch, who at 112 busily weaves rugs somewhere near the Hopi mesas; but, judging from a bleached picture in Baird's museum, in her long purple skirt and traditional blouse she's his formidable counterpart.

Baird an hour ago shed his hunting vest in the heat and is sitting this one out. His granddaughter instead does the requisite interpretation. "Are you folks tired?" he now asks through our truck's rolled-down window. Suffering sightseeing burnout, my wife and I have returned while the rest keep milling about.

"Just eager for the big stuff," I reply unmindfully, referring to this petroglyph obsession of mine. That seems to hurt our host. "It's all big stuff," he says, as if my focus questioned his dusty decades, his Latter-Day-Saintly inheritance.

At long last, we park at the lip of Chevelon Canyon, a Coconino Sandstone gash cleaving this brittle expanse. Sixty-foot walls with bluish-black patina bracket the willow-lined creek, stretched out as a canvas for one of the Southwest's most thrilling alfresco "art" galleries. For its creators, a permanent spring five miles upstream multiplied the cliff bay's appeal. Before their survey, anthropologists budgeted roughly five months to find and document every petroglyph panel there. It took eight years instead. More than three thousand glyphs pecked with hammer stones into mineral patina span a period of six thousand years. Clustering most densely along a quarter-mile bend of Chevelon Creek called "The Steps," they represent different cultures: Archaic, Anasazi, Navajo, and Puebloan—Hopi and Zuni. Unsurprisingly, Baird's Chevelon Steps is listed in the National Register of Historic Places.

Baird considers this natural breach, the sole access within miles, "a place the Good Lord made for these people to get down into the canyon." Making it easier yet for modern, less nimble visitors, Baird constructed metal stairs and railings to the bottom, a footbridge across the creek, and, jutting from the rim, a roofed viewing platform with picnic tables. A sign at the gate warns that you enter at your own risk. "We haven't lost too danged many," the site's steward assures the timid. Still, a rattler buzzing my wife at the parking lot reminds us to pay attention.

The granddaughter introduces the rock art below from the observation deck but does not escort us downstairs. We're told to take as much time as we want and of a shortcut to drive back out when we're done.

Sand trails probing thick vegetation end at panels named Holding Hands, Cinderella, or The Birthing Scene. Inspecting their details, I climb ledges on which lean engravers worked up good sweats. I ford the creek, waist-deep here, because of beaver activity, to reach my favorite panel. On this rockslide a rake with wavy tines, thought to be a rain symbol, scores lustrous varnish next to an antlered, triangular guy, and meanders and mazes that still grace Navajo rugs, Hopi pottery, and rubber-treaded hiking sandals. Elsewhere, six-foot darts signpost a vertical crack, a forbidding exit. Deer and bighorn sheep, a few superimposed on older marks, mingle with bipeds ranging from stick figures to patterned bodies sporting antennae. There are enough strange-looking morphs here to give any sci-fi fan fainting spells.

What do they signify? What is the message I cannot decode, while, equally unintelligibly, birds chirp in the mesquite and the creek gurgles at my back? The shamanic scrawls invoke essentials—fertility, exodus, death, epic hunts, shape shifting, and the magic of water. Perhaps these seers, kin to tipsy, nectar-siphoning sphinx moths, primed for the sacred by ingesting hallucinogenic datura. "Archaeologists don't know what these symbols mean," Baird has said. "They're trying to figure it out, same as us." He gleans the best insights not from the Heard Museum or Smithsonian Institution but from Native Americans who tour the ranch.

Their forebears filed into this cleft, migrating, trading, or raiding. Seasoned desert dwellers, they preferred its shade to sun-struck grasslands bristling with cacti and enemy spears. Chevelon Canyon, whose name commemorates a nineteenth-century French trapper killed by poisonous "parsnips" (probably hemlock), linked the White Mountains' Grasshopper Pueblo and Mogollon Rim headwaters with the Little Colorado River's Homol'ovi settlements, a gaggle of Hopi ancestral sites close to Winslow. The third largest of those, Tsakwavayu, or "Blue Running Water," boasted five hundred rooms and was renamed "Chevelon Ruin," for its proximity to this creek. The four-story pueblo was one node in networks that encompassed Flagstaff's Sinagua, "Without Water" people, merchants of obsidian, an inky, volcanic glass for tools and arrowheads that still cut like scalpels. The web expands even farther. Little Colorado River Puebloans reworked a Pleistocene hunter's spear point, which later surfaced again, eleven millennia after first being honed, near Chevelon Ruin.

The canyon in its entirety today is seldom traveled. A two-hundred-acre, ponderosa-rimmed, ultramarine reservoir in the Apache–Sitgreaves National Forest, "Arizona's most scenic trout-lake"—filled by damming the creek—presently feeds the gorge. Few kayakers dare facing class IV rapids, shooting past three-hundred-foot ramparts at monsoon levels. Wall-to-wall flows in the slot's lower reaches prevent scouting those bucking-bronc runs.

The ranch's future as a tourist mecca hung in the balance when Baird fell gravely ill after his wife and dog died. Worried about liability, his sons were loath to continue allowing strangers in. Luckily, the old-timer got right back into the saddle, or rather, his truck seat.

Once he is gone, who will parse the local past with such quirkiness, such gusto and depth? Who will connect his era to the present? "It's important to let people know how special this place is, and how rich in history," he's said in an interview. And, "My grandkids ask if we had running water and I'd tell them yes. We'd take the bucket and run to the well.... Nowadays, it's a completely different world, completely."

Solitude

FITNESS IS AN EDGE all too easily blunted. Despite car camping and excursions throughout the winter, Melissa and I are ill-prepared for our first backpacking jaunt every spring. Like rookies forgetting to bring sunscreen and lip balm, we get blitzed. We learn anew how many ibuprofen or "vitamin I" pills maintain our knees and hips. Each passing decade requires upping the dose. Yet, I *must be still and still moving / Into another intensity*, in T.S. Eliot's phrasing. *Old men ought to be explorers / Here or there does not matter,* he believed. Shoulders and lower backs become chafed on such vernal outings, heels and toes blistered, thigh muscles sore, and egos bruised. As an acquaintance, the writer Scott Thybony, says, "Muscle memory may be real, but it's short term."

An April trek to the Grand Canyon's Cape Solitude suits us for reasons other than relearning backpacking routines. Arid and largely shadeless, the route drops and ascends moderately—an old jeep track, which fades now and then or contracts to a footpath. It's about thirty miles round-trip, a taxing all-day venture. However, you'd miss glorious dusk and dawn, the low-raking sun at the point, and solitude best enjoyed after sightseeing flights stop in the evening. So we've decided to spend the night there.

Like our bodies, our navigation skills have grown a bit rusty. In Melissa's truck we orbit between the park's Desert View entrance, the campground, and the gas station, looking for the dirt road to Cedar Mountain. Ignoring the *DO NOT ENTER – RESIDENTS ONLY* sign at the ranger compound, we finally score.

Solitude starts where the pavement ends, in this case on marvelously eroded switchbacks that drop 600 feet and tease with glimpses of the Great Abyss. Nothing deters Sunday strollers more than a couple of rutted miles to a trailhead. Scenic pullouts along the nearby South Rim drive boast toilets and picnic tables, as well as the under-the-rim buzz hikers feel on inner-canyon trails, but not here. It partly explains why so few visit Solitude. On this whole hike, we don't find any trash besides one crinkled Mylar balloon skin, a ubiquitous nuisance, snagged on some sagebrush.

We park under piñons at the top of the hairpin turns. The truck could get us to the trailhead at Cedar Mountain—a perfectly symmetrical red-sandstone-and-shale flattop, an altar of giants—but walking the three miles is just as fast. Besides, we love finishing with a climb, truly earning that frosted brew afterward.

In the off-season, even our sweat glands cease to function. Now we perspire freely beneath our loads, which include five quarts of water each, the minimum for dry camping at the cape.

Around Cedar Mountain, the road exits the forest, straddling blond, grassy ridges, probing bony arroyos, the Navajos' "Graylands." The Little Colorado weaves across dun plains, bottom concealed, joining its burlier sibling at our headland destination.

Together with the Rio Grande and San Juan River, the Colorado (female) and Little Colorado (male) gird the Navajo homeland Dinétah as sacred boundaries. Holy Beings dwell in these waterways, and travelers crossing into foreign, dangerous territory—lands of the white men, Pueblos, Spaniards, or Núuchi-u (Utes)—sprinkled corn pollen and recited prayers for protection on their journey. Compare this to the stance of Dominguez and Escalante, who, having tried to ford the Colorado at three places over thirteen hard days, named their camp, at what later became Lees Ferry, *Salsipuedes*: "Get out if you can." Upon succeeding, they fired off muskets "as a sign of the great joy which all felt at having vanquished a difficulty so great." I daresay that most drivers reenacting the feat with a press on the gas pedal, hurdling the river on the only highway crossing between Page and Hoover Dam, Marble Canyon's Navajo Bridge, don't give it a thought.

We no longer see Desert View Watchtower, Mary Colter's neo-Puebloan exclamation mark on the South Rim, or Flagstaff's snow-tipped Humphreys Peak peeping over a cloudless horizon. Deep in the topography's folds, it's difficult to envision the sudden precipice one upslope mile to the west, Palisades of the Desert, the eastern rim's coves and prows that plunge twice the Empire State Building's height to the Colorado River and reminded the mapmaker-geologist François Matthes of timbered defensive walls. "Be careful whom you ask to point the place out to you," Mary Austin complained in *Land of Journey's Ending*, "lest you be answered by one of the silly names cut out of a mythological dictionary and shaken in a hat before they were applied to the Grand Cañon for the benefit of that amazing number of Americans who can never see anything unless it is supposed to look like something else." There's Gunther Castle, Siegfried Pyre, and Freya Castle, Wagner fans will rejoice to hear. Rama, Krishna, Vishnu, and Zoroaster set up shop. Temples were dedicated to Sheba, Solomon, Venus, Apollo, Jupiter, Juno, and the Egyptian pantheon, more shrines than crowned Rome's Capitoline Hill or Jerusalem's Temple Mount. (Secular saints of evolution—Huxley, Wallace, and Darwin—warranted only a terrace, a butte, and a plateau.) A park map or roster of name donors makes even the canyon's boondocks seem crowded. Countless toponyms by the peoples who truly worshiped this stone went unrecorded, or their meaning was lost. Like the obsolete regional terms for topographic features Barry Lopez and his wife Debra Gwartney gathered in *Home Ground*—bosque, break, comb ridge, box canyon, and rincon, to list but a few Southwestern examples—Colorado Plateau Native coinages suggest "the vastness and mystery that lie beyond our everyday words." Linguistic time capsules, they condense the spirit of locales steeped in longstanding knowledge and lore.

Near Comanche Point, a cone-shaped hogan bakes in sage flats, its logs polished by age. Beyond hills sprawls the Painted Desert, an open book of gullies and rainbow mounds legible to those versed in Earth's history. Branching cholla cacti, the odd juniper, and tall agave stalks signpost the route. Dark brown, furry caterpillars pursue arcane business while black olive pits on legs—darkling beetles—perform headstands. After the drab months, splashes of brilliance buoy the soul: electric-red Indian paintbrush and tiny fuchsia stork's-bill stars thriving in sand, yellow-blossomed pincushions wedged into crevices.

Ignore not the minuscule miraculous for the grand view, the track for the portent, the sign for the pattern. The aforementioned beetle, one of the most commonly encountered desert insects, is conspicuous throughout the Southwest. Twenty-seven species enliven the Grand Canyon's soils. After hatching, the larvae burrow into the dirt, where, like Egyptian scarabs, they transform into beetles and surface as if resurrected. Some roll over on their backs, feigning death, when disturbed; others live for ten years. Even when they hide under rocks, logs, or in detritus, or, buried in sand, escape the noon heat, you can spot their zipper spoors on dunes or in alcove dust. One of the great walkers of the beetle world, this seasonally nocturnal, flightless migrant seems to wander at random, finding food—fungi, decaying plants, animal dung—by its odor. It hustles about with its head to the ground like a black Lab on a scent. Its hard wing covers are fused together, which reduces evaporation, and it metabolizes all needed water from its diet. A few kinds, when they're approached, can spray noxious fluid from the tip of their abdomen while doing their acrobatic "headstand"; hence their other popular names: "stinkbug" and "skunk beetle." Undeterred by defensive posturing, grasshopper mice pin darkling beetle rear ends against the ground and eat the more palatable front parts.

Popular Anglo attitudes toward this amazing critter have found expression in Clint Eastwood's movies, where gunslingers crush them under boot heels or douse them in well-aimed spurts of chewing tobacco juice. The Latin designation of the family (*Tenebrionidae*) suggests shadows and darkness—things obscure, secretive, underhanded. According to some Hopi elders, bad people, likely including the desperado spitters, are reborn as darkling beetles. An anthropologist with the tribe considered beetles that had fallen into the pit of an old kiva "the perfect picture of lost souls as they lumber about, futilely looking for a way out."

We lose our way where the curves skip through a gate in a fence onto Navajo land, failing to pick up faint parallel ruts on the adjacent hill. Suckered down a drainage instead, following the path of least resistance, we reap unexpected rewards. A pictograph by a cowboy's shallow-alcove camp smolders orange, crisp, as if drawn decades, not centuries ago. An even-sided cross, twice outlined and taken to represent our sister planet Venus, brightens the shelter's ceiling. Zunis and related Pueblo dwellers link single and double spirals like those finger-painted on the wall with water, emergence and quests in search of the Center. Watched over by celestial bodies personified, the ancient ones, migrating as clans, working the fields in family groups and appeasing the spirits communally, may not have known solitude even outdoors at night.

Following the fence, we reenter the park, and the double-track soon doglegs toward the rim. The route's crowning mile skirts the abrasive-limestone lip, some twenty skydiving seconds above the Beamer Trail and the Hopi salt mines. Their sacred deposits—a crumbly crust—mark the place where Changing Woman, traveling west from the Echo Cliffs, met Salt Woman, who rose there to the earth's surface. Everywhere you step in this country, this so-called "wilderness," it seems, you step on a half-buried story or memory. "Landscape is a work of the mind," the historian Simon Schama reminds us. "Its scenery is built up as much from strata of memory as from layers of rock."

Solitude you may find here, yet in a time when all things were animated, it was impossible.

Standing on the brink of Cape Solitude is like sitting in a fire lookout: things to weigh up unfold below, screened only by hazy, pulsing space. Crucially, however, your feet touch the ground, connected to the sights, unlike the disembodied in a plane.

The cape's fauna greets us with exuberance. White-throated swifts chitter and dive-bomb, scythe-wings swishing, slicing air. Their Latin name, "Rock Aeronauts," perfectly sums up their cliff-bound existence. Sailing by overhead, a peregrine and later a turkey vulture survey the void. Two ravens tail a third that clamps a corpse limp in its bill. Chipmunk? Lizard? I cannot tell as the hounded one is speeding by. The gang wheels about vertical bays in a dogfight—cawing, clucking Mustangs and Messerschmitts. Who needs skywalks or cable tramways? Mentally trading places with the rascals thrills me as much as the out-of-body levitation practiced in dreams.

Before the light leaves, I peer down from the peninsula on submerged golden sand bars, on the blending of liquid, bottle-glass green and milky-turquoise—the latter a tone unlike any other on the Plateau. Excepting Havasu Creek, ninety-five miles to the west. A ranger I know described that as of "a color you'd only find inside the glass of a Las Vegas cocktail or as a gummy worm candy." Half a dozen rafts bob downstream, colored beads threading to camp at Carbon, Lava or Tanner beach. Pea-green, freshly leafed cottonwoods in upper Lava Creek catch my eye, or it could be the rill glinting there.

Sulfates, magnesium, and tiny reflective crystals of broken-down calcium carbonate, the stuff that forms corals and seashells, give the Little Colorado its surreal color. Its main, perennial source, Blue Spring, surfaces thirteen miles from the confluence. There, a transparent eye with still only an aqua paleness and the volume of 50,000 showerheads wells up from the ground. Three-fourths of the stream's flow, fed by over one hundred springs, stems from the San Francisco Peaks volcanic field and the rest from a 20,000-year-old, or older, aquifer on the reservation. A Blue Spring dive in 2020 hinted at a "vast subterranean world" behind its entrance. The expedition caver Adam Haydock believes Blue Spring could be part of one of the country's longest submerged systems. Grappling scalloped walls studded with chert nodules—material otherwise flaked into arrowheads—he inched forward against the gin-clear current tugging at his mask, into which water quickly seeped. Whenever he strayed into the central jet, it spit him out into the gateway's gravel bowl in "a fast and fierce tumble." One hundred and twenty feet in, played out, with the cave continually widening, he called it a day.

The Coyoteway stories of Chinle, a community at the mouth of Canyon de Chelly, say that Holy People, a Diné version of the katsinas, have a home at Blue Spring. One wonders what they and Navajo tradition-bearers might say when the next crack scubanaut enraptured with this "boiling resurgence," ready to "penetrate" the unknown, knocks on their door. *Hataałii* "singers" still fill flasks for curing rites at Tó dootł'izh, "Turquoise Water." A herder lost some cows there to a flash flood that scoured the narrows.

It's precarious country, demanding respect in more than one way. Of three difficult routes into the gorge, the easiest ends near Blue Spring and starts on the West Rim northeast of Cedar Mountain and Desert View. That "trail" (it deserves the scare quotes), a vertical leap of faith with "significant exposure and unforgiving route-finding," and a rope needed for lowering packs, and pink rattlers basking on ledges less than a foot wide, makes even bighorn sheep dizzy. Quicksand gums up stretches of the canyon. Water above Blue Spring is scarce when ephemeral Grand Falls lies silent. The well-known Flagstaff photographer and maverick George Mancuso, cut from the same dark cloth as the Kolbs, died with his modeling friend Linda Brehmer in a branch vis-à-vis Blue Spring. The canyon had been his life's "single-most important love affair." August monsoons had unleashed a lethal tide that swept it.

The rim can be equally dangerous. In 2007, a German physicist went missing at Hellhole Bend, near the Cameron trading post and highway bridge; despite an extensive search, he was never found. The entrenched loop where he disappeared may have been named for the sinkholes in the area's porous Kaibab Limestone.

We hear soughing, like wind in pines, at Cape Solitude's lip, the impatience of water with river boulders. The junction is sacred to Zunis and Hopis, to the Havasupai and the Navajos, even to a *bilagáana* such as myself. The Hopis' ancestral clans that created the pictographs we saw earlier shimmied up a reed to this present world. Angered gods had destroyed a previous one. The survivors exited through the Sipapu, a whale-size domed mineral spring four miles from here. The Y where the two canyons met spelled the final leg of a salt pilgrimage their descendants often undertook. During that rite of passage for boys, men gathered healing stalactites that the Tapeats Sandstone—cemented beaches of a Cambrian sea—extrudes at the river level. In this sere quarter, the Little Colorado, let alone the main stream, channeled more water than a Hopi raised on the mesas would encounter in a lifetime. Considering that two gallons a day will keep you from dying, here was life eternal for entire clans. A man who had journeyed there as a boy recalled that pilgrims, upon arrival, sipped of the brine and left prayer feathers on the riverbank. Pisisvayu, the Colorado, "River of Echoing Sounds," flowed through stories of emergences and migrations. The Rattlesnake Clan still keeps stories about Tiyo, a youth who, wondering where all that liquid bounty went, embarked on a journey in a hollowed-out cottonwood trunk with both ends sealed with pine pitch. In the words of the anthropologist Jesse Walter Fewkes, a Powell contemporary, Tiyo "floated over smooth waters and swift-rushing torrents, plunged down cataracts, and for many days spun through wild whirlpools where black rocks protruded their heads like angry bears," to the "Great Water" (the Gulf of California) and the "place beyond the horizon" of myths. Diné myths feature a similar character, "The Dreamer"—like Tiyo, an archetype of daredevil, starry-eyed river runners of today. If either were to try his descent today, he would end up dragging his dugout canoe across cracked mudflats in Mexico where a parched land absorbs the last trickle, the river's final, agonized breath.

At this point in time, we lack physical evidence of pre-Columbian river running anywhere on the Plateau. No paddles or pieces of hull have been unearthed, and rock art that might show watercraft is ambiguous. People must have had ways—floatation devices like wood rafts or inflated deerskins—to wet-commute when traveling on trans-canyon trails in the high-water season. Nagged by this blind spot and the emphasis on Powell and his Anglo successors, the amateur river historian and guidebook author Tom Martin built a raft made from tules. Like the Pipa Aha Macav, or "People by the River," whom we know as the Mohaves, other lower-Colorado and California tribes used the buoyant reed for millennia. They braided or wove this relative of papyrus into baskets, nets, mats, skirts, cordage, baby cradles, water bottles, bowstrings, sandals, shelters, and boats. This wetlands plant was a pre-Columbian plastic but a renewable resource if the roots were left intact. Martin and his wife cut (with permission) and sun-dried ten-foot rushes, which they then bundled and lashed together as Lake Titicaca fishermen do. They christened their canyon Kon-Tiki *Lotsaknots*. After flipping in the Paria Riffle, a kayaking-novice friend straddling the brush-bowed sit-on-top with a Walmart paddle propelled it for thirty wintry days through the gorge, though he swam a lot, too. The ranger at Lees Ferry had let him launch after a quick demo of the craft's river-worthiness near the ramp. To Martin and the test pilot's surprise, *Lotsaknots*, the Little Broom Boat That Could, not only swept through all rapids without coming apart but also kept up with the flotilla on flatwater stretches during twenty-mile days. They propped her upright each night to let the reeds drain and dry. Martin worried that beavers might consider her dinner. He'd given her "odds to Soap Creek, just 11 miles downstream and assumed it wouldn't be long before *Lotsaknots* would be draped over the back of one of the big rafts, next to one of the kayaks. That never happened." For the paddler, the Colorado tree-ring researcher and novice kayaker Peter Brown, it had been a very wet, "intimate" ride.

So, indigenous boatmen and -women had the means; they had the artisanal skill, the gumption—we know from the placement of some rock art and granaries—and, by living with the river daily, the knowledge, motive (see Tiyo), and opportunities. Modern embodiments nowadays ply these waters: Diné and Hwal'bay (Hualapai, "People of the Tall Pines") guides.

I next scan the plateau of the Little Colorado River Gorge opposite the dirt patch where we've pitched our tent. In 2009, an Arizona developer promoted a resort that would perch on the caprock upstream, an amphitheater below the rim and a gondola lift and boardwalk to the confluence. Up to 10,000 visitors per day, the capacity of two large cruise ships, would shuttle to the holy place. Environmentalists feared that the resort's groundwater pumping and sewage would threaten Blue Spring and the humpback chub, an already endangered fish species at the confluence. Sounder minds prevailed, swayed perhaps by aquatic spirits. Activists and traditional Navajos fought this "Escalade" project, and it was shelved. The name said it all. An Escalade, also a brand of Cadillac luxury SUV, was the scaling of a town or fortress's walls with siege ladders—think Battle of Helm's Deep. "The old world will burn with the fires of industry," Christopher Lee's Saruman intoned in *The Two Towers,* in anticipation of modern times.

The developer-orcs based in Scottsdale, Arizona, had argued the usual. Jobs for the locals. Quick, easy access to first-rate scenery for many, as opposed to its jealous safeguarding by an elitist minority—kayakers, hikers, and assorted wilderness nuts.

I'll stop rafting this river section if that atrocity is ever built. The defilement would be too painful to witness. It could happen if resolve on the reservation were to weaken.

A duo of different developers has been seeking permission for an atrocity upstream from the Sipapu that makes the Escalade look like child's play as far as environmental consequences go. In this Big Canyon Pumped Storage Project, four dams would contain reservoirs prone to evaporation, three situated on top, on the Painted Desert's Blue Moon Bench, and one that would flood the linked pools, falls, and narrows of the Little Colorado tributary for which the project is named. Billions of gallons sucked from the already dwindling aquifer that feeds Blue Spring would fill the reservoirs; a hydroelectric plant nearby would supply the Tucson and Phoenix grid, so that that sweltering masses can run their ACs and spoon their gelatos and comment on the latest fads online. The vivid branch might turn into the Rio Perdido—another "lost river." In lockstep with melting ice sheets, groundwater pilfering and eventual transfer to the oceans has shifted Earth's tilt and spin; more worrisome, it boosts sea level rises. In addition to desecrating cultural sites, the scheme would deprive local corn and watermelon fields as well as livestock and alter habitat for wild plants and animals, including the humpback chub's. Meanwhile, one in three of the reservation's Navajos, still living without running water, haul their supply on truck beds from distant wells to the hogans.

The area's Sleeping Beauty repose, as an irresistible challenge, irks princes of finance, those captains of capitalism who love to deliver their kiss of death. It's a colonial way of doing business, unchanged since the 49ers and fur trade: cajole, or just barge in. Take resources. Unmoor communities. Leave a mess. No matter if the loot is Malabar spices or Black Mesa coal, seafront property or uranium, the Navajos' "yellow dirt."

"If trouble comes when you least expect it, then maybe the thing to do is to always expect it," Cormac McCarthy wrote in his pre-COVID, post-apocalyptic novel.

John Wesley Powell in the Grand Canyon would have done well to heed this advice. On August 10, 1869, he and his crew huddled under a rock ledge by the river, with a view of this promontory, because the afternoon had been drizzly. They stayed two days to patch boats, dry out rations, and most importantly, fix their position. They craved decent drinking water, as cloudbursts had silted both rivers. Powell's head boatman, Jack Sumner, considered the Rio del Lino, or "Flax River," a name then seldom used, "as disgusting a stream as there is on the continent," estimating half its volume to be solids. To local cowhands, it was "Poison Canyon," not for the stream's alkaline tang but because one drop *off the rim* could kill you. Sumner thought the confluence "a miserably lonely place indeed, with no signs of life but lizards, bats, and scorpions," on a level with hell's first gates. Meanwhile, up on "Tree Grove Point," a cluster of junipers 3,400 feet above Bit'íís Ninéézi, the "River of Neverending Life," a Diné healer may have chanted Blessingway prayers for protection.

After ten weeks of travel, Powell's party—grumpy from lack of whiskey, sound footwear, and sleep, tired of weevils in the flour, grit in the coffee, and bacon green with mold, constantly haunted by weather, by carries that bruised ribs and ankles, by rumors that somewhere the Colorado dips underground, and harried, too, by gantlets of rapids (the major refusing to run several of these), and by comrades equally fractious, the men cooped up in boats together in the resounding depths—either had had enough of solitude or else not enough. "He is contented and seems to think that biscuit made of sour and musty flour and a few dried apples is enough to sustain a laboring man," Powell's assistant geologist-oarsman, George Bradley, griped. And that from a guy whom a fellow crewmember characterized as being "tough as a badger." (It was Bradley who'd belayed Powell with his drawers in Echo Park.) Yet little could darken their leader's mood. Forever intrigued by geography, John Wesley praised the Colorado Chiquito. He thought it "a marvelous river," a "broad but shallow torrent of mud." One wonders. How would he have gushed had he seen it in its turquoise mood? The next morning, his brother Walter grabbed a barometer and scaled the north side of the tributary gorge at its mouth, summiting near the site that generations later was earmarked for development. "We could see him as he reached the top. He looked like a mote in a sunbeam," Jack Sumner wrote in his journal, quite smitten for a mountain man–trading post owner.

In dusk's peach-blossom light, the swifts, unbothered by human affairs, make room for the insectivore graveyard shift: bats. The last chopper has landed at Tusayan. Quiet settles in, almost a physical thing. In the canyons, better yet on a rim, you notice that night does not fall but rather rises, a lavender mist welling up from the bottoms. The ribbon of silver below Nankoweap briefly duplicates Redwall cliffs before it gleams like blued steel and then dulls. Shadows mantle both arms, snuffing out distance and their arteries' glow. The Kolb brothers called this empty grandstand "Cape Desolation." What were they thinking?

We've waited to cook dinner until sundown. Venus, meanwhile, has risen, bright as a small moon. Satellites and furiously blinking jets transect the Milky Way's arced diamond dust. Flashes streak the Desert View neighborhood—did they remodel the watchtower into a lighthouse? Luminous smears on the skyline betray Grand Canyon Village, Flagstaff and Page. Clusters like an army's distant campfires or crashed constellations show that Tuba City and the Hopi mesas share our cities' megawatt blight. This coruscation might seem cozy to some people, an echo of home, hearths and TV screens. Curmudgeonly, I take the hermit's stance. Sardined in an airliner, I often imagine a lucky soul bedded down in darkness expanding below the plane's wings. I envy him, and the switch of perspective helps me endure endless flights. Kin to the Zen-recluse poet Ryokan, I don't dislike people. Rather, "it is just that I am so very tired of them." Solitude soars above the din of city days like this cape above thundering rapids.

Seeking the backcountry's balm, Edward Abbey recuperated from a year of book tours and speaking engagements at this roost. Weary, discouraged, "still smelling of nervous sweat," he tried to mend, to live sanely for a time. In his cryptic, often circular way, he left readers wondering about his chosen retreat. "Call it—Cape Solitude," he wrote. "I like the name. A fictitious name, of course, but the place is real. Or a real name for an impossible place." His description pretty closely matches the scenery my wife and I are taking in. He played his flute butt naked, because in this high lonesome he could do so without repercussions. A fellow desert scribe, the late Ellen Meloy of Bluff, Utah, believed that, "In solitude you strip yourself bare, you rest your mind on what is essential and true." (She meant nudity as a metaphor, surely.) "The mind is sharper and keener in seclusion and uninterrupted solitude," Nikola Tesla elaborated, with originality thriving "free of outside influences beating upon us..." Apart from society's trappings, we draw on inner resources or confront a lack of such. Mystics and dropouts discovered a flipside, alas. In prolonged solitude, we court annihilation. We defied short-faced bears and saber-toothed cats by roaming in bands. Language was the bonding agent. It binds us to each other, to the world of things, to ideas. Deprived of human company without the promise of relief, castaways become mutes or mutterers, solipsist, slobbering idiots.

Homebound the next morning, we cross paths with a Japanese hiker. Double-poled, fanny-packed, he zips past Cedar Mountain and us. Then, at the blasted switchbacks, we meet a rosy-cheeked, otherwise pallid couple. She leads a black Cerberus that eagerly eyes me; he piggybacks the millennials' cradleboard, a canopied baby carrier.

"You're not supposed to bring dogs into the park," I growl, short of breath.

"An employee told us it's okay if we keep him on a leash," she replies, hiding behind shady authority, perhaps a concessionaire.

Solitude starts where the pavement ends. Except where it no longer does.

No Walk in the Park

"YOU CANNOT SEE THE GRAND CANYON in one view, as if it were a changeless spectacle from which a curtain might be lifted," John Wesley Powell wrote in 1874 in *The Exploration of the Colorado River and Its Canyons*. To really see it, you instead "have to toil from month to month through its labyrinths. It's a region more difficult to traverse than the Alps or the Himalayas...."

Having finished a fifty-eight-day Arctic traverse the previous year, and glutton for beauty and punishment that I am, I lusted for more. I'm aware that this makes me sound hairy-chested or like a flagellant. My scourges would be ocotillo, the "Devil's Coachwhip," and catclaw, my hair shirt a quick-wick tee, my cross to bear a sixty-pound pack. A lengthwise Grand Canyon traverse on the north side, always below the rim, at a leisurely pace with layover days, should take only slightly less time than that tundra excursion. Food, fuel, and extra socks, stored in rodent-proof five-gallon plastic buckets we'd schlepp in and stash in alcoves and thickets beforehand, would make this feat possible, we hoped. The full distance is 575 to 750 miles, from Lees Ferry to Pearce Ferry, at Lake Mead, with the lower estimate being conservative. Colin Fletcher, a '60s guru for ambitious ambulators, walked about half that far before the park's extension, which incorporated the whole canyon. The Welshman trekked through deep time by moving upstream, from Hualapai Hilltop to the North Rim's Point Imperial, supplied by parachute airdrops, often holding on tight to "the thin and immediate present" and dogpaddling across, with his pack and beloved hiking staff, to a little green air mattress. There are, on this tortuous route that ties eons and weeks together into a seamless rug underfoot, "a lotta ins, a lotta outs, a lotta what-have-yous." It would be like tramping through England from end to end. That is, if England, unpopulated, lay near the equator, had wildlife and rains that could kill you, and terrain hacked up, denuded, and rumpled by giants. Only nine miles on the Clear Creek Trail near Phantom Ranch is maintained. Everything else, in the words of one long-distance junkie, is "cross-country, user trail, climber trail, sheep trail, deer trail, scrambling, scaling, crawling, creek walking, boulder hopping, ledge walking, tight-roping, cliff tip-toeing, chute sliding, and any other form of precarious foot travel."

A mere ten people had completed the thru-hike in a single push when we set out, far fewer than have dived to the deepest part of Earth's oceans, the floor of the Mariana Trench. Why, I wondered? A few days in, I no longer did.

I was on my third pair of boots, my second pair of shorts, and my air mattress was leaking—the canyon's abrasiveness had taken its toll. Ravens had hacked into my clear-plastic water bladder, thinking perhaps that its content was gin. I had busted a hiking pole and lost a lens from my sunglasses when a wind gust skittered them off a Redwall Limestone rock bench, stranding them three stories below. My hiking bud Andrew, a herpetologist built like a fire hydrant, swarthy of looks, choleric of temper, opinionated as myself, had climbed down a rock chimney to retrieve the now useless eyewear. At the same camp, a custard-colored scorpion scuttled from my ground cloth when I folded it up in the morning. I liked that Andrew cared about "herps" to the degree that he returned a baby bullsnake he'd cupped in his hands for us to admire to where he had picked it up, the environment with which it was familiar.

Somewhere on the high saddles route, Andrew's camera got yanked off when we lowered our packs with a rope. His bargain sombrero had frayed the first day, and he now wore a bandana headband-style. His shirt hung in tatters, reinforcing his Rambo appearance. The shirt was a precious memento. He'd worn it on trips with his wife, who fell to her death from these Redwall cliffs less than two years before. Our intended seventy-day thru-hike—largely off-trail, on the canyon's north side—in part sought to honor her, her short life, her zest for adventure, her dream of walking the length of this gorge.

Introduced by an acquaintance, Andrew and I had jointly hiked for four days the previous spring, to check our compatibility. We were both spellbound by long quests in this convoluted yet simple place, an obsession we shared with certain math teachers, photographers, backcountry rangers, geologists, and river rats. The canyon and the river that carved it have a way of consuming—or centering—lives. Normally, only faith calls forth such devotion.

Otis "Dock" Marston, a California boatman and amateur historian of the Colorado–Green River watershed, sleuthed for three decades—talking to people, tracking down documents and even abstruse leads, amassing enough to fill 420 boxes, fifty-four microfilm reels, and 189 photo folders—in an attempt to compile a chronicle of the first hundred river runners through the Grand Canyon. Caught up in the "splendid misery," as the naturalist David Petersen calls the packrat behavior of a writer's research, Marston never felt the manuscript was ready for publication. (It saw print posthumously.) The "Last Lone Ranger," John Riffey, passed up promotions and civilization's dubious offerings, settling in sixty-five miles from Fredonia and a thousand from the world's cares. For thirty-eight years, he manned the Toroweap post, near where we'd lay over on day forty-five; after suffering a heart attack on the job, he was buried there. "A place good enough to work at is good enough to die at," he believed. Or to die *for*. Riffey once critiqued a monkey-wrenching technique that Edward Abbey had fictionalized as being ineffective. Abbey's protagonist should have poured sand—cheap and ubiquitous—into the D9 Cat's fuel tank, Riffey thought, and saved the syrup for pancakes. The heretical warden, always quick to host a stranger or help out a ranching neighbor, vowed to use every trick in that book to keep asphalt off the dusty single-track to Toroweap, if it ever came to that. "And if that doesn't work," he'd told the stripling Moab ranger Jim Stiles, "they'll have to pave the road over my dead body." As with the Burr Trail, blacktopped now to the remote, western foot of the Waterpocket Fold, the DOT's vision, and our civilization's as a whole, is vintage Isaiah: "Make straight in the desert a highway for our God"—our supreme god being Mammon—and thereby "the crooked shall be made straight, and the rough places plain."

"And fast," one might add. Riffey would be happy to hear that the Toroweap road still is fractured limestone, gypsum, and shale, and impassable after a downpour or snowfall. Riffey never had to make that ultimate sacrifice of putting his body between progress and the canyon; he rests on a hillside near the ranger station, a stone's throw away from the road, in the uniform he seldom wore.

A few of those whom the canyon hooked paid dearly, gone missing or drowned by wretched flash floods. One self-destructed after hiking both sides of the canyon, unable to cope with reentry into what people kept calling "the real world." Here, the view alone could kill. When first exposed to it, a tourist at Yaki Point fainted and tumbled 500 feet to end up looking like a rag doll.

The abyss stared into us and we into it.

It did not spare our bodies, either. Blackbrush, locust, agaves, and carnivorous limestone gouged my forearms and shins. (I was saving my long pants for the cool days ahead.) My knees and lower back ached, embedded spines festered, and the pack's hip belt left plum-colored bruises. The narrow toe-box of my boots pinched the contents like Chinese foot binding. A gash running from Andrew's elbow to his wrist, from a wipeout on an unstable stone slab, had barely begun to scab.

Some stretches along the river resembled a booby-trapped jungle gym. Precariously balanced, car-size rocks alternated with tamarisk thickets and snarls of mesquite and aptly named catclaw acacia, "Wait-a-Minute Bush." (You better *do* stop when it snags you and unhook the curved thorns that otherwise rip your clothes and rake your skin.) On the canyon's Tonto Platform shoulder, bayonet-leafed agaves and extensive prickly pear forced us to high-step as through a minefield. Saddle Canyon had bigtooth and Rocky Mountain maple, whose crimson and gold pierced the heart, and New Mexico locust that pierced the skin. We got rattled at a few times, but mostly, with winter pending, the sssnakes were silent, lethargic. The midges that on a few occasions drove Andrew buggy did not bother me much. I've had worse, in Alaska.

Once in a while, rewards for our workouts came in the form of full, scratched-up cans, "river booty" from the bags that rafts dragged to keep drinks cold, which we fished from driftwood-clogged bays. If the ravens scavenged, we could too—"When in Rome..." We soon excelled at spotting a glint or color amid the debris, as sometimes the journey had scoured off paint. We never were sure what we sighted or, with labels rubbed out, what we'd caught. Other treasure bobbed in the eddy stew, tantalizingly out of reach. Coke and Sprite were a bit of a downer, since we carried enough sugar. The beers were lukewarm, and I've seldom had better. One that Andrew was saving for dinner in the outside mesh-pocket of his pack got punctured when he put down his load. I still smile at the memory of him sucking beer suds spraying from the hole, cursing between sips.

The four kinds of dehydrated pouch-dinner in my pack never got old, though the bloating they caused quickly did. We looked forward to mashed potatoes or Pad Thai as if they were four-star cuisine. "Mi-so happy," Andrew would pidgin-crow, slurping Japanese instant soup like Buddha, on a rolled-out sleeping bag.

Just when the weight of our packs was getting bearable, we'd reach one of our food caches; fully loaded again, we felt as if gravity had doubled overnight. Despite meals that could fatten a galley slave and treats guest hikers delivered (salami and cheese; oranges; a half-gallon of vanilla ice cream on dry ice), our waistlines receded. The midnight snack in the sleeping bag had become routine. Our beards, meanwhile, were filling in lavishly, streaked silver-gray. We rinsed our T-shirts and socks in potholes or eddies whenever we could but nevertheless looked feral and smelled like ringtails in heat.

We enjoyed luxuries at Teddy's Cabin on Bass Canyon's Muav Saddle, one of the few huts in the Grand Canyon. Laying over there for a day, we carried water up from the spring to do laundry, and I dashed to the rim for a six-pack of beer that hiking strangers, impressed by our quest, had promised to leave for us. Worried about the rodent-borne, lethal hantavirus—a river runner may have contracted it in an alcove camp known as Poncho's Kitchen, and several Navajos did at sheep camps—and by now used to sleeping under the sky's dome, I moved one bedframe outside, where the wind swished through long-needled ponderosa boughs all night long. Dreaming among waltzing trees was as good as dreaming rocked by the river's waves on a raft 5,000 feet below. There, too, I've felt connected to a huge vascular system, buoyed by its heaving, its breathing. And waking up to sunlight kissing pine tops or cliffs simply is priceless.

Most days, though, we balanced on boulders, traversed talus, spread-eagled through limestone maws, edge-walked, bush-whacked, switch-backed, stream-waded, scrambled, bled, swore, laughed maniacally, thirsted, and pined for our women; mine luckily joined us at South Canyon for two weeks. We struggled on each geological layer between the river and rim, from the yellow-gray Toroweap to the black, titanic, glowering Vishnu schist. We cautiously shuffled along the chasm's brink, sometimes on treacherous ball-bearings gravel, going where bighorn sheep fear to tread. When we were hauling up water with a rope from a pothole to which we had to rappel, a hardcore, visiting canyoneer tore a tendon. That put him out of commission for close to a year. We had his number and in a pinch called him on the satellite phone for route information or replacement gear. But at least we'd avoided a full-blown search and rescue—for now. "No news is good news," we had briefed our safety contact in Phoenix.

The weather gods rather smiled on us. We eased the blistering heat by soaking bandanas and T-shirts and by sitting with lizards under their rocks when the sun beat down most brutally. In a few places, water-pockets or springs we had counted on greeted us dusty and barren. Elsewhere, we left the river for a better route higher up, but long, chalk-dry miles convinced us that hiking onshore wasn't so bad after all. Cliffs often kept us from the vital fluid when we changed our minds and wanted to descend. A Paiute name for the Colorado translates as "Long Way Down to Water" or "Water Deep Down in the Earth." It teased us with ampleness, high-hanging fruit that we could not grasp.

I particularly remember the afternoon when, after a long day on the Redwall rim, we dropped into Rider Canyon near the sweet beach at House Rock Rapid, the day's destination. A huge natural stone-table by the stream there—the "House Rock Hotel"—promised respite with cool breezes. Our water bottles were empty, my face was burning, the smooth sandstone baking, and the death-star hung overhead, torturing flesh and ringing like a giant brass gong. When we finally reached the river, I dove into its emerald curl as into a lover's embrace.

A series of gully washers that had scoured the North Rim had refilled the water pockets in late August, in time for our hike. An ultra-light backpacking shelter I'd decorated with my totem—a carefully painted bear-paw print—turned out to be overpriced junk. At Clear Creek, when staccato fat raindrops pocked the dust, weaving hazy sheets behind which the canyon walls blurred, its Silicon-bottom tub collected half an inch of water. Squalls had roared through the gorge all night long, caged beasts that threatened to drop cottonwoods, "widow makers," on our pup tents. By morning, snow filigreed the South Rim's upper layers. My gear and sleeping bag were sopping wet. Another time, we bedded down in an alcove in the dust of millennia, watched over by painted sheep and skeletal shaman figures, while a drizzle glazed bedrock outside of our chamber. We also nearly got lost in a sand storm on our return to camp, after dinner with river runners below Nankoweap Rapid who'd invited us. The pale fingers of our headlamps stabbed the night as we tipsily threaded through several washes, spotlighting ghost bushes and cliff faces confusing us in their sameness.

That was it, as far as vagaries of weather were concerned—the rest of our days shone robin-egg blue, shimmering uniformly, luscious pearls or forget-me-nots on a string.

We *did* ride out a perfect bureaucratic storm: the park shutdown, result of a stalemate over the federal budget. I first heard about it through Andrew's inReach, a satellite-serviced texting and GPS device. Rumors circulated that rangers would intercept us or detain us at Phantom Ranch, where we had placed a cache, and escort us out. Because Andrew daily posted our whereabouts, they would know where to find us, just as they would radio-collared sheep. This would have been somewhere near Glasgow, one-third into our hike.

Downstream of East Clear Creek, we noticed signs of abandonment. No more river trips passed us; trails and campsites lay vacant. Descending through the stacked-deck Tapeats Sandstone, we could not see any hikers or mules on the South Kaibab Trail. The gossamer footbridge vaulting the river linked to a beach and corrals, to a campground, lodge, and guest cabins, all eerily quiet. Had I not known about the shutdown, I might have suspected a new 9/11 or mysterious plague. Word finally reached us, as digital text, that after a high-echelon meeting, the Park Service decided to let us continue, consistent with its treatment of river runners, who were allowed to proceed if they had launched before the closure. Suspicious by nature, I still was prepared to sneak onto the ranger cabin's porch to grab my food bucket under the cover of darkness.

I need not have worried. The ranger on duty released our supplies and told us we could pick any tent site. The Park Service had even made arrangements to bring in my replacement boots and Andrew's cold-weather gear with the last mule train to leave the South Rim. It was "a safety issue," after all. With Townes Van Zandt moaning from Andrew's iPhone, we sipped single malt whiskey at the campground's group site at a picnic table close to a bathroom with water taps and electric outlets, but the post-apocalyptic vibe lingered. What a rare, historical moment. We were the sole humans in the normally busy inner gorge, holdouts on closed public lands. We were the last legal hikers within 2,000 square miles. When I saw off Melissa at the Bright Angel Suspension Bridge, it felt like a scene from *The Road*. A ranger would meet her at the top and drive her to Tusayan, near the park boundary, because shuttles were no longer running.

It's an old saw that a good deal of the troubles of wilderness travel can spring from group dynamics. Tension may lie coiled below the surface, the prank clown in a box, yet never explodes. In our case, it did. Things started coming apart between Andrew and me on day thirty-eight, things that could not be fixed with our well-stocked repair kit. I could blame clashing views about culture, about science, the outdoors—but ultimately, it was personalities. Like some old couple, we knew where to aim knife words to draw blood. It was as if the canyon's prickliness had rubbed off on us.

He became angry when, prodding him in his comfort zone, I called evolution "the creation myth of biologists." He understood "myth" as being synonymous with a lie; I did as a foundation story that explains the workings of the universe. He thought I was doing science a disservice by extolling the beauty and deep truths of myths. I accused him of not having a poetic bone in his body. He, pointing out that he owned volumes of poetry, rightly accused me of "ad hominem attacks." He also believed that some languages are "more primitive," less complex than others. It was the same as deeming an abstract pictograph or one reduced to essentials crude when compared to a Botticelli. Being bilingual and having taken classes in two Alaska Native languages, I knew that languages emphasize relationships and facets of existence differently, that their vocabularies flourish in fields that matter to the speakers, that it is harder to express some things than others in *every* language, and that these differences make each people who they are. I wish I had known then that some geophysicists use Inupiaq phrases to capture nuances of snow and that one quantum physicist described the behavior of matter with concepts he borrowed from Navajo grammar because English lacked adequate words. (Not a new trend. India's ancient Vedic texts in the 1920s helped Schrödinger & Co. in formulating hypotheses.)

Verbal squalls between Andrew and myself often precipitated from me relaying tales, practices, and beliefs of the groups that considered and still consider the land on which we hiked to be home. One example I mentioned to him near the Colorado-Little Colorado confluence was the Hopi emergence from three previous worlds into the current, final one through the Sipapu—for the Navajos, who count a total of five, this is "the Glittering World."

In summary, he was a mule-headed empiricist and I a pig-headed creative-nonfiction writer with a penchant for qualitative science, like "thick description," which the anthropologist Clifford Geertz had popularized, at least for my academic circle. In this method, narrative, detailed ethnography provides context, not just "the facts" of physical behaviors, to let outsiders see the world from the insider's perspective as much as that is possible. The observer-participant-writer acts as a middleman or -woman in this, not as an expert but as a translator of culture.

Except that I did feel expert relative to a herpetologist, since I'd studied these matters for years. Call me conceited. But I would never have challenged Andrew with passé or gut-instinct sweeping statements about snake evolution, biology, or taxonomy. He had co-edited *Snakes of Arizona*, after all, an impressive doorstopper.

The white noise of civilization Andrew carried in his pack

bothered me most. Electronic chatter asserted itself day and night to the point of distraction. On this, I was with Mark Twain, who, apropos of the newly invented telephone, snarked that the human voice carries entirely too far as it is.

I had witnessed the deleterious effect of such intrusions once, at Phantom Ranch. Always, when we landed to refill our drinking-water jerry cans at the pump near the beach, clients wandered up to the lodge to buy iced homemade lemonade, mail postcards stamped "Delivered by mule," or call home from the public phone by the restrooms. On one occasion, a client had received news of matters that needed attending to in person—an estate issue, I believe. He decided to leave the trip then and there and hike to the South Rim in the oppressive midday heat. The trip leader tried to convince him to wait until the next morning, or closer to sunset at least. She had no guide to spare as an escort. The client, overweight, rubicund, out of shape, could not see reason and grew combative with a ranger the trip leader called on for assistance. They argued for hours in the tamarisks' feathered shade, with the client complaining about being babied and bossed, the trip leader and ranger fretting about the man's safety, and the rest of us wondering if we'd make it to the intended camp that night. The brouhaha broke river time's flow, the spell canyons weave, leaving a bitter taste, graying the mood for days.

On a different trip, in Alaska's backcountry no less, a client at a lunch spot where he had cellphone reception informed us of yet another mass shooting. "There's no there there," Gertrude Stein famously wrote about her California childhood home, which had changed beyond recognition. It appears that there's no longer an undiluted here here either. (But a cliffrose is still a cliffrose, its scent everlasting in memory.)

With sat phone, iPhone, and inReach, Andrew tried to stay updated, yoked to his city existence. Though some messages clearly upset him, he'd respond to texts, sometimes while on foot. The inReach's green eye watched over his sleep; I watched the coursing of satellites that kept us ensnared. When, at the crux of a climb through the Redwall, the inReach in Andrew's pack began chirping, a line between here and back home had been rudely breached. "You cannot escape from your life," Andrew had said— but I wanted a break from it, from the buzz-saw whine of the news cycle, the clanging and roaring of anthill life. I wished for a few weeks to concentrate only on this barebones place, to absorb its air of splendid isolation, to revert to an older, elemental mode of existence, one closer to the land. Like the curmudgeonly Edward Abbey, I found my contemplation of nature compromised when too many people were contemplating it with me at the same time. I had come for the silence and "silences," those spaces on maps, ever more rare, left blank by cartographers. I welcomed drop-ins who hiked with us for days at a time for their contributions to our larder, less so for the news they brought of the outside world. With each contact with new people, the dynamics subtly shifted; there was never a sense of cohesion, of a core of friends that grew closer with the miles they traversed. Each social shake-up felt like another throw of the dice. Just when I got used to visitors, it was time for them to leave.

Andrew, conversely, enjoying new people, hailed each passing trip, even from the Redwall a thousand feet above river level, and visited every camp, loitering in the kitchen area, hoping for dinner or company or a pat on the head.

I cannot say in good conscience that the chronic dehydration from which we both suffered had nothing to do with our crabbiness. The kangaroo rat is one of my role models. It never has to drink, not in a lifetime, but instead metabolizes all necessary water from the seeds and succulents nibbled. What you don't need, you don't have to carry (or find). Despite outdoor expert advice to keep your urine flowing "clear and copious," and guzzling more than a gallon a day as a precaution, I did not imbibe enough on this trip. But brains that had shrunk into dried figs cannot serve as an adequate excuse for our spats.

After one more argument, we parted in an alcove with six-foot skeletal ghosts painted on its ceiling. I pulled out the climbing gear I had carried and told Andrew I was leaving. I nearly had run out of food—we were going to pick up cache number seven the next day near the rim. The route up there was not straightforward, marked only on the map inside Andrew's pack. Too proud to ask for a look at it, I shouldered my load and took off.

An hour later, cornered by bulging Supai Sandstone, I conceded that I had veered off-course. Rather than risk falling or wasting more daylight, I decided to exit the long way, at the Tuckup Canyon trailhead. But at this time of year, there might be no traffic on the spur dirt road leaving that canyon. The best option for catching a ride required a sixteen-mile walk from Tuckup to the Toroweap Road, from "Tuckit" to "Tuweep," as cowpunchers said.

My final dinner under the stars consisted of a snack bar and orange fizzy drink. Powell at this point only had bacon so "badly injured" that he threw it away and "musty flour for ten days and a few dried apples but plenty of coffee." He considered calling it quits. On any river trip, food assumes the role of the hearth fire around which the tribe gathers. The solitary meal is simply for nourishment.

The next morning, before dawn enflamed The Dome, I was climbing switchbacks to the trailhead. From there, I followed the rutted track that rolled through piñon-juniper forest and sage flats. My empty belly rebelled, but I was not quite ready to quaff olive oil, the only calories left in my pack.

Eternities later, after trudging on autopilot, salivating through daydreams of pizza and cheesecake, I approached the corral near the Toroweap Road. Two pickups and a Polaris—an ATV on steroids masquerading as a golf cart—were parked there. Perhaps these belonged to hunters or ranchers, with whom I could ride to fair Fredonia.

As I drew closer, to my surprise, I saw the Toroweap ranger

perched on the ATV's roof, radio and map in hand.

"There he is," said one of the guys by the pickups. It was our go-to canyoneer, who had helped place our cache and who'd met Andrew there this morning. When they realized that my food bucket had not been touched, they'd grown concerned and talked to the ranger, who happened to be there for a routine check. He was about to call for a search-and-rescue helicopter when I sauntered up. Even when I thought I'd escaped, I never slipped the dragnet net in the ether.

Hiking out prematurely, reluctantly, with a rancorous head of steam, I forfeited my seat in the hall of heroes. I may or may not finish this traverse some day, adding the missing miles to Pearce Ferry. Even if I did, my accomplishment would never rank among those of the exalted winners of tougher-than-thou pissing matches. I've lost my shot at becoming a "contiguous thru-hiker," unless I started from scratch. I would forever be branded as a "segmental guy." Backpackers, too, can be a competitive lot, which sorely grieves me. Nature offers our best chance to leave behind the measuring-up. Rivalries. Hierarchies. Animosities, except toward those who destroy the places we love. Yet we manage to waste that opportunity with the petty insecurities carried over from our everyday lives.

Sour grapes, you may say. But I'm confident that, physically as well as mentally, I could have finished this. Incompletion can be an act of acceptance, an admission that we don't come here to conquer. Beginnings matter most, it seems to me. And I'll always have a reason to return, if in fact I need another one, to begin again. I never liked the term "thru-hiking" anyway. It carves out chunks of terrain as something on the way to somewhere else, not as land worth dwelling in and on. Call it "long-distance hiking," if brag you must.

Back home for hibernation—my scratches and blisters mend nicely, and I'm putting on pounds. I briefly muse how wilderness brings out the best and the worst in us, how the desert glare throws flaws and passions into relief as no other light does. How it asks that you surrender your ego without guarantee of returns. I may only have made it as far as Coventry, two weeks short of our finish line. But, bent over maps, already forgetting, I start planning my next walk in the park.

A River Now and Again

WHEN WE EXIT THE TRUCK, applause greets us, ringing frenetically from the Little Colorado River gorge. Near the overlook, it swells to a crescendo, a roar with a droning bass note, foot stomping in the bleachers. The streambed and Grand Falls, which lie barren or reduced to a runnel for most of the year, have sprung back to life.

Thrilled by the high flow levels the United States Geological Survey posted online, we drove two hours from Flagstaff, on paved byways, across reservation washboard, through pine woods, and past volcanic cinder cones, with not a drop of water in sight. Time passed quickly as we chatted and hashed out the logistics of shuttling cars between the put-in and takeout.

At the overlook, speechless, we face a mirage: an off-color Iguaçu in the desert.

Gravity rules at the lip, while farther down, the canyon-cutter writhes like a coral pink, glossy worm. Cascades leap from the falls' outer edges. The main current charges with biblical force over tiered, beveled limestone ledges midstream. Falling, it unravels in frothed dizziness, forming massive, ragged jets. It would be a feat to track any flotsam after it slips off the brink. Distended to an eddying lake, the plunge pool at the bottom trembles with chop but calms near the outlet. Water vaporizes in the impact zone, lashing tamarisks on shore, pushing a scent of freshly mown grass. Driftwood carpets a beach in the cove; more spins on its flood in a miniature logjam, enough to build pyres or rafts.

Innocent and incongruent, a thin, blue sky arcs above everything. I shudder as much from the spectacle as from the sharp March air, expecting to feel vibrations through the soles of my feet. We would have to shout to be heard, but our faces say it all.

Grand Falls is as much a quirk of hydrology as one of geology.

Some 20,000 years ago, lava from a vent known as The Sproul oozed across the flats and into the Little Colorado's trough, plugging it with a basalt dam. The river, compelled to detour, spilled over the dam, and Grand Falls was born. At 185 feet, the falls stand taller than Niagara. Their range of moods illustrates that a stream at heart is a weather phenomenon. In droughts, there is not enough flow to buoy a duck. In flood, the wash channels runoff from monsoon cloudbursts or snowmelt from Arizona's White Mountains, near the New Mexico state line. A good portion of the Painted Desert—friable siltstone, sandstone, and clay—ends up rebuilding eroded beaches in the Grand Canyon.

The Spanish missionary Francisco Garcés called it *Rio Jaquesila*—the "River Unruly." The Navajos called it Red Water. A river *muy macho, muy colorado*, indeed. The men on John Wesley Powell's first expedition deemed it "so filthy and muddy that it fairly stinks." They guessed half of its volume and two-thirds of its weight to be muddy silt. It could carry worse things, however, and it has. In 1979, in the biggest radioactive spill in US history, 100 million gallons of waste slopped from the tailings pond of United Nuclear Corporation's Church Rock uranium mill into the Puerco River, an upper fork of the watershed. Toxic guck reached the Navajo reservation, where traces can still be detected today. Children played in pus-yellow puddles, and elders who waded the river to gather their sheep lost their legs later or died from the hellish effluent's burn. This legacy may seem remote in space and time, but as the biologist and cancer survivor Sandra Steingraber reminds us, we all live downstream of some headwater. Just open a tap in your kitchen for proof.

In drier conditions, the lower Little Colorado runs shallow and leisurely, in no great rush to join the main stream. Laced with minerals from Blue Spring, it glows like Curaçao liqueur near its Grand Canyon confluence with the Colorado. The Mormons and other settlers had difficulties crossing it even in its serene state. Their teams and wagons often bogged down in quicksand. It was easier to ford at Grand Falls and the smaller Black Falls, ten miles below, where water slides over bedrock.

The initial spell has broken. Shouting above the din, we point and laugh and shake our heads in disbelief. Melissa, who stands next to me, works as a public health nurse and visits homesteads throughout this part of the Navajo reservation, routinely driving across a little upstream of here, sometimes without wetting the truck's tires. Were she to try today, she would get swept to her death. At the flow gauge near Cameron, the river registered almost six feet deep, passing more than the load of a twenty-foot freight container every second.

A half-mile-long trail winds steeply into the seething cauldron, and we hump down two Hypalon toys plus gear: paddles, daypacks, an air pump, and life jackets. Eager to launch, we inflate our "ducky" inflatable kayaks on a sliver of beach. Christa and I are going to look at the chocolate-milk rush from up close. As a desert geologist and Grand Canyon raft guide, she cannot resist its siren song, and neither can I. Melissa chooses to stay on shore because we did not bring drysuits, and the spray looks as if it could drench you in a minute. For the same reason, she decides to walk around the pool's outlet, a boulder-flanked funnel with a pour-over boiling in the middle—a Class II rapid, easily. She's always been smart about this sort of thing.

Christa and I sit ten yards from the monstrous wall, dabbling to keep our distance. We don't want to get pushed under it by the gyre; it would destroy our crafts. "The world is rough and surly," wrote Ralph Waldo Emerson, "and will not mind drowning a man or a woman." Or a man *and* a woman. Except for stampeding wildlife, few things in nature move with the mass and speed of a river in flood: clouds, twisters, avalanches, tsunamis...but you can join none of these, or only at risk to life or limb. If you manage to do so, precarious empowerment is your reward. Still, to truly understand any river, you have to be in it, not on it. Spray blasts us, and my clothes start to soak through. It is even chillier here, in the river's mist plume, that twilight zone between water and air. Seen from this close, the falls seem to rotate horizontally, like a huge cylinder, causing moments of trance. The motion suggests a perpetual mobile; it's hard to imagine this silt conveyor could ever slow down, or stop.

When we've had our fill, we paddle toward the outlet. Christa runs it first. Not watching her line, not bracing, and not shifting my weight forward, I hit the center hole. The bow goes up and I go flying. Gasping from the rapid's punch, I swallow a sediment-laden pint—at this time of year, snowmelt from the high country feeds it. My kayak races ahead, wrong side up, but I manage to hold on to the paddle.

In passing, I catch a glimpse of my wife snapping candid shots from shore.

There are two kinds of river runners, we say in my trade: those who have flipped and those who will. This is my fourth upset. My baptism took place in Rapid No. 5 in Cataract Canyon, on another private trip. There, the instant my fourteen-foot raft dipped into a gnarly hydraulic on the left side I had realized I wouldn't make it. Before I could so much as yell "High-side!" to have Melissa balance the boat by throwing her weight on the rising tube, we had turned turtle, and the maelstrom churned me under. While she popped up right away next to the raft, crosscurrents tumbled me like clothes in a dryer, near the river bottom. I could not tell up from down, at once subjected to mayhem and the muffled quietude of the womb—or the grave. Seconds or rinse cycles later, I was pardoned and ascended toward twilight. I surfaced, sucking air with the yen of a bicycle pump. After assuring myself that my companion was alive, clinging to the hull's "chicken line," we tugged the raft into an eddy to right it. When our friends arrived, lending a hand, they told us that all they had seen of two duckies that had followed us blindly over the lip into that hole were paddles airborne above spray.

At this water level, on the Little Colorado, there are few eddies to pull into. Luckily, Christa is parked in one, with my ducky in tow. I crawl from the shallows winded and not quite clear yet what happened. I'll have to look at the pictures later to figure it out. Not anticipating a swim, I hadn't dressed for one. I shiver immediately, my teeth clacking castanet-style.

Meanwhile, Melissa has joined us, offering dry layers from her pack. My stuff is still there, strapped into the boat. But it's sopping, and I've lost my favorite ball cap. I'll now have to wear a girlie knit hat.

After a quick snack of trail mix and cheese—fuel for the faltering engine—we shove off, Christa in one boat, Melissa and I in the other. I'm shaking so hard that Melissa, in the front seat, feels the kayak vibrating.

Let the fun begin. With the river hushed between here and the landing, we hope to spice up adventure with a dash of archaeology.

Wet or dry, this gulch has attracted people for at least 11,000 years. Some Ice Age hunter lost a leaf-shaped, fluted spear point on the prairie close by, a dandy blade for killing mammoths; the bones of one surfaced not far from here. The obsidian came from many miles away. The lower gorge enfolds the Sipapu, a travertine dome spring from which the Hopis climbed after three previous worlds had been destroyed. Cut loose from this umbilicus—their most recent place of origin—they were set adrift in the fourth and final world. After they settled down, the Little Colorado connected Homolovi and the Hopi Mesas to the north with Wupatki, the Grand Canyon, and points south. Goods, individuals, and ideas trickled both ways, according to season and want. Tokens of far-flung trade—Mexican copper bells and scarlet macaws, seashells from the Pacific—traveled as far as Wupatki. The hundred-room pueblo squats on a rock knoll near our takeout and the Black Falls Road, which crosses the river. Its Mesoamerican-type ball court is the northernmost of its kind. Between 500 and 1225 CE, when they permanently abandoned Wupatki, evicted, most likely, by drought, thousands of people lived there or within a day's walk, in outliers such as Wukoki and The Citadel.

Wupatki must have been famous too, drawing pilgrims, as the home of the Hopi wind god, Yaponcha. Near the pueblo, a large tectonic fissure, one of several in the region, inhales and exhales through a blowhole only a few inches wide. As the outside temperature and barometric pressure change, air rushes through the opening at up to thirty miles per hour, forceful enough to levitate a plastic bag or to whip back the long hair of a person bending over the subterranean gale. An excavation team found remains of prehistoric habitations at many such earth cracks within the national monument. Surprisingly, these dwellings often lay closer to the blowholes than to crucial water sources. This makes it likely that, at least sometimes, religious concepts trumped practical considerations in the ancients' choice of a residence.

At these bustling crossroads mingled Sinagua, Cohonina, and Kayenta Anasazi, ancestors of modern Puebloans. They pecked evidence of their beliefs and preoccupations into rock varnish alongside this river. It's an outdoor gallery hard to match, even on the rock-art rich Colorado Plateau.

I cannot get warm, despite wearing hat, gloves, and life jacket, on our strolls to the petroglyphs. There are simply too many to check out each one if we want to make Wupatki before nightfall. Engraved in the cliffs' manganese-iron skin are spiders, bears, turtles, bighorn sheep, birds, lizards, and joyous dancers. Flute players and "traders"—figures with packs and hiking sticks—march solo or single-file. A throw-dart sprouts from the back of one traveler, an ambush or act of revenge, perhaps. I show Christa, a sworn cat lover, the glyph of an archer who aims at four felines. (Though they could well be rodents.) The animals seem to be tied together by their tails, pulling in directions that correspond to the four compass points. I tell Christa, whose cats to my dismay every so often zap hummers at her birdfeeders, that

I'll call this the Animal Control Panel. She does not think that is funny. In another scene, nine sheep have been speared with missiles launched by a throwing-board or atlatl. Each bend brings a new discovery. Against the red dirt, flint chips and potsherds with black-on-white lattices shine like bone scatter in the sun. We find hewn spirals, waves, sun and star patterns, lozenges, and checkerboards also common in ceramic or textile designs. We find psychedelic amoebas and cerebral mazes, hoof marks and foot-prints, archives embossed with lichen or crisp as new pennies. We find no watercraft, no swimmers, no sign that the ancient ones entrusted themselves to this shifty highway; but some scrawls might celebrate clan migrations, or the river's curved detours.

Biased, perhaps, by the shape of our journeys, we perceive rivers as finite, linear, stretched source-to-sea. We name their main stems, sections, and tributaries. We speak of waterlines, waterways, river left, river right, arteries, forks. We envision them as vascular, muscular, serpentine, braided, branching, threading, or ribboning. We rank them by length and plot GPS points to cairn remote float trips for others to follow. Some people tally the rivers they've "done," sometimes in logbooks or lists. Others rhapsodize, praising them with story or song, with a fluency of their own.

To the naturalist John Graves, a river is, like a body, "one of the real wholes." But lines of our doing dissect rivers—dams, locks, and weirs, wheel ruts, bridges, and cables, pipelines and power lines, and invisibly, lines that split the liquid asset or "re-source" between counties, between upper and lower basin states, lines that sever what should be inseverable, perhaps even sacred. Neighboring groups through whose lands great rivers wind not only knew them by distinct names but also sometimes had sever-al, including ceremonial ones, as if in acknowledgment of water's many moods. Some knew neither the source nor the destination. Just the rolling, majestic, reassuring presence they witnessed, notwithstanding its fluctuations, which spoke of the seasons.

A Navajo locution for the Colorado, "Life Without End," imparts a deeper truth, an ecological understanding. Cyclical, dynamic, rivers shift in space and time. They are channel surfers, opportunists, quick-change artists—topography's transients or mayflies. Rain or snow falls, gathers in rills, then rivulets, and rolls on, past confluences, into reservoirs, through deltas, to ocean shores, and into marine depths; it ascends and joins clouds, to be held as insurance against future shortages. And so on, ad infinitum. Every sixth grader knows this. Yet we chart river-flow graphs, map bowknot bends. Circles and spirals much better encrypt the nature of water—any water. We forget, viewing rivers as we view life: vectors to be gauged, not miracles to be mulled.

It is getting late, and the gorge slowly wraps itself in shadows. Once in a while, the stream wells up a gurgle. In the deep quiet, I hear paddles dripping and silt hissing against the tubes. Already the falls have become hearsay, unreal.

At our last stop, we climb to ruins that stand on the north rim like broken teeth. Touched by the westering sun, blond sandstone glows peachy. The river's grinding yields clay, the mortar that once kept these walls from crumbling. One building block bears a fossil imprint. The crocodile ancestor's three-lobed track lends to the ruin an aura of time beyond time, a time before humans were even so much as a thought in the mind of creation. There is permanence of a sort next to this western wadi, this fickle flow that has channeled pilgrims and settlers, locals and travelers, a place that draws worshippers to this day.

Still cold, or cold again, I initiate the descent to the boats. We've got a long way to go, and a portage around a diversion dam yet ahead. We'll be looping back to the truck at Grand Falls in the dark. But we don't mind. It's another day with the river, another circuit completed. At home, in our easy chairs, it will be good to remember that silt happens now and again.

Dancing the Rain

A DRUM STEADY AS A METRONOME announces the procession. The still February air buzzes with anticipation, and my goose bumps are not from the cold. I am packed shoulder to shoulder with raven-haired people on a flat roof in Muh-oon-qah-pi, the "Place of Running Water," waiting to fall out of time.

Owl hoots join the drum, and then hail on flagstones—rattling from deer hooves, seeds, turtle shells. Here they come! A crush of masked bodies clad in the land's minerals, bright as humming-birds, feathers and furs swaying, pounding bare ground with bare feet, inflating cloud bellows and bringing up seedlings with each stomp. This is Powamyua, the start of the Hopi ceremonial year and first appearance of the katsina spirits since their winter re-treat to the San Francisco Peaks near Flagstaff.

I am in Moenkopi with a few river guides and Grand Canyon National Park staff as part of a collaborative arrangement between the park, river outfitters, and tribal groups. Through cultural immersion, this program seeks to increase our understanding of tribes affiliated with the canyon. Its practical goal is to enrich the interpretation of a cultural landscape by including First Peoples' perspectives.

Fortunately, we are not on our own. William Talashoma, a river guide and interpreter from Moenkopi, shepherds us through the maze of Hopi etiquette and beliefs. For a change, we guides are the guided ones, feeling like babes in the desert. On our way to the village, we briefly stopped at Cameron, near the lip of the Little Colorado River's gorge. There, William recounted his people's emergence from previous worlds, destroyed by ice, fire, and flood, into this present and final one. The place of emergence lies down canyon, near the confluence with the Colorado, where a travertine dome housing a spring swells from the riverbank like an earthen breast. Its Hopi name, Sipapuni, translates as "navel" or "umbilical cord." William thinks of it as symbolic, a reminder of rebirth and the fact that we come from the earth. It evokes our ascent from primordial muck to consciousness. Fittingly, the souls of the dead return to this gateway for their journey home. As a navigational landmark, the Sipapuni pegs the tribe's surfacing from the canyon's depths onto the mesa tops after epic migrations across the Southwest that followed its last emergence.

At Moenkopi, we parked our van bumper to bumper with cars by the side of a congested dirt road. Down that road, single-story houses hunkered between tan bluffs and the wash's dormant cornfields. We followed a trickle of visitors toward the lower village, to the cottonwood-shaded spring that gave the village its name and still gives it life. Offerings had been left in a shrine-like niche: Turkey feathers tied with white cotton string. A broken rattle. Yellow cornmeal. Carved prayer sticks, both male and female kinds, painted turquoise. I stooped to pick up a gray, corrugated potsherd that could have been a thousand years old. Though Moenkopi only dates back to 1870, the Hopis' Motsinom ancestors probably worshipped there.

As portals to the spirit world, springs did and still do hold meaning for people of the corn.

We shared lunch with William's family, eating in shifts, as the house was bursting with guests. On the porch, a boy played with a painted bow, a gift from the elemental beings, the katsinas. We sat at a lunch counter where we were served *piki*—phyllo-thin blue corn bread baked on a heated stone slab. A girl with almond eyes and a shy smile warned me of the batch spiced with chilies. There was fry bread and beef soup with bean sprouts grown from heirloom varieties for the occasion in the underground secrecy of kivas, the clans' ceremonial chambers. I was reminded again how food should nourish the soul as well as the body, how much we ignore the spiritually wholesome for the merely nutritious.

The Powamyua, or "Bean Dance," concludes a sixteen-day ceremony of creation. The katsinas have arrived in force, helping the Hopis prepare for the growing season, and if the rites are performed humbly and correctly, they will bring rain from the sacred peaks to the south. It also marks the initiation of young children into the entry-level Katsina Society, preparing yet another generation for growth and maturity. The Hopis, for whom the world teems with sentient beings, would not be surprised to hear of scientists' recent findings that tomatoes and tobacco plants shaken by drought or suddenly wounded emit staccato ultrasounds resembling bubble-wrap popping. The audible response likely is physiological, stemming from cavitation in the plants' tissues. But is a person's gasp of fear any less physical? These "distress cries" differ depending on the cause and may even affect nearby insects and other animals.

Laughter erupted from the table around which elders and close family sat. In a dimly lit corner, an old-timer with mahogany skin reclined in a hospital bed, part of the proceedings.

Like the planet's progress solemnized in this hilltop community, my journeying has come full circle. New to the country in 1983, I was hitchhiking across the Southwest when a Hopi who offered a ride invited me to visit with his family on Third Mesa. I stayed at his grandmother's house for a few days. A potter from the renowned Nampeyo lineage, she fired pots the traditional way, burying redware smooth as calabashes and webbed with black geometric designs to smolder on cedar logs inside a mound of dry sheep manure. Her grandson painted watercolors of katsinas in lifelike poses, and I bought a set, which now hangs in my study. That Hopi family's hospitality helped kindle a decades-long love affair with the Colorado Plateau and fed an interest in the continent's first people that eventually led me to anthropology and north, to Alaska.

From the rooftop, I see initiates wearing nothing but blankets, who stand with their godparent sponsors, sleep-deprived and hungry from their ordeal. Their near-nakedness signals humility, their bare feet a debt owed to the earth. They spent last night curled fetus-like in the kiva's womb, below a cornmeal line painted on the wall—the path that Maasawu, the Creator, expects them to follow. On the previous day, the katsinas had whipped them. When tears flushed their eyes, their godfathers had traded places with them, receiving the blows in their stead. This, too, a promise: if you walk the straight path, Maasawu will take on part of your suffering. Blood shed in this covenant is thicker than water.

The Mudhead chorus now marches past with its dried-clay masks, heads smooth as urns, eyes and mouths O-shaped, as if in constant surprise. Their big-bellied drum hums in the pit of my stomach. In tune with the fertility theme, clown katsinas pretend to hump old women in the crowd. Black ogres chase Hopi tough guys, trying to blacken their faces with soot. Other monsters go from door to door, demanding fresh meat, threatening to eat children who have misbehaved. Spectators who line the streets pluck feathers from the procession's wake, blessings the katsinas left in the dirt. Humor and horseplay, mixed with awe and reverence, take me by surprise. What I witness reminds me that the sacred and the profane are as much part of a continuum in an eddying universe as the seasons and generations.

Katsinas circle the village four times, always, *always* following the sun's daily and annual course. (We'd call it "clockwise," but abstract time, time detached from the body, has no function in feasts linked to the earth.) The dancers stop on every kiva roof, where the clan priests consecrate them with cornmeal, "feeding" the spirits that have traveled so far. With each round, I recognize more characters in the melee of colors and forms.

A Kokopelli Katsina—"a nympho," according to William— sports a woman's kilt and the Hopi woman's twin-whorl sculpted "butterfly" hairdo.

A Mocking Katsina latches onto bystanders and the ranks of

fellow katsinas, mimicking his target's every move. Dressed in cutoff jeans, modern footwear, hippie pendants, and a beaded vest, he resembles certain White Men.

A Guard Katsina in a checkered kilt points its yucca wand at me. Guards punish any transgression on the katsinas' path, and it takes me a few seconds and the example of others on the roof to understand the request to remove my cap.

A Heheya Katsina with a lasso tempts children by holding out woven baskets, katsina dolls, bundles of *piki*, or cookies on a string, snaring them when they reach for his gifts. This tempting with riches, and the white-plumed, spruce-ruffed Snow Katsina, bring to mind a controversy that embroils my hometown, Flagstaff, an hour from here as the vulture soars. A ski resort operator plans to use wastewater to supply the barren slopes of the San Francisco Peaks with snow there. Concerned residents, environmental organizations, and Hopi representatives have protested such waste and desecration; but it looks as if the city will go ahead anyhow.

Could the multi-year drought that squeezes the West signal our straying from ground truths, from the straight path? Have we lost sight of priorities in a desert? Dancing for harmony in the world, the pueblos are dancing for all of us.

Toward evening, we drive on to Shongopavi, perched on a spur of Second Mesa. Residents of Old Shongopavi relocated here after the Pueblo uprising of 1680, fearing Apache marauders and reprisals from the Spanish. Outside ideas, diseases, and trappings have taken their toll, but this village remains a stronghold of Hopi tradition. We shiver in sweaters and pile jackets, while the supplicants brave the late winter chill bare-chested. There is less levity here, less chasing and teasing. Despite our lighter skin and self-conscious poses, nobody pays us any attention. A different cast of katsinas shuffles through Shongopavi's still frozen mud, dwarfed by the wing-helmeted, somber Crow Mother. Yowe, the katsina that beheaded the Franciscan priest more than 300 years ago, wields an old saber. Memory runs deep on the mesas, as does the desire for restoration. A few people in the audience ask for canings, to be cleansed and healed. It feels like a foreign place at the heart of America. But no. This *is* the ancient heart of America—wounded but resilient, vibrant, enduring, powered by and powering immemorial cycles.

In a handout for the trip's participants, William had summarized the Hopi worldview. "We must have constant prayer in our hearts, from the minute we are awake till the time we are asleep. We must respect both the spirit and the creation."

"Hopi," William said at one point, "is not a tribe, but a state of being."

At last light, the main kiva swallows the host of katsinas. One by one, their feathered silhouettes shrink into the roof hatch. Eventually, only the tip of the ladder that they descended protrudes aboveground, angled at the first stars. The rooftops and streets quickly empty. As we walk back to the dirt parking lot, a TV like a blue eye flickers from a dark house with a satellite dish.

The Last Fifteen Miles

THIS IS A PILGRIMAGE OF SORTS, and like all good pilgrimages, it starts on foot. After the convenience of air-conditioned, motorized travel in a contraption whose model and brand convey status as a trek to Mecca or Jerusalem once did, I set out for the sacred place humbly, in sturdy leather boots.

Trudging through deep red sand, past a gutted mattress and shards of whiskey bottles that glitter like broken dreams, I search for the route into the canyon, down to the Colorado's lobed shores. I weave back and forth on the rim in sight of the power transformer station, the metal industrial orchard selling the fruit of the river's harnessed liveliness to the Four Corners states and Nebraska, Wyoming, and Nevada. After avoiding "Lake" Powell and its dam for decades like a hanta-haunted shack, I finally decided to visit what is left of Glen Canyon. Over the years, I sifted through stacks of bleached photos and accounts by travelers lucky enough to have seen the Glen in all its glory. A succession of luminaria, local patches, like the naturalist Helen Macdonald's "glowing with memory and meaning," had been put under, snuffed out.

With those historical fragments and my knowledge of similar canyons, I've tried to reconstruct loss—a loss felt possibly even deeper because I neither knew the thing lost nor would have a chance to reclaim it. Those from whom it was taken at least have their recollections. The last of that generation soon will be gone. The damming feels like personal trauma, as there is no other landmark I care to know that has been so completely corrupted while almost staying within reach. I am curious how the place I imagined compares with reality. There is middle-age stocktaking also, which casts its long shadow. I am past sixty now, and the likelihood of seeing the reservoir drained or dried up in my lifetime is slim. Is my desire but selfish, a different, slightly refracted form of possessiveness? I think not. The Glen should be restored for its own sake, that of the life that unfolded there and downstream, in the Grand Canyon. Hoping the drought persists so that Glen Canyon may yet again shine compounds the moral dilemmas that plague our age.

After a tour of the concrete blade that guillotined the river and now marks Mile Zero, the little-used Ropes Trail to the river seemed just the cure for a case of civilization blues. When I had asked about the trailhead's location, a volunteer at the Park Service information desk refused to provide that information, because "it's too dangerous." I guess the agency thinks that rescuing a few cliffed-out, dehydrated hikers or retrieving the bodies of those who, looking for a way down, haplessly slipped on the edge is less trouble than facing a liability suit.

I was sure I could find the trail on my own, but, apparently, I had walked from a hard place into rocks—plenty of them.

Beyond turtleback outcrops, sandstone yields to sheer space. Peering over the edge, I cannot see an entrance gully or lower ledge to reach safely. No markers, no cairns. Instead, steel pylons march overland, two-headed robotic grotesques of the mythical Navajo warrior twins. They hum with the river's life force, and cables droop from their raised arms into the abyss. On the far rim, the town of Page sprawls across hot rufous flats, still improvised blight, but now catering to golfers and house-boaters rather than dam builders.

Across from town, upstream from where I am scanning the cliffs, the Carl Hayden Visitor Center sticks to Glen Canyon's West Rim like a modernist cliff-swallow nest. I had opened its mirrored-glass doors with trepidation. Would anybody there recognize me as a dissenter, a deserter from the American Dream? Morbid curiosity compelled me to take that guided tour—*Know thy enemy!*

Bureau of Reclamation personnel at the dam try hard to

keep undesirables from infiltrating the site. Waiting near the desk for the tour to begin, I learned from a cardboard sign that nail clippers and binoculars were among the items forbidden to bring, for security reasons. "Any mentioning of bombs, sabotage, etc., will not be tolerated," the back of my ticket stated. Did a black, tapering Visqueen "crack" in the dam face—the one Earth First! famously unrolled on the 1981 spring equinox—qualify as sabotage? Plaques mounted below panorama windows vis-à-vis the dam instead bombard visitors with stats, as if the view alone weren't enough. "Height of dam above river level: 583 feet. Maximum thickness at foundation: 350 feet. Generating capacity: 1.3 million kilowatt. Cost: $145 million..." The film schedule at the auditorium listed *Desert Oasis*, a cultural and natural history flick about the reservoir, second largest in the United States. In the exhibition area, posters with diagrams and historical photos further trumpeted our species' accomplishments. Strangely, the pageant of progress included a fish tank in a corner. Boxed-in behind panes, flannelmouth suckers and humpback chubs—streamlined by the turbid Colorado, now endangered by sediment-trapping dams—hung between neon green plastic plants, suspended in unnaturally clear, filtered water.

The Bureau would be hard-pressed to add another to that listless display of riverine royalty: the Colorado pikeminnow. The six-foot, eighty-pound muscled torpedoes were known as "white salmon" also, for their migrations. Pikeminnow fisheries once thrived throughout the Colorado River Basin. A Vernal old-timer remembered that one such fish was like a crop that, cut into steaks, produced "not just one meal, but quite a few meals for the family." Dams, agricultural runoff, and introduced sport-fishing species like trout long ago put the pikeminnow on the endangered list—three million years of locally grown "organic" food and diversity circling the drain. But at least the survivors are no longer saddled with the ignominious moniker "squawfish"; it is no longer appropriate, like the overharvesting of wild foodstuffs, or the settlers' name for three-leafed sumac, "squaw bush" or "sourberry," whose tartness fills in for red-zinger tea in my water bottle whenever I come across them.

"When the earth is cleansed and nourished, its purity infuses me," writes one of my role models, the deer-hunting, fishing ex-anthropologist Richard Nelson. Conversely, "A fouled molecule that runs through the earth runs through me," he laments. This is not a flight of fancy or New Age mysticism. Pregnant women have been advised not to consume fish from "Lake Foul," this reservoir. Archeologists routinely use bones and tooth enamel to reconstruct human paleo-diets and migrations through isotope analysis. While we grow up, our bodies accumulate chemical elements—carbon, nitrogen, strontium, oxygen—from the foods that we eat and the water we drink, which relay mineral traces of the specific soils from which they sprang. These fingerprints of place stay with us throughout life and even afterward, for a while, locked in our skeletons. We hold the places that first sustained us, as we hold our memories. We are not only *what* we eat but also *where* we eat.

Having passed through the airport-style security checkpoint, our motley band stepped into the first elevator and quickly fell to the dam's crest. Our tour guide, Duane, a gray-haired gent with high-riding chinos, probably meant well. Originally from Salt Lake City, he had worked at the Page power plant for thirty years and now enjoyed shepherding tourists for the Glen Canyon Natural History Association. As it turned out, we would not hear much natural history. "Lake Powell gets 2.5 million visitors per year," Duane said with a lisp that at times made him hard to understand. He told us about a dam visitor who, when Duane mentioned that in dry years no Colorado River water reaches the Sea of Cortez—a sea that "does not really need it"—commented, "Good. We're using it all up."

I wish Duane had taken the time to find out and explain that, before the construction of dams, the Colorado River supplied one of the world's largest desert estuaries. Fed by freshwater and nutrients, these coastal wetlands teemed with deer, beavers, coyotes, numerous species of fish and waterfowl, even jaguars—*los tigres* to Central Americans. Farther out, whales, dolphins, and California sea lions cavorted in the fertile mixing of waters. "The river was nowhere and everywhere," Aldo Leopold reminisced about the delta he'd canoed in 1922, for it "could not decide which of a hundred green lagoons offered the most pleasant and least speedy path to the Gulf." In front of his bow, "Fleets of cormorants drove their black prows in quest of skittering mullets; avocets, willets, and yellow-legs dozed one-legged on the bars; mallards, widgeons, and teal sprang skyward in alarm…"

The Kolb Brothers had ended their 1,200-mile journey in January 1912, after 101 days and 365 big rapids, at Needles, California. Seeking closure, Ellsworth, a "wandering spirit" and the dreamier of the two brothers, completed it the following spring, without Emery running 400 miles on highwater in eight days. "So ended the Colorado," he said, taking stock after reaching the gulf. "Two thousand miles above, it was a beautiful river, born of a hundred snow-capped peaks and a thousand crystal streams; gathering strength, it became the masterful river which had carved the hearts of mountains and slashed the rocky plateaus…"

Where Aldo and Ellsworth once drifted at leisure, today an impoverished void sprawls, baking mudflats cracked and coated with alkaline. On aerial shots, the delta's feathery tree of life appears withered.

Our tour group first stopped on the dam's crown, at one of the van-size concrete pouring buckets, a memento of construction times. "Five million cubic yards of concrete were poured," Duane boasted, while a uniformed guard loitered nearby. "Cement blocks were cooled with ice water for fourteen days before the next block was set into place." A heavily made-up German woman in a stars-and-stripes vest and straw cowboy hat worried about "ze kracks on ze side of ze dam." She should have seen the 300-foot black polythene one that Ed Abbey and Earth First! unrolled from the dam crown in 1981, decommissioning this engineering marvel in an inspired bit of political street theater and optical illusion. Two years later, Nature almost accomplished the real thing. Unprecedented speedy masses of snowmelt had threatened to overtop or unmoor the dam from its "solidified sand dunes" foundations.

Duane assured the worrywart tourist that those cracks were the seams of the concrete blocks and perfectly safe. I was more concerned about the lush hanging gardens and tapestry seeps on both canyon walls downstream of the dam. To Duane's credit, he admitted that the reservoir's leakage through porous Navajo sandstone—the dam's anchoring rock—caused those. Fifteen feet lie between Lake Powell's high-water mark and the dam crest; Duane mentioned the 1983 snowmelt, which almost crested and threatened the dam and everybody downstream. He recalled the 5.5 magnitude earthquake of 1993. (A precision earthquake "to shake that dam loose once and for all," for which Abbey and his pal Jack Loeffler prayed on their knees, had failed to materialize.)

Our tour guide moved on to praise the lake's fishing, its annual contests, citing record striped bass that weighed in at forty-eight pounds and eleven ounces. Not a word about the dam's impact on the finned natives downstream, in the Grand Canyon. When I leaned over the parapet on the reservoir side, the side formerly considered "upstream," I spotted an introduced trophy fish near one of the intakes, floating belly-up. Biodiversity was not all they had squandered. As if in a fugue state, I saw long-ago people leaning against sun-soaked walls, coiling clay pots and braiding rope, watching naked children splash in a creek bed below. Silt now settled on the kiva roofs. Carps and bass swam through windows and doorways, bug-eyed alien home invaders. Images drawn onto an alcove wall, praising the life-giving power of rain, dissolved in the twilight depths next to crumpled beer cans and hovering plastic-bag jellyfish. Gone was the fluted cascade of canyon wrens, the machine-gun *rat-a-tat* of northern flickers. Gone was the swishing of cattails and willows in the breeze. Down there, murk and the wrong kind of silence now reigned absolute. Even in the unlikely case that the reservoir would be drained or fully dry up, it is thought that the alcoves would have been scoured clean. Pots and granaries would have further disintegrated, arrowheads and metates long been buried under hundreds of feet of sediment. But at least for now, the ancestors' bones lay undisturbed.

I have been accused of hypocrisy. During one pre-trip rig at an outfitter in Fredonia, the warehouse manager—seeing an *Undam Glen Canyon* sticker on my personal ammo can (a guide's idea of a purse)—scowled at me. "If it wasn't for that dam, your river season would be pretty short."

"I'd take that any day," I replied, "because it's not just about what we want or think we need." Having missed the epic flood of '83, I'd in fact give a pinkie to see the Colorado in a spate.

After pausing at the merry-go-round of a display turbine, we entered a second elevator, bound for the belly of the beast. Bridging the silence in the tight cubicle, Duane informed us that we were passing several inspection galleries on our way down, each equipped with instruments that measure the dam's flex under varying pressure from the reservoir. "It's a living creature," he reminded us. In exiting, I looked up the concrete elevator shaft, slightly woozy. We followed a neon-lit, echoing tunnel chilly as a bunker or meat locker. *More than 100 feet of concrete lie between you and the waters of Lake Powell* read a sign near some drafty hole, and a gray sample polished like gemstones was displayed to be touched. Comforted by its smooth solidity, we emerged on a gallery at the dam's foot. Between the generating station and the dam stretched a buzz-cut, incomprehensibly green lawn—a space level and wide enough for a game of golf—planted, according to Duane, "to make it look nice."

Bulging against the river's might, the blinding white act of defiance stolidly linked brick-red canyon walls. At this shrine, a society worshipped technology, its own cleverness, but despite the overwhelming gigantism it felt like veneer on the masonry of the ages—a child's stick barrier in a gutter.

I wondered how many in our motley band had read *Encounters with the Archdruid*. In this hard-hitting triptych, the essayist John McPhee recounts Bureau of Reclamation commissioner Floyd Dominy's comment on the pre-dam river: "The unregulated Colorado was a son of a bitch. It wasn't any good. It was either in flood or in trickle." The federal water tsar, confronting Sierra Club director Dave Brower on a joint Grand Canyon trip the writer had arranged, admitted that from an engineering perspective, he'd as much enjoy deconstructing the dam as he had putting it up. Wags named the lake sediment that the drought has exposed and hardened the "Dominy Formation." They hope that, before long, after silting up the reservoir, a river resurgent overtopping the dam will turn it into "Dominy Falls." Vaughn Short, the horse-packing, river-running bard, fingered the culprits in "Floyd's Void":

> There's a breed of men who sit at their desks
> And they like their water tame...

What was being reclaimed? One definition that dictionaries are spitting out for reclamation is "the cultivation of wasteland or land formerly under water." The BuRec beavers flipped this on its head, wasting formerly cultivated land, land the ancients and homesteaders had been gardening, under water. Other meanings, such as "reasserting a right," or "revoking something granted," codify the entitlement to trash a living river in this case, though what right or grant existed there in the first place? The term, an outgrowth of biblical primacy and Manifest Destiny, ignores prior claims, whether human or other-than-human, the latter of which, in Henry Beston's pithy phrasing, constitute "other nations, caught with ourselves in the net of life and time." True reclamation is currently happening in the resurgent side canyons of a drought-stricken puddle in freefall.

In a way, that concrete atrocity had turned me into a writer. After reading somewhere that 120 canyons drowned as the reservoir level rose, I'd decided some years ago to explore an equal number of canyons on the Colorado Plateau to understand the magnitude of this eradication. Journals I kept during these treks morphed into a bigger story and then into my first book—strange to think that five million cubic yards of congealed hubris have been my muse.

Inside the generating station, from a bridge like that of a ship or a spaceship, we admired a row of eight buttercup-yellow, spinning generators, each the size of a small two-story house and fed by a penstock ("fifteen feet in diameter") that sluiced water down from eight reservoir intakes. An overhead video screen spouted more techno-propaganda, and a sign reminiscent of Soviet-era factories praised *Reclamation—108 years of serving the West.* Thank you for your service! The uneven, hand-drawn number *8* showed that it had been proudly updated each year.

The desert, as it always has, serves up famine or feast, now mostly the former. This millennium's first two decades have been the driest spell in the Southwest in 1,200 years. The Bureau of Reclamation's reign in comparison is the lifespan of a housefly. Scant snow cover in the Rockies from this megadrought has lowered the reservoir to 27 percent of its capacity, a level barely above the intake pipes essential in power generation. Were those to be exposed by the line dropping further, sucking air instead of water, the dam's turbines would stop spinning and a colossal hiccup in the system could damage its generators. That condition, which also strands marinas high and lonesome, is "dead pool," officially and appropriately.

A new menace thus surfaced downstream, joining the rapacious trout feeding on chub eggs and fry: smallmouth bass, until now confined to the reservoir's warmer upper layers. Their life zone now sits near the intake tubes, through which some have escaped to wilder pastures beyond. In 1962, Utah and Wyoming fishery managers poisoned more than 400 miles of the Green River with the pesticide rotenone, to wipe out the odd "undesirable" native fish species in favor of trout to be released below Flaming Gorge Reservoir. The lethal bloom drifted downstream, into Dinosaur National Monument. Sixty years later, the Park Service dumped rotenone in a slough behind a cobble bar below Glen Canyon Dam to save humpback chubs hanging on by the tips of their pectoral fins from non-native sunfish and bass appetites. Different times, different priorities.

On the upside for us cactus-huggers, floods have cleared fifty-foot lake-sediment beds from the ends of Glen Canyon tributaries, like angioplasty freeing a stagnant gourmand's arteries. Wildlife, willows, and cottonwood seedlings do nature's work again. The falls at the Cathedral in the Desert plunge pool have been resurrected. Thirty archaeological sites not seen since the 1960s resurfaced. Museum of Northern Arizona researchers found at least a fourth of those listed in a pre-dam survey have survived inundation. Among them are sturdy stonewalls, stairs, rock art (diminished), metates, flint tools, potsherds, and one intact pot with its yucca-fiber carrying cord. There the artifacts sit, on dry land, resurrected from their watery grave but exposed to visitor vandalism and the urge to own.

Reservoir fluctuations give up other things, more reminders of our own kind's short tenure, in the Navajo sandstone—things older than golf balls, petrified diapers, and houseboats crusty with minerals, things that even predate Anasazi artifacts. In 2023, they bared tracks and bones of Jurassic burrowing herbivores, mammal relatives that looked like badger-lizard crosses and that overlapped with the dinosaurs.

At long last, I spy a black-and-white-banded metal post pounded into slickrock slightly below the rim, in line with several others. Rubber-kneed under my heavy pack, I seek traction, shuffling down an exposed sandstone ramp with the posture of a stubborn mule. A chainsaw's nasal drawl rises from the canyon bottom— tamarisk control or firewood cutting for a fisherman's camp? After passing an alcove with cowboy inscriptions, I approach the last and steepest pitch above the river. Here, a steel cable, the trail's "rope," runs through eyebolts in the wall. Avoiding frayed strands that could draw blood from my palms, I lower myself hand over hand, feet planted firmly against naked rock.

I now have descended roughly the same distance I "traveled" by elevator from the dam's crown to the power plant, but the two trips couldn't be more different.

At the bottom trailhead, the hiker faces a shithouse half as big as some cabins I've lived in. It sits smack-dab in a site of worship. Millennia ago, out of the rock varnish, Desert Archaic hunters chipped beanpole, latticed figures with light-bulb heads, bug eyes, and "antenna" appendages. The bullets of imbeciles "killed" the panel's bighorn sheep, the mainstay of people who entrapped spirits in stone, who appeased and bound animals to themselves by magic. The crack of the nimrods' shots must have resounded like rams' clashes, head butting that the Diné thought produced thunder. I'd pay admission to watch such ritual violence.

Lightheaded from the heat and the climb, I loll in tamarisk shade, glugging tepid water. Midges whine and a raven talks to its own echo. Below the cliff rim across the river, I notice four test pits for dam sites that engineering geologists considered but ultimately rejected.

I get up and walk upstream to an old cable car, a relic of more optimistic days. The dam that goes with it lies around the bend, out of sight, which is just fine.

Looking for the beach behind the shrubbery belt, I stumble into a squirrel's nest of a camp gouged from the tamarisks. Two geezers in folding chairs puff enormous cigars among coolers, solar showers, and fishing paraphernalia. A chainsaw sits on the ground. They thinned the green canopy to make room for their

Bedouin tent, hiding from the sun and the world.

On the beach's sand crescent, I unroll the packraft I had strapped to my pack. As I inflate it with an ingenious nylon air-bag, which I squeeze like Scottish pipes, two pontoon motorboats are pulling up, disgorging gear and kayakers who will paddle downstream to Lees Ferry. To get a head start and perhaps a camp to myself, I push off right away, wedged into my raft.

This is my little tub's maiden voyage, and I enjoy its ma-neuverability—it turns as if on a swivel—and the freedom and ease of travel it affords. Working my shoulder muscles also feels good after the punishing hike. The spark of self-sufficient discovery galvanizes me, as it does after every launch. I stab my double-bladed paddle into the river, watching water pearl from its edges and momentarily dance on the surface like droplets on a hot stoveplate. Little whirlpools follow each stroke, hand-blown miniature waterspouts. Fish jump. A cormorant rakes through the afternoon, a stumpy-winged crow. A red-necked grebe dives, leaving haiku pond-ripples. About a quarter-mile downstream, a spring splashes from a fern-bearded rock crevice straight into the river, calming as a courtyard fountain. Already, most of the canyon lies wrapped in shadows, but occasionally, low-angle light sheets down a defile, igniting fall willows and tamarisks on shore. Between sightseeing planes and motorboats that chop into the Glen's tranquility, I can peer through cracks in the present, glimpsing what it must have been before. Heeding Abbey's rec-ommendation, I rediscover "sights and sounds a million years older and infinitely lovelier than the roar of motorboats...a small and imperfect sampling of the kind of experience that was taken away from everybody." Even the few pockets of recent civilization in Glen Canyon's bottom could charm; a farm at Hite boasted cherry trees and a vineyard. The Dandy Crossing ferry was a modest, old-timey affair, a wooden platform pulled across on a cable by the engine of a Ford Model A mounted on deck, an Al Capone-style car that already was an antique then. Abbey foresaw that Hite Marina, Bullfrog Marina, Rainbow Bridge Marina and, eventually, Wahweap would be abandoned, though he fingered the wrong cause: siltation instead of the planet's meltdown. I wish this cesspool's end were just a regional, erosional symptom.

I cannot help but imagine what we would have done regardless, to wring lucre from Glen Canyon's allure. Jet tour boats would ply the river, as they now do below Moab and above "Lake" Mead. Helicopters would shuttle the rushed rich to and from the canyon. Private permits would be hard to obtain, rock art would be vandalized, riverbanks trampled, campsites overrun...yet another quiet place loved to death. Beginning in 1948, Arizona business pioneer Art Greene *did* offer motorized trips from Lees Ferry, upriver to Forbidding Canyon and nearby Rainbow Bridge, spearheading industrial tourism's assault on the canyon country. In a way, the Glen seems safer now, ensconced in our memories, our dreams, untouched by crowds or bureaucracy.

At the Honey Draw riffle, the current accelerates; fronds of weed and river cobbles rush by underneath the raft, some Lewis Carroll netherworld, as I get sucked onto the glistening tongue. Blowing down the chute, I flinch at licks of icy water.

It is getting late, and I look for a camp. At Ferry Swale, a veritable tent city has mushroomed with lustily burning fires, and so I continue. Tamarisks choke the banks, and where they did not find a foothold, erosion has gullied other possible tent sites. Eventually, I make landfall at Mile Nine, near the apex of Horseshoe Bend, where the river doubles back as if to meet with itself.

The canyon's east rim flares like burnished copper before it turns leaden gray. Warm and cool air currents caress me while I fix dinner. Mourning doves mourn what once was. When a breeze combs the tamarisk thickets, the expiring day sighs. Silhouetted walls amplify water shushing across gravel bars, cicadas shrilly pulsing in the bushes, and later, stars shining bright as lit dust motes. Never mind the scattered bottle caps, the hobo hearths of metal-ringed fire pits, or the camp's sign fluorescing in the beam of my headlamp. Fifty thousand boaters a year change a place.

I awake to some yahoos hollering on the Horseshoe Bend overlook. It has now become an Instagram hotspot, requiring a much bigger parking lot, and several followers have plunged to their deaths off its prow. Sticking my head out of my tent, I see ants on the rim, with camera flashes going off. I briefly consider showing my butt but instead wolf down breakfast, break camp, load up, and go.

The gorge has a Sunday morning feel to it—as a matter of fact, it *is* Sunday. I rest on my elbows, paddle athwart, and surrender to the river. Like me, herons inertly survey the scene. In an eddy, mallards chortle as if at some private joke. A raven sculls past, alighting on yet another sign, where he throws back his head and slides some limp thing down his gullet. Twirling on glassy boils, I glide past Finger Rock's pillar, which slips through my field of vision. In some places, blind arches texture the cliffs like walled-off tunnels. Elsewhere, buttresses plunge directly into translucent green crystal, leaving no beaches whatsoever. I did not bring a camera this time, as that can be distracting. Though photos serve well as mnemonic crutches, as a writer, I try to paint word pictures and would rather not squeeze grand landscapes into a tiny viewfinder. My photos aren't good enough to hang in galleries, but they serve as writing prompts. Last but not least, the camera does not capture other sensations: cliffrose vanilla, liquid raven mutterings, sun and water on skin, the radish sharpness of cress, or the iron in alcove spring water.

When on occasion I flip once again through the color plates of *The Place No One Knew*, Eliot Porter's photographic elegy for Glen Canyon, I cannot help feeling a mix of despair and nostalgia, or "solastalgia," as this kind of affliction, this grief for places erased, is nowadays called. Too young to have experienced this gem of the Colorado Plateau before it was flooded, yet old enough to have heard grizzled river rats talk of its splendors, I almost wish these photos did not exist, that they would not evoke the riches squandered. And yet, Lake Powell draws vastly more amateur and professional photographers than the gorge it submerged ever did.

Transcending mere documentation, Porter's lacquered vignettes, which the Sierra Club published to undermine planned Colorado River concrete stoppers, together with titles like Philip Hyde's *The Last Redwoods*, Hyde and Ansel Adams' *Time and the River Flowing*, and the illustrated anthology *This is Dinosaur,* supported campaigns to preserve iconic Southwestern landscapes. Porter, a student of Adams, was aware of the camera's clout. He described it as "a propaganda device, and a weapon for the defense of the environment." The relationships that interested him were "both biological and aesthetic, ecological in the broadest sense: interactions between living things and the physical environment, which includes rock, water, and ambient light." The light also entranced Georgia O'Keeffe, who joined Porter on a couple of guided trips through the Glen. In-between sacrificing people to trees, the "Archdruid" and Nobel Peace Prize nominee David Brower had visited three times. As the Sierra Club's director, electrified by Porter's prints, he'd conceived the masterpiece that of course should have been titled *The Place Not Many White People Knew*. Brower, not knowing what was there before he went there and when it was too late, had let Glen Canyon Dam go unopposed in exchange for scrapping plans for dams in Echo Park in Lodore Canyon on the Green River, and in the Grand Canyon's Marble Canyon and Bridge Canyon. Brower regretted this Washington horse trade for the rest of his life. Glen Canyon's light struck him, too; he listened to its harmonies:

> The inner world of the side canyons, walled in shadows, will never know the sun but may catch reflected hues from a high opposite wall. The thin crescent of blue is the inner world's only fragment of sky, and any shiny place in the depths will mirror but distort it. The reflected light cannot be conventional when the incident light is not...

What would the soundtrack for this gorge be? "Thus Spoke Zarathustra," or something more intimate, less grandiose? A non-human tune, perhaps. The birds' dawn chorus. Our planet's humming. The music of orbiting spheres.

Before this float, I'd lingered over a set of repeat photos of a rockscape somewhere in canyon country. Except for the quality of photographic lenses and film stock, the passage of fifty-some years had made little difference. My eyes snagged on a juniper hunched in the foreground, gnarled like an arthritic hand. The tree looked so fragile. Barely hanging on in a parched land, it remained virtually unchanged. It inspired humility, awe. It stirred me to try to help it survive those photos of it.

Visitors often comment on the reservoir's Kodachrome aqua color. "The river is so dirty," people in my raft, on the other hand, sometimes complain. I tell them it's the sediment that gave the Colorado its name. And that "humus" and "human" have the same root (Latin *humi*: "on the ground") and that in creation myths throughout the world original people were shaped from clay. I tell them how, once we've used up the tap water we carry on trips, we'll let river water settle in five-gallon buckets overnight, and then decant and filter it. We should not worry about dirt but giardia, I say, a parasite hiding in cow pies and human crap, a waterborne bug you don't wish upon your worst enemy. And, "I'd be more concerned about what you cannot see": traces of radioactivity from the Atlas Mine tailings piles or that company's brazen, We-dare-to-rub-it-in-your face "Pandora" Mine, both near Moab, upstream; or from naturally occurring uranium in the Grand Canyon's Horn Creek; or petrochemicals from the boaters recreating on Lake Powell; plus wastewater from the reservation. "It's not dirty enough," I say when I feel especially pesky downstream from the dam, referring to the good kind of dirt. By the end of each trip, with the sun having done its dehydrating work, clients swig the Colorado as if it were forty-buck bubbly. With that drinking water, the river circulates inside us, its restlessness ours, causing some of us ever to return to its silky bosom.

I must take a minute or two or five here to sing dirt's prais-
es. Born from a Norse word for excrement, the word teems with
negative connotations: "dirt-poor," "dirty work," "dirty jokes,"
"getting the dirt on somebody," and the related "muckraker"
and "mudlark." (Among river runners and desert rats, however,
"dirtbag" is an honorific.) It runs the gamut from tan to brick red.
The catchall contains multitudes: sand, clay, loess, volcanic ash,
minerals, molds, plant debris, and—yes—excrement. But dirt is
ambivalent. "Grit" and "sand" dirt represent mental and physical
fiber. For the original inhabitants of the Colorado Plateau—human
and non-human—dirt has been home, wealth, paint, crockery,
and medicine, the stuff of creation. It shelters animal life: worms,
insects, rodents, reptiles, amphibians, burrowing owls, bears, and
badgers. You can measure and rate biodiversity by sampling soil
from different locations and taking a species headcount. Playing
in dirt helps children to literally bond with the earth. And not
only that; exposure to dirt may boost mood, along with the im-
mune system, even in adults. A friendly soil bacterium has been
linked to the increased production of serotonin, the "happiness
hormone," in mice.

As pervasive as it is, dirt also holds absences, from animal
tracks to the Grand Canyon's mile-deep chasm. The grist that the
mill of erosion removes gets swept to the Gulf or piled against
Hoover Dam. Arroyos and fluvial terraces testify to the dustbowl
years that broke pre-Columbian cultures. Mudstone and shale
keep tactile evidence of fossil dirt: the washboard ripples of ancient shallows. In geological and archaeological layers, dirt preserves a record that reaches back without rupture over hundreds
of millions of years. It is easy to wax downright philosophical
about dirt. We are stardust, dust in the wind, residue of the eons.
Ashes to ashes; dust to dust. We are dirt.

Before the dam, the Colorado hauled more than half a million
tons of silt and sediment per day past Bright Angel Point. Clyde

Eddy, commanding a guide, a gaggle of Ivy-League students, a hobo who'd fallen off a train, a mutt (Rags), and a black bear cub from a traveling circus on the first successful Grand Canyon high-water run, saw water "so heavy with suspended sand that it rolls along like a river of quicksilver, sweeping everything irresistibly before it. When men are thrown into the stream their clothing fills with sand and the very weight of it drags them down to death." Then, he wrote in *Down the World's Most Dangerous River*, "The cruel and cunning river hides their bodies in backwaters in its lonely canyons and covers them with sand, burying them there forever."

Well—not exactly forever, in most cases. In 1975, a hiker downstream from the South Rim's Tanner Trail near the mouth of Cardenas Creek found a skeleton nestling amid driftwood, soon determined to be the remains of Bert Loper, the "Grand Old Man of the Colorado." The Glen Canyon prospector, homesteader, and scout leader had died rowing, in 1949. In the tumult of 24.5-Mile Rapid, Loper slumped, from a stroke or heart attack, and his boat flipped and he vanished, despite the life preserver he wore. The seventy-nine-year-old had embarked on his last adventure against the advice of not one but four physicians. His was an end many a boatman envies, the next-best thing to a Viking sendoff.

Across from Waterholes Canyon, fly fishermen enact age-old foraging rituals; casting spider silk from the shallows, they offer time and hope to some wild, pagan river god. Waterholes is one of only two side canyons spared partial or full flooding by the reservoir, one of over a hundred that accounted for Glen Canyon's particular charm. Near Cave Canyon, a skipped piece of slate skims the still surface—a belted kingfisher patrolling for fingerling trout. A peregrine spooks a raft of ducks, which scoot with a sound like a sloughing cutbank. After a failed attempt to bushwhack to Hislop Cave, I watch its black yawn sail past high on river left. In the late 1800s, Navajo raiders who'd killed a rancher in Utah drove his sheep across the frozen river here after sprinkling sand on the ice. They hid the flock behind the cave mouth's perfect Roman arch. Where the cliffs recede above the more widely eroded Chinle shale and volcanic ash of the Echo Cliffs monocline, an old roadbed to Lees Ferry dips and swerves along the left bank. On Powell's second, follow-up expedition, a teen with a pencil moustache, who would not stick out in a Starbucks, had climbed a sand slide the size of a ski slope and then a peak on the opposite shore and fired a revolver at the river, ruffled perhaps by what lay ahead or by the grand silence. "When I pulled the trigger," he journaled, "I was positively startled by the violence of the report, a deafening shock like a thousand thunder-claps in one.... Next, from far away there was a rattle as of musketry and peal after peal of the echoing shot came back to us." The echo, which he timed in a repeat performance, was delayed by a full twenty seconds. Let us not judge Frederick Dellenbaugh's noisemaking rashly. Who has not toyed with the bodiless voice in the wilderness, not listened to it bouncing off sandstone walls, clipping syllables from words, to eventually fade back into silence? There's magic in this form of play, and we assert our aliveness thus in hostile surroundings that dwarf us. The desire to be heard in, to be known by, this titanic gorge, to assure ourselves that we have substance against the desert's vacuum of mute indifference, weighs heavily on many a visitor. It may weigh equally on the dam engineer. Writ large, it's our species loneliness in the cosmos.

Less unsettled by the unknown—enthralled, you might even say, with being overwhelmed—Grand Canyon guides entertain clients with flute playing or a cappella singing in Blacktail Canyon or Redwall Cavern, as they once did in Glen Canyon's Music Temple of fame. They choose these sites for the reverb and intimate coziness. Music Temple, a grotto in a wet tributary three miles below the San Juan River confluence, was sanctified Navajo land. Its historical visitor log, removed before the flooding, resides in the University of Utah's Special Collections. A magnificent grove of box elders and cottonwoods screened the mouth of that feeder canyon. The eponymous chamber, in Powell's description, was "more than 200 feet high, 500 feet long, and 200 feet wide," with "a narrow, winding skylight" a thousand feet above. His brother Walter sang a favorite Civil War ballad in a fine bass voice there on the first expedition. The major, in a spell of animism, writing that the hollow was "doubtless made for an academy of music by its storm-born architect," bestowed the name under which it was afterward known. A one-second note, they say, resonated for eleven Taj Mahal seconds in this temple.

Ancient peoples would have had no scientific paradigm to explain such auditory effects as invisible pressure waves that stack up into echoes. To them, voices seemed to issue from within the rocks. Some archaeologists think that the sonic properties of certain sites may have influenced the placement of rock art there, marking portals to other worlds. Stone surfaces appeared permeable, as in the case of a boulder on Lime Ridge, near Utah's Valley of the Gods, a hogan that a Diné deity had petrified. When people approached it, they could hear the wailing of wayward children trapped inside. A Paiute legend tells of witches in snakeskin who hide among rocks and delight in repeating the words of passersby. In a worldview differing from ours, echoes did not reflect the needy self but the powers of Earth. Diné holy men made Talking Rock medicine from scrapings they gathered in an echoing cave. Mixed with plant matter, it was used to cure illnesses and the symptoms of witchcraft. The Singers believed that the echo ingredient doubled the potency of their healing songs. In a similar vein, prayers in an alcove near Bluff petitioned Monster Slayer, or "Killer of Enemies," on behalf of servicemen going to war; the attendant echoes increased the plea's spiritual range.

"The ear is an eye," the poet Wallace Stevens wrote. (So is the tongue, and by extension, the written word.) Acoustics define a place unmistakably, with each sound announcing an action, a presence. The more my eyesight relaxes, and the more vision rules everyday life, the more I find myself drawn into the audible world. As it becomes quickly impoverished, the voices of animal species drop out of the chorus one by one.

Too soon, wall stumps of local stone and the Paria Riffle's unvarying pitch, a ringing that makes me homesick, spell the end of Glen Canyon. And thus commences the Grand Canyon, grandest of all, Abbey's "conveyor belt for baloney boats," which I shall leave for some other time, some bigger baloney boat.

Duly impressed, a bit shell-shocked, we had resurfaced in the busy visitor center: The teenage couple holding hands as if on a date. The Euros, always chic, seeing the best 'merica has in store. The *Jurassic Park* fan getting kicks from nature engineered into amusement. And the dad holding the hand of a four-year-old boy with a dozer emblazoned on his T-shirt. As I was preparing to dodge bodies in the lobby and beeline for the exit, a tall, bald-headed punk rocker turned to me: "Not too bad a tour, huh?"

Not at all. Not at all. Not if you like nature transformed into techno or metal or grunge. One number had been missing, drowned out by Duane's rote citation—the number of miles between Hite and the dam, the true measure of Glen Canyon before its undoing: 186. It took days, sometimes weeks, to string them together with paddle strokes and with elbow grease, and each mile was miracle-filled. Surviving names evoke mossy grottoes and phallic rocks, ruins tucked into cliff seams, petroglyphs, stone-cut hand-and-toe trails, corkscrew narrows, dripping springs, cottonwood groves, solitude, mystery, history, romance, the poetry of moon-shadow and resonant halls. Twilight Canyon, Tapestry Wall, Klondike Bar, Last Chance Creek, Iceberg Canyon, Cathedral in the Desert, Hole in the Rock, Hidden Passage, Crossing of the Fathers... I curse the sins of *our* fathers (our mothers' to a lesser degree). They sacrificed too much beauty for what they mistook for progress. Born too late, I have nothing of the dear, crippled stem but these names and the last fifteen miles.

Vermilion Light

WHAT ATTRACTS US TO NEW PLACES? What compels us to stuff our car trunk or backpack, to once again brave marathon drives, truck-stop fare, or the Byzantine requirements of land managers for a backcountry permit? The trigger can be an aside by a friend. A snippet of history stumbled upon. A rumor of rock art or refuge. Or simply a name.

As first snow dusts the ashen peaks that front my hometown and the sun's arc flattens, Arizona's Vermilion Cliffs promise light glorious and exuberant, a last taste of summer. In these waning days of the year, I long for the palette of canyon light, for pastels refracted by smooth facades, for arches and alcoves, towers and buttresses varnished and richly aglow.

Fall is my favorite time in the canyons. The mosquitoes and deerflies are gone, and so are most tourists. Clear, tranquil days succeed each other, gleaming like childhood memories. Beneath vegetal decay, I sense a sweet feeling of loss in the air, which pinches the heart. Gold briefly ennobles box elders and cotton-woods before winter's rude disrobing.

The hardest part of each morning is stepping into the icy stream, soaking my socks and boots. Knee-deep in the Paria, I resign myself to numb feet and a sunburned neck before reaching camp in the afternoon, where a cup of mud will take off the edge. Aside from the water and air temperature, in the upper canyon the season's advanced stage is not obvious. Growth is sparse here at all times—rabbitbrush, coyote willow, and tamarisk cling to shallow soil pockets. The odd box elder has not yet shed her serrated leaves or even changed color. Pillars and crosshatched whalebacks rise above the still canyon rims, sentinels from the past watching over the present.

Upstream of the famous narrows, waves of Page sandstone

and the red Carmel formation abut the wash with swirled ice-cream flavors. Strawberry. Butterscotch. Pumpkin. Vanilla. The variegated rock chronicles floods that alternated over millions of years between muddy, tinted and sandy, clear. More recent runoff has sculpted eccentricities from this material, hourglasses and Swiss-cheese perforations, cracks, niches, and lattices, and eye sockets filled with polished pebbles high water left there—perfect hideouts for lizards or gnomes.

"At the end of a day of walking," the filmmaker Werner Herzog wrote, crossing the Alps, "the wealth of a single day is past counting."

Backpacking was my first outdoor love and, despite the forced marches of army days, remains my preferred mode of travel. It provides a sense of self-sufficiency and independence I rarely experience in a world hedged with constraints and demands. As a snail carries its house, I carry all essentials—food, extra clothes, and my shelter—in a package on my back. Except for spiritual nourishment and the miracles of chance encounters, I expect nothing but water from this place. Ecstasy is always welcome, a bonus. My pack even has room for some luxuries: a folding chair, a pint of Scotch, flip-flops for camp, *War and Peace*. I never read about the desert while I venture there, afraid that another writer's view would cloud mine. The plight of Napoleon's Grande Armée in Russia's snowy wastes keeps me cool and, by contrast, comforted. It is good to remember: ordeals can be so much worse.

True, each additional pound is paid for with sweat; but the longer I hike, the lighter the load becomes. Provisions dwindle, stamina grows, and the desire to finish fortifies me. (As does the occasional sip from a flask.) Besides, like much ecstasy, complete exhaustion wipes out the self, which can be a blessing. As long as I feed this engine and maintain its parts it will serve me well, and cheaper than one made of steel.

I do my best thinking while walking and find myself in good company. "I can only meditate when I am walking," Rousseau confessed. Kierkegaard composed all his literary works on foot, he insisted. "You must walk like a camel," Thoreau counseled, "which is said to be the only beast which ruminates when walking." And I do. An entire school of sages, the Greek Cynic philosophers, lived vagabond lives, berating the settled that stooped in the market places. (Diogenes, who might have slept in a wine barrel, thought Aristotle's legs were too skinny.) A walk down memory lane is not just metaphorical, either—Charles Darwin acknowledged the mnemonic edge sauntering gives.

Topography structures cerebral cadences. Deep breaths perfuse thoughts. Footfalls beat a rhythm for language and song. In walking, the mind unkinks for its dialogue with nature, and the longer the walk, the deeper the dialogue. There is scientific truth to all this. Regular walkabouts improve memory and reduce depression, anxiety, and the risk of dementia. They keep you mentally spry. The semi-automatic, repetitive act leaves the creative part of the brain free to go gallivanting. Another bonus of thinking afoot, a pain-relieving side effect, is the distraction it offers from blisters and creaky joints.

One last advantage of backpacking as a form of locomotion comes from its leisurely pace. Human perception is attuned to, and evolved at, walking speed: three miles per hour. Walking, upright and long-distance, is the one physical skill at which we alone in the animal kingdom excel. It made us who we are. But from the "Devil-Wagon" of yore to the writer-curmudgeon-my-cologist Lawrence Millman's "two-ton wheelchair" to supersonic passenger jets, the increasingly hectic pace with which we have altered ecosystems and the entire planet has hastened the "Great Acceleration." It would behoove us to decelerate, as individuals and as a species. "For untold thousands of years," the historian and geographer John Brinckerhoff Jackson writes, "we traveled on foot over rough paths not simply as peddlers or commuters or tourists, but as men and women for whom the path and road stood for some intense experience: freedom, new human relationships, a new awareness of the landscape." With slapping sandals of braided agave fiber and pounding cowhide boots, on the tracks, often, of mule deer or bighorn sheep, humans have spun a web of ground truths. Compressed soil snaking between plant islands, across slopes, over desert intaglio, on ridge crests, and through washes links the South Rim and North Rim, the canyons and California's coast, us with the earth and each other. Throughout history, *Homo sapiens* has left trackways like tangled storylines on the land. We first walked out of Africa around 180,000 years ago, to the ends of the Earth, for whatever reasons, and have been unsettled ever since. Some of us, feeling that itch, are not yet ready to stop.

Proceeding down-canyon, I pass through hot and cold air currents. With them come whiffs of cow and juniper berry backed by notes of stale water. A tarantula hawk ghosts by, raising the hair on my neck. Anything this big should be a bird. It is actually a kind of neo-tropical wasp and looks the part. Driving, you would miss such gems. The only insects you're likely to see explode bile-green on your windshield, now, by all accounts far fewer than there used to be. Males of this bruiser wasp are content to siphon nectar from flowers. Females, which can become as big as my pinkie, look very attractive with their glossy black rump and amber wings. You expect them to buzz, but their approach is silent as an owl's, which makes them even more eerie. They are ruthless predators, true femmes fatale, but also good providers. No. They are what they are and should be: utterly alien despite any labels we pin on them. After mating, the female locates the inhabited burrow of a tarantula or trapdoor spider. Twanging strands at the entrance, she summons the spider, an assassin ringing the doorbell. She then sinks her stinger into the homeowner and drags the paralyzed prey to her own lair, where she lays a single egg onto it. After hatching, the wasp larva feeds on the interred body until the time comes to transform itself, cocooned in silk. Perhaps, another terrible beauty will be born. If female, the young wasp will unfurl cellophane wings the following spring and take off on her own life-giving search-and-destroy mission. This way of propagating may seem brutal, but it's part of the magnificent cycle that holds all living things. Compassion is a little icing nature put on our consciousness cake. Of course, it is also what made us social, successful, and become invested in public welfare.

Near the junction of the Paria Narrows and Buckskin Gulch, afternoon gilds the shallows. Navajo sandstone folds into tight goosenecks in the stream's repeated attempt to break free. I pass Slide Rock, a silo-size chunk spalled from cliffs. The Paria has sanded its base into a dainty pedestal, allowing hikers to walk underneath the slanted roof between the rock and the canyon wall. Considering this smorgasbord of impressions, I wonder how *pedestrian* acquired the negative meanings "commonplace; prosaic or dull." A colorful walker of Abyssinia's desert, Rimbaud was "a pedestrian, nothing more."

A little later I drop my pack at the cavernous confluence to stroll up the lower end of the gulch. From Wire Pass, a slit in the Cockscomb's incline, it unspools more than twelve miles toward the Paria, as the longest and most spectacular and therefore most popular slot canyon on the Colorado Plateau. It has claimed hikers' lives. The body of one flash-flood victim was found ten miles below the junction, in the Paria's main stem. In some places, squeezing your shoulders, Buckskin Gulch soars 500 feet overhead. In others, you wade cesspools or fight quicksand. Its roseate walls funnel me to a boulder jumble, which I pass underground by crawling through a cubbyhole instead of climbing over it. Suddenly, a feline face stares at me from the sand in front of my boot tips, eerily disembodied, a mask. Closer inspection reveals empty eye sockets, the muzzle, intact and with delicate whiskers, and patches of fur clinging to the browned skull. It's a bobcat, surprised and dismembered, possibly by ephemeral torrents. Here is another of the desert's many stories that will go untold for lack of witnesses or clear evidence.

Time dissolves as I move up the canyon. In a fit of "the bends," I want to peek around the next bend, and the bend after that, and always one more. I keep walking, under a spell.

Too soon, shadows lengthen inside the gulch, urging me to return to my pack and look for a tent site beyond the confluence. Before I reach camp, bats wing-stitch curlicues into the fabric of tangerine twilight.

The following day I enter another, much shorter side canyon breaching the Paria's palisades. Its spring splashes emerald across a sere canvas, spreading reeds, scouring rushes, and mosses under box elder and cottonwood canopies. Countless leaf skeletons rustle on the twigs—spoil from some caterpillar invasion. Yellowing tamarisk filigree and a few daisies colored like faded lilacs betray the year's waning. Coral light caresses the gorge, glancing off planed, tilted stone.

The trail ends under Wrather Arch, a colossal portal sprung from striped walls at the head of this box canyon. Freezer-size chunks of its ceiling litter the incline, crude chips from time's workbench. In all my canyon sojourns, I have witnessed rocks falling only a few times, normally heard rather than seen—the geological clock beats at an inhuman pace. More reason to slow down and behold, to listen to your heart beat, to measure your own pace against that of the ages.

Until the Paria begins to grind down through Kayenta sand-and-siltstone, the walking is easy, a constitutional along a beach, not a strenuous canyon scramble. Instead of crushed seashells and kelp, juniper berries and pine needles limn the wrack line. Summer's thunderstorms swept them from the edge of the Paunsaugunt Plateau, the Southern Paiutes' "Home of the Beavers," though you can spot them in the Colorado as well. Its Pink Cliffs thrust up as the topmost of topographical tiers known as the Grand Staircase. "These cliffs are bold escarpments hundreds and thousands of feet in altitude—grand steps by which the region is terraced," John Wesley Powell prefaced a geological survey he had commissioned. The oldest, upholding the Vermilion velvet cake near the ferry, sound absolutely delicious: Chocolate Cliffs. No less impressed, the pioneer whose name Bryce Canyon bears glossed that candy-cane badland as a "hell of a place to lose a cow." Paiutes Ghost-Dancing with their faces and hair painted white regretted that, by way of earthquakes, it didn't gobble up all the newcomers.

I set out on this trip into the cleft in the lower, red-blond formation after the monsoon season, to avoid pouncing surges. When I stoop by the river—a creek really, at this water level—frost rime on its margins turns out to be salt crystals blooming from the ground.

For half a mile, the staid streamlet perks up, hurdling across purple Kayenta ledges, pretending to be a rambunctious mountain brook. Squeezed by jagged terraces and talus, it ricochets between house rocks, forcing me to look for a dry route on the slopes. Hard to imagine that in 1871, sixty head of cattle were herded down this gash in the earth. How the walls must have rung with cows bawling at the land's bitterness! The first Anglo to stare dumbfounded at these features was John Doyle Lee, after the Mormon church ordered him to establish a Colorado River ferry at the Paria's mouth.

Lee had been scapegoated for the Mountain Meadow Massacre, during which a wagon train of settlers had been attacked and all adults killed. Reluctantly, the renegade obeyed his call of duty: to stay out of sight. He disappeared for a spell into No-whiteman's and No-white-woman's Land, secure between scalloped reefs, and started the ferry business with a boat Powell had abandoned. US marshals wanted him also for polygamy. In the course of an eventful life, Lee married eighteen women, cohabiting, they say, with as many as five at a time.

Lee's exile ended in 1874, and three years later, excommunicated by then, he faced a firing squad for his involvement in the slaughter. His need for female companionship had tripped him up. He was arrested while visiting one of his wives. Emma Lee, wife number seventeen, who had walked 1,400 miles behind a handcart from Illinois to the Great Salt Lake, kept operating the ferry until 1879, and then sold it. After three men drowned in a crossing in 1928, the ferry shut down and a bridge replaced it—one more step in the domestication of the Southwest.

Even in those paired steel arches, a semblance of wildness abides. Each time I pass underneath in a raft I crane my neck for the California condors that sometimes roost on the girders below and on shelves in the abutments. Birds bred in captivity have been released at one clifftop site for over twenty-five years. Reared by hand puppets, they still struggle with human wiles, dying from carrion poisoned with hunters' lead bullets. Some now hatch in the wild, augmenting the one-fifth of the world population that makes the canyon country their home. Some have surprised me by swooshing low across the escarpment whose thermals they ride. The broad back and white tags of one I saw from above while I traced the rim of the Redwall on my attempted traverse. I've heard a day-tripper on the South Kaibab Trail comment on how big the "vultures" there are when one on an outcrop unfolded its nine-foot shadow wings coded with white-number tags, to take off with the gravitas of a count spreading his coattails while settling into a chaise. I heard that another condor collapsed a backpacking tent, mistaking it for a dead cow; but that could be mere guide lore, the equivalent of an urban legend.

Where the stream weasels past a final constriction, the scenery changes once again. Saltbush dapples the wide and parched valley. Soft hills of Chinle simmer rainbow-striped, wrinkled by rain. A subtle splendor infuses the strata transected by Utah Highway 89 and the Colorado's lazy loops, each layer responding in its signature way to the touch of erosion and light. Flesh peels away, revealing Earth's skeleton, her innermost, fine-grained secrets.

Petroglyphs scarring rough-and-tumble colossi in the lower

Paria testify to the canyon's importance as a route to the Colorado long before Lee set foot on its banks. Only half of the images on one at the foot of the slope face right-side-up. Sometimes in rock art the dead are depicted head-down, topsy-turvy in limbo. But most likely this patinated giant rolled before pre-Columbians had finished engraving its sides. Or a different bunch (antipodes?) later came upon the toppled block. Its symbols and pointillist figures baffle us. Modern interpretations fail. The wild-sheep hunters that first combed these hollows did not distinguish between art and religion, between humans and non-humans, between the natural and the supernatural, or a rock and the world. They incised in stone what came to them in visions or dreams, what they saw or what they had heard in old stories, it did not matter which. If additional proof for the difference in mindsets is needed, consider which traveler now would chisel scorpions and centipedes into monoliths, and with flint burins only. Ours is an age of impatience, of destinations. To us moderns, Aldo Leopold wrote halfway in time between Lee and myself, that land is "the space between cities in which crops grow," and we bridge that space by car or plane. To the first people, the land upon which they walked was a source of strength.

So was the light. Equated with the rainbow, the hogan's ceiling protected residents like the multi-hued fringe of a drypainting does patients, who during a healing sit at the design's center, absorbing its powers. The doorway faced east, the direction where people prayed and made offerings, where the sun blossomed orange on the day construction began. It framed dawn's honeyed light, promising that all was as it should be. As a practical benefit, this orientation helped warm the house on high-desert midwinter mornings. Many anthills are aligned that way for the same reason. The quality of natural light inside a hogan changed with the sun's position throughout the season and day.

For the Hopis, the world's great awakening is an act of creation. They distinguish three phases: purple dawn (when you can see a person's shape); yellow dawn (when you can see a person's breath); and red sunrise (when a person is fully visible).

The Grand Canyon, destination of the Paria River, has been called a "House of Stone and Light." Both elements also rule at the Vermilion Cliffs. A patient person might sit all day and gaze at the serrated scarp, just to catch all nuances. Late fall afternoons yield the longest and most profound illumination, with a splinter of sadness embedded as the year dies. Sunrise stirs the Navajo sandstone's iron oxide, which also bands mounds of The Wave nearby. Rose-fingered indeed, the goddess rises from the opposed Echo Cliffs, daubing the landscape in permutations of loveliness. But early morning doesn't need a Greek deity; it has its own katsina, Talavai, rayed with a head-fan of eagle plumes. Formerly singing from rooftops, it woke up the villagers, who would not want to miss his gift. A perfect dawn, you realize, does not "break." It sweeps with incremental brushstrokes. Noon's crucible robs the colors of subtleties, casting the harshest shadows, except in Buckskin Gulch, other side canyons, and the Paria narrows, where sun shafts spear the depths and charged walls return a warm blush. That light has almost a tactile presence. Porter called it "enveloping," of all the phenomena of Glen Canyon's transepts the one "that evokes the ultimate in awe." It enlivens the mind and body on a wintry day, when you're immersed in shade or wading the stream. At dusk, shadows march up the canvas from the talus slopes, a third parapet growing from the ground. Pools and the stream during this hour brim with molten metal. Again, finally, tops ignite, flaring up golden-red, copper-plated more intensely than at dawn. After the sun seems to have sunk into the Kaibab Plateau, you drink in the canyon afterglow as rays the atmosphere scatters and bends briefly touch cliff crowns. A little later, when Venus winks on, the bedrock has grayed. Its bulk sits lifeless now. A hint of mauve lingers close to the horizon.

You yearn for the light sometimes for reasons beyond mere aesthetics.

On a spring day years ago, I'd chugged up an old route in a cleft, to the clifftops that outline the Paria Plateau. Spiral and sheep glyphs oversaw my ascent. When I stopped to gulp water high above blazing badlands, two condors slipped by so closely overhead that I could hear feathers soughing. I'd dropped my pack on the piñon-juniper tableland for a leisurely afternoon of exploring.

The forested plain, lacking significant features, kept throwing me curveballs. Whenever I thought I was back where I'd started: no pack. I tried retracing my steps but could not escape the maze of my boot prints in the red dirt. Dusk quickly intensified. Wind moaned from the abyss, pushing cold air. I bedded down under a grandfather pine, my blanket the prickly green of some boughs. Soon, clouds blotted the stars out. Raindrops penetrated the canopy, hitting my duvet, pitting the sand. I sought better shelter.

Curled into a niche in an undercut boulder too shallow to screen out the rain, I tried to reassure myself. *Each year, fewer than 100 Americans die from lightning strikes*. It was as dark as under a raven's wings. Ten miles from Page and Lake Powell's houseboat scene, and I couldn't see a single light.

But wait, *ZAP—BOOM!!!*

Spidery electricity split the sky, the atmosphere's white-hot temper raking the plateau. Every few minutes, a magnesium bolt leapt from the clouds, searing afterimages onto my retinas. Lightning is the antithesis of the warm radiance bathing these cliffs. Once in a while, a blinding tendril rooted in clouds spiked ground within sight. Thunder chased lightning ever more closely; the almost instantaneous claps told me that the storm was now milling straight overhead. I was wearing hiking boots, shorts, and a T-shirt, stretching the T like a miniskirt over my knees for a semblance of warmth.

Traditional Navajos consider lightning to be animate and

strike sites sacred, bull's-eyes of supernatural power. They observe taboos, some of which match Anglo weather wisdom. When it rains, a person should not stand in it, be in an open area, or carry guns and knives (or, in the White Man's case, umbrellas, golf clubs, or selfie sticks). He should remove his weapons, sit down, be quiet, and maintain a reverent mood. In the Navajo universe, lightning guards mountaintops against the ritually unprepared, climbers who fail to show proper respect. Perhaps the atmosphere roiling around me hinted at something.

Sitting humbled, in silence, was easy. Reaching deep enough for that reverence? Not so much. I knew that fate's scorching finger stabs the park—sometimes simultaneously points ten miles apart, or with lapis sky visible—on average 25,000 times a year. Concomitant flash floods kill more people within its boundaries, but that did not put my mind at ease. "The fear of lightning," Mark Twain wrote, "is one of the most distressing infirmities a human being can be afflicted with. It is mostly confined to women, but now and then you find it in a little dog, and sometimes a man." My dad's mom would wait out thunderstorms with her visiting grandchild on the lowest cellar stairs; the flash-bangs induced flashbacks to World War II bombings in her. Blasts from an anti-aircraft battery had rattled her windows as phosphorus and TNT blossomed among the row houses, and she'd survived a firestorm rung in by "Christmas tree" glaring markers that had clawed my birthplace for a week.

It was turning into the longest night of my life. Think school detention on a sweltering summer afternoon, but with added doses of terror.

I should have found solace in the fact that the Kolbs withstood worse. In the fall of 1930, Ellsworth and his brother Emery tried to enter the cave at the head of Clear Creek, above the inner gorge, not too far from Phantom Ranch, that gives birth to mysterious, intermittent Cheyava Falls. A tour guide acquaintance at a distance had mistaken it for "a big sheet of ice." After verifying by telescope that it was unfrozen water, the Kolbs rigged up a boom-and-pulley system above the North Rim's Redwall to access it. As the elder brother, Ellsworth decided he'd take the plunge. A heavy storm was brewing, and they were out of food and water, so he took a canteen. With him only halfway down, a spider on a silk thread a thousand feet above Clear Creek's bed, one of the most terrific rain and hailstorms either had ever experienced struck. The wind was so strong that Emery feared getting blown off the cliff. Following a search-and-rescue truism that a rescuer in a pickle becomes another casualty, Emery, tying the rope to a gnarled piñon pine, left big brother hanging midair. Since the cliff was undercut, he later recalled, Ellsworth could not steady himself against the wall. "This permitted the wind to whirl him round and round until the three wet ropes became one."

During a lull Ellsworth managed to "gradually unwind himself," pushing against the cliff with a pole Emery lowered to him. By dark, the top man had the dangler back up on the belay platform after suffering an "uncomfortable rupture" from the strain of pulling. Ascending in the pitch-black abyss, they spent the night in another cave, hungry, tired, and wet, like myself. Knowing what I know of the brothers, they probably posed and grinned while Thor snapped their picture.

I, strobed by ghost light, counting seconds between flashes and cracks in my Vermilion stone hideout to gauge the storm's distance, missed my sleeping bag, tent, and hot-chocolate nightcap. I feared that, come morning, the plateau would be socked in, that even with daylight I still wouldn't find my pack. I had been hypothermic before and knew how quickly coherence unravels into daft bumbling and coma.

I set out stretched terribly thin, half the man I used to be, as soon as first light painted cloud tatters. Methodically skirting the rim, I finally spotted my pack's red bulge. I vowed to *never, ever again* roam without essentials in a daypack—a space blanket, some trail mix, fire starter…and a first-aid burn-kit.

Near sunset I arrive at Lonely Dell, John Doyle Lee's old home-stead. The name still feels appropriate. Tan adobe melds with the desert. Crosses in the ranch cemetery lean into the evening. A nearby dugout, cobwebbed and dark as an animal's den, barely seems fit for human habitation. Past hopes, dreams, and cares, past hatreds and fears crumble in the shadows of ruins. The bob-cat again vacantly gazes at me, another trailside *memento mori*. I wonder if Lee ever questioned the striving of a world, or the doctrine of a church, he'd temporarily left behind. I wonder if, in a chair on his porch, feet propped on the railing, he sometimes was simply content to watch the light on the cliffs change.

At Home in a Hole in the Rock

IN THE WESTERN GRAND CANYON, when the mercury hits 100 degrees, shade becomes a destination. Water curbs life in this hardscrabble place. Dryness shrinks slickrock pools, condemns tadpoles and fairy shrimps, wicks away sweat. Moving or simply breathing depletes your inner well. If you cannot find water at the end of the day, you will have to backtrack to it on the next.

Halfway down through the region's sequence of Gaia's ages, I walk on the pumpkin-colored, level Supai Group, feasting my eyes on the scenery. Its constituent strata, topped by Esplanade Sandstone, bear the names of Havasupai families: Watahomigi; Manakacha; Wescogame. Silt-bearing streams and advancing seas, from 285 to 315 million years ago, built this ruddy Reuben of shale, limestone, and sandstone. The Vishnu schist and Zoroaster granite in the canyon's basement, exposed in the inner gorge marbled with rapids, are an incomprehensible six times older. As summer radiation parboils my neck and pack straps dig into my shoulders, I scan the Esplanade benches for refuge. Below, on a natural patio next to an outcrop, an old horseshoe snags my attention. I drop the pack to scout and discover an opening, stone gaping like a whale's throat.

This alcove housed people once. Its centerpiece, rodent-ravaged bedding, is folded neatly and weighted with a rock. It looks as if the most recent cave dweller stepped out to attend to his horse and never came back. There is juniper firewood, a Dutch oven, a torn bag spilling flour, a can of lard and another of Calumet (the baking powder with the hatchet-nosed chief)—it could have been a biscuit or a pancake day. There's a tin of Prince Albert tobacco, sporting His Highness, frocked and ramrod-straight. There is coffee, of course, and a coffeepot, a glass jar of pitch or molasses, a box of matches that look like they would still light, a double-blade ax, and blackened silverware. Against the wall, two wooden panniers, painted midnight-blue, with rope handles and a carved stock brand, in which to haul all this stuff, sit beneath a rough-scratched date: *1942.*

I picture the lone buckaroo dodging summer's inferno while another, manmade hell raged in the South Pacific. Clearly, he had meant to return.

Brick-red marks smudge the back wall, which flakes with age. "Dramatic forms in enclosed spaces," a doyen of Southwestern archaeology called such pictographs. Up close, they sharpen into centipede shapes that hunter-gatherers painted eons ago. While rock art at times loudly proclaimed the people's title to these lands, it elsewhere lay sequestered, known only to the initiated or those about to become such. The same need pulled us all here— nomads, sun-blasted, sore, looking for rest or for answers, snug in Earth's embrace.

I've escaped to this back of beyond from yammering neighborhood dogs, from the fracas of Route 66, from my town's narrowness and contentions. When I left there, the peaks had gone from green to gray, and the industrial outskirts huddled around a pet-food plant tower bleaker than usual. My two-week retreat into the Grand Canyon thus also marks a last hurrah in the sun before I crawl into winter's deep cave.

The ground outside—the same slickrock that roofs the alcove—is smooth terracotta, randomly pitted and cracked. Routes here do not lose or gain much elevation but, by skirting each side canyon, add miles to distance as the surveyor sights. Progress through this terrain is always painful and seldom straightforward. Limestone chunks from the layers above the Supai abrade hiking boots and shins. Catclaw, bear grass, brush, and agaves lacerate skin. June can roast marrow, January freeze your brain.

This Back Forty, the Arizona Strip, split off from the rest of the state by the canyon and which Utah formerly claimed, is infamous for its lack of water. Only during the monsoons do potholes form a lifeline of fleeting reservoirs. But it's often a jungle in there, another eat-and-be-eaten world. Predaceous diving beetles hunt tadpoles of red-spotted toads and of canyon tree frogs, as do backswimmers, single sculls stroking after small fish even, which they stun and suck out with their beak, and tadpole shrimp, which add their siblings and fairy shrimp to the menu. On the surface skate cannibal water striders and whirligig beetles—watermelon pips playing bumper cars—both cruising for ripples that hurt insects cause.

Permian winds laid this pavement, grain by crystalline grain. The fossilized dunes cap a terrace 200 yards to a mile wide, the Esplanade. Two thousand feet above the Colorado River and roughly the same distance below the canyon's North Rim, it winds drunkenly around nooks, springs, and peninsulas, from Crazy Jug Canyon to the Toroweap viewpoint and beyond. At points in between, the Esplanade juts into space in balconies above silent depths. Every once in a while, when the air does not stir, the whispering of rapids reaches an overlook.

Water that gnaws at sedimentary rock carves out hollows that, in size and acoustics, range from cubbyhole to concert hall. At Mesa Verde in Colorado and near Arizona's Navajo Mountain, vast alcoves harbor entire settlements: tiered citadels, apartment hives, towers, and plazas that buzzed at the same time Europe was building cathedrals. The Grand Canyon's alcoves are smaller, less noted, but their secrets keep me coming back. In theory, on all public lands, federal laws protect cultural relics more than fifty years old, be they cowboy paraphernalia or ancient rock art. Pothunters and vandals, however, blight the land, and I'm always surprised to see such treasures in place, undisturbed.

With soot on the ceilings, dust tracked by generations of mice, and rusty-tin middens nearby, the Esplanade's abodes differ drastically from the romanticized chuckwagon camps of John Ford Westerns. Spend a few hours in one and you'll taste not campfire wistfulness but hardship and hardheadedness, the hermit's self-imposed exile. Dents in a washbasin. An ax handle mended with wire. One-gallon glass jugs with crudely sewn burlap or blue jeans covers meant to keep them from breaking. "Patched over-all," Bessie Hyde wrote in a poem, "and minus guns, just ordinary men you'll find." A wilted keratin shell of a hoof with a horseshoe attached, and leg bones, sits on slickrock like an oracular throw of the dice. The remains bring to mind advice for travelers inscribed on W.B. Yeats' gravestone in Sligo, part of Ireland's wild, sparsely peopled west:

Cast a cold Eye
On Life, on Death
Horseman, pass by!

Packy—No Eats, signed *The Hungry Boys from Jump*[-up Point?] some hands in the 1930s messaged their horse packer in a shaky inscription, imploring him for supplies. Elsewhere, they simply recorded the date, plus *Snowing* or *Hot*. Three horseshoe "ringers," collaring a rusty stake in the ground, speak of downtime.

Edward Abbey, who sometimes cowboyed while he worked as a backcountry ranger at Arches, grumbled about canyon cattle "making things more difficult than was really necessary. In the cool of the morning they were feeling lively; also, not having seen a man or horse all winter, they were half-wild."

You can still trace an overgrown trail that cattlemen in the early 1900s blazed from the North Rim to Crazy Jug Spring on the Esplanade, named not for moonshine but for an oddly shaped rock. It's an ancient route, as pictographs testify. A fencepost and barbed-wire corral and cement watering-trough revert to the earth. Mormon settlers summered cattle and sheep on the Kaibab Plateau near the rim starting in the early 1870s. That land barely supported ten horses or cows per square mile, yet one rancher ran 1,000 head on the public range, seriously overgrazing it. A hunting companion of Roosevelt, Edwin Jessop Marshall, "the last true cattle baron," owned the largest tract of ranchland in the US at one time, the Grand Canyon Land and Cattle Ranch, with holdings on the North Rim. One of Brigham Young's sons had managed the company initially. The National Park Service, at first allowing grazing within park boundaries, gradually phased it out. Disgruntled stockmen smeared cow shit onto the walls of Toroweap Valley's ranger station. Strays kept lumbering in. In December, when heavy snows forced mavericks from the high country to the canyon's edge, hands with pack stock patrolled the points, rounding up the wayward. They carved dendroglyphs into pale aspen bark—signatures, poems, caricatures, dates reaching back to the 1890s, and busty women—woodland archives the decades sealed as dark scars and bloated, often to the point of illegibility.

Elsewhere in the Arizona Strip's rim country, hikers follow livestock steps hacked into steep slickrock, or loose-rock bridle-ways shored up with logs on the cliff faces. One rancher's daughter recalls her dad having to coax a lead cow down the trail in Son of a Bitch Canyon (a Grand Canyon offshoot labeled "Hundred and Fifty Mile Canyon" on maps) with a bucket of cottonseed meal. Some mules and horses, due to treacherous footing, have met their maker before retirement. A packer related an incident from the 1920s in which the hind feet of one of the string's animals on the switchbacks above him went off the trail; upon impact, it first broke its neck right in front of this rider, who'd "never heard such a noise and such a crunchin'." The mule bounced once before going over the edge. "Couldn't even see where it went.... Just disappeared entirely," that hand told an oral historian. Those mounts were something else; one evacuated an appendicitis case on a litter; another carried a washing machine down to Phantom Ranch; still others did Black Bridge, the Kaibab suspension bridge, piecemeal. (Forty-two Havasupai men walked the one-ton cables down switchbacks, a human-steel snake.) Given the severity of the terrain and the amount of horseback traffic between the rims and enchanted inner-canyon garden and tourist lodge, it's a wonder only one person on record was ever killed riding. Oblivious humans atop foolish beasts are a bad combination, and the cast of both kinds of characters seems identical. They range, I know from experience, from the spunky, the daft, the senile, the sluggish, mad, or obstinate, to those with a short attention span. The person who died, however, was a pro. A muleskinner for the Fred Harvey Company—the canyon concessionaire in those days—had doubled up with a partner. Mules in the pack train crowded them and pushed their mount, which fell and crushed the guide. The second rider survived.

Feral horses continue to haunt the Esplanade, as if in search of owners long gone. I once spooked an unkempt band sucking from freshly filled potholes in Chamberlain Canyon. They took off, bug-eyed, snorting, tossing their manes and tails, kicking up dust on the talus slope.

One room-size sandstone undercut holds the headgear of a bighorn, full curls chipped in duels, tips filed down to stubs on sharp rocks, "broomed" when they interfered with the ram's peripheral vision. Calcium-starved rodents nibbled the skull plate. Did he die of sickness, injury, or old age, comforted by the shade?

Did a mountain lion drag him in, feasting concealed?

Did a hunter 800 years ago honor his life there, or perhaps all life, with some private ritual? I find no additional bones close by to untangle the riddle.

Mummies and human bones now belatedly being repatriated for burial with indigenous descendants speak of calamity and privation in this place. The lifespan of Ancestral Puebloans, skewed by high infant and child mortality, extended to somewhere between twenty-nine and forty years. Lower leg fractures were common, as could be arthritis, malnutrition, atherosclerosis, anemia, parasites, and teeth worn down to the gum line from sand in the food, a result of the grinding stones used to prepare it. A young woman between 1090 CE and 1280 CE, near present-day

Farmington, New Mexico, fell, or was pushed, from a considerable height, breaking both long bones in her left forearm, cracking some vertebrae in her lower spine, and dislocating her hip on that side, likely suffering internal injuries too. She received more than just palliative care. A healer set six wooden splints to stabilize her forearm, in what the archaeologist saw as the first evidence of surgery in the Americas. Signs of infection at the splint sites showed that she survived the trauma for a while. In southwestern Colorado, fractured ribs and noses and dented skulls, suggesting blows from stone axes or clubs, in about four in ten skeletons from a settlement near Sleeping Ute Mountain had fully healed. My own body, by this fourth quarter of the journey through life, displays a map, with its frailties frayed paper, its wrinkles the contour lines, and its scars storied landmarks.

Recesses in this bolthole for people fatigued by our cities were places of final rest not just for wildlife or the pre-Columbian dead. A dynamite blast during the construction of the South Kaibab Trail dislodged a boulder that crushed a crewman; fellow workers and rangers interred him in a vaulted chamber near Phantom Ranch.

At least one alcove served as a weatherproof setting for Mormon conviviality. A large amphitheater in a butte by the Hole-in-the-Rock Road, during a two-month hiatus, became a dancehall for a wagon train that pioneered a shortcut from Escalante to "Bluff City," which it founded on the banks of the San Juan. Scouts bringing news of the route descending to the Colorado River dampened the square dancers' and fiddlers' mood. Wagons groaning under the weight of water barrels, cages of rabbits, chickens, and ducks and even beehives tied to their sides had to be lowered by rope, with their rear wheels locked and brakes set, after the portal notch—the "Hole in the Rock" on Glen Canyon's western rim—had been widened with blasting powder, chisels, pickaxes, and shovels. Draft horses balked when they first saw "Uncle Ben's Dugway" (named for the Welsh miner who had spearheaded the construction) and the river sliding past the crossing, 2,000 feet below. The engineering took six weeks on a journey of six months.

In this stark landscape, alcoves screen the mind as well as the body. Bedded down on slickrock under star-strewn infinity, far from rainfall or rescue but near the abyss, even the hardiest soul shivers. Cradled by stone instead, you ignore what could keep you awake. "You are the canyons you nestle into, each year deeper than the year before," Derrick Jensen has written, addressing the disgruntled, the resisting, the awakened, by way of a river metaphor. I feel this in the fiber of my flesh.

A seep above the Supai, which a stockman with a dynamite stick had supposedly tried to enhance and which I hoped to tap, turns out to be barren. Luckily, as the rim's shadows flood the patio, bringing chills in their wake, I find a gallon of rank effluent a stone's throw from the alcove, where runoff has guttered the bedrock. This must be part of the shelter's timeless appeal: the only potable water for miles around, with "potable" being a relative term. Quite frequently, on my backpacking trips, tomato-soup, algae-scum miso broth, or a chocolate-milk colored slop is the only water around. Untreated, these concoctions are too thick to drink and too thin to chew or mold into pottery. But I grit my teeth anyway, imbibe the good earth, and truly partake of the essence of a place.

Water and weathering sculpt these alcoves, as they do natural arches. Rain and snowmelt seep into cracks and filter through porous sandstone. Freezing, the water expands, slowly prying the rock apart. Repeat the cycle enough times, and it will weaken, with gravity taking charge and sections caving in. The fracture planes, normally smooth because of the uniformity of the grains, make excellent canvases. Just hope you're not snoozing inside when a big collapse happens. There is rock art on the underside of some slabs that used to be part of a ceiling.

Signage at many alcoves could say *Harvey Butchart Slept Here* or *Harvey's Hotel*. Over four decades, the Flagstaff math professor, obsessed with Redwall breaks, ferreted out a whopping 108 off-trail approaches to the river. He logged 12,000-some miles—but hey, who's counting, right? Built of hardwood chopsticks and guitar wire, powered by inexhaustible batteries, wearing glasses and a knotted bandana instead of a hat, he became the granddaddy of canyoneering. Beware of routes he classified as "sporty." Among backpackers, "butcharting" became a synonym for "roughing it in the canyon," with minimal gear and provisions and maximal verve. Harvey has joined the illustrious few whose notoriety transformed into verbs: Thomas Bowdler, Charles Boycott, Joseph Ignace Guillotin, Angus MacGyver...

The cozy crannies that offer respite also attract ant lions with sickle jaws that crater the sand (not a problem if you're not a slipping ant); deer mice whose urine, droppings, and saliva spread the hantavirus; glossy, pea-size black widows guarding eggs inside web funnels; and ringtail thieves, one of which I faced off with on another Esplanade excursion not far from here.

On the threshold of night, before dawn pinked the sky, I had been loading my backpack to beat the incipient heat. The canyon lay still as a pool. Only the beam of my headlamp danced across its slickrock bottom. Suddenly, awakened by the light, two pale-green discs fluoresced in the dark. When I focused on the shine, a foot-long raccoon tail and slim body of the same length took shape. The creature had frozen, keeping its eyes trained on me. I'd never seen one of these cat burglars before. Their reputation preceded them. A friend had told me how, once, in Cataract Canyon, he awoke in his sleeping bag with a ringtail on his chest.

Known also as civet- or miner's cats, ringtails are not cats but endowed with true feline stealth. Easily tamed, they made competent mousers for miners and settlers who kept them also as pets against loneliness; some cabin owners today swear by bullsnakes or even rattlers instead. Although ringtails are carnivores, these raccoon relatives pilfer hikers' and river runners' food stashes indiscriminately. Even hanging your grub or wedging it high into a crevice does not guarantee it will be there in the morning. When there are no people around, ringtails make do with mice, packrats, rabbits, snakes, lizards, and birds, and won't turn up their nose at carrion or fruit. The most agile of canyon acrobats (my apologies to all bighorn sheep), ringtails use their stole-like appendage as humans would a rudder or balancing pole. They reverse gears instantaneously, descend or ascend cliffs, shimmy up between boulders, tiptoe on ledges, go out on a limb.

The specimen I'd encountered made a move, *coming closer.* Its fearlessness was surprising, its silence a bit eerie. Concerned that it might be rabid, I threw pebbles, which drove it off—momentarily. Each time I turned, it slunk back from obscurity. This dance continued until first light sketched my surroundings. Before I hoisted my pack and left, I feinted once more and the grayish-brown shadow scurried away, trailing that night's dreams.

About a week into this trip I have seen neither humans nor four-legged animals. I enter a fissure that starts in the Esplanade and entrenches deeper and deeper toward Kanab Creek. The largest Grand Canyon lateral on the north side and one of few major water sources in the Arizona Strip, Kanab Creek runs only sporadically. It feeds netleaf hackberry, singleleaf ash, seep willows, coyote willows, and western redbuds, the trees that put out gorgeous magenta edible blossoms before they do leaves. And it beads hanging gardens of flowers and maidenhair fern, misted respites from drab blackbrush and cactus fields. I plan to follow the creek for a while before exiting its canyon and climbing back to the Esplanade. I long for its soothing touch, which will cool my scrapes and rinse the dust off my body. Only last spring, I camped under the cottonwoods on its banks, lulled by the water's soliloquy.

Where the tributary widens into Kanab Canyon, I do a double take and again check my map. But I haven't made a mistake—the creek has been silenced; dust cloaks its bed. Mud crunches under my steps with the sound of unfired clay. My boots grate on cobbles where the current once slid across gravel bars. I'm in shock. Is this the result of drought or of siphoning for irrigation by ranches in the creek's upper parts?

There is a third culprit, I realize as I trudge between thickets: tamarisk, the scabrous pest that bleeds the Southwest. The lacy-leafed growth crowds out native willows and cottonwoods, concentrates salt in the soil, and sinks taproots that lower the groundwater table.

This land minted by water often withholds it. You see water, water everywhere, and not a drop to drink.

After an hour or so, I arrive at a pool of Butchart's "pollywog soup." Ringed with mud, it checks my progress in the creek bed. An agave tip long ago punctured and drained my plastic water jug, and the bladder in my backpack has only a pint left. But the dregs of this stream in retreat are too thick to be filtered into drinking water. Disappointed and dehydrated, I bushwhack around the gunk hole and push on.

Toward noon, keen to leave this husk of a waterway, I nose up a side canyon that could lead to the Esplanade. One of its forks soon ends in a sandstone balcony three stories above. A second fork beckons like a mirage: sinuous, wavering, promising. Muscular walls block the sun's stare, and lenses of clear water gleam in a floor smooth as a sidewalk. I fall to my knees and kiss one greedily, not bothering with filter or cup.

I round what I hope will be the last bend before the drainage tops out but am stopped by a rock fall. Cabin-size boulders lie poised on edge, stacked into a lethal gym, a disaster zone riddled with crawl spaces. A possible route through this mess starts with stemming between two angled monoliths. I place one foot and both hands before pushing up and into the chimney in one quick move.

The sickening sound of wrenched gristle—of a rotisserie chicken being disjointed—registers an instant before the pain in my right shoulder does.

I slide back to the ground. Something is seriously wrong. The limb is useless, not part of me. I am suddenly light-headed, which masks the black ache. This is the fourth time I've dislocated this shoulder, though never before so far from a companion or outside help. By now I know the drill. Let your arm dangle, muscles relaxed. Rotate your upper body, carefully, back and forth. Avoid any grinding of bone on bone. When the humerus head and the torso's socket align just so, the limb will slip into its joint, smooth as a chambered bullet.

And it does, after several tries. Never mind all the TV shows you've ever seen in which a patient's joint is realigned violently, with a cracking sound, like an ineptly shifted gear; such force does more damage than good. Trust not Mel Gibson but a hiker for whom this has become routine. I'm an old hand at this, you could say.

The first time it happened to me, I was hiking up lower Chinle Wash, a feeder stream of the San Juan River. I had hooked my thumbs under my backpack's shoulder straps, my elbows angled out, chicken-wing style, when my boots lost traction in a mossy runnel. The impact drove the long bone out of its socket. Dizzy with waves of pain, clammy sweat slicking my brow, I'd mumbled a mnemonic I'd learned in a Wilderness First Responder course for realigning parts where they belong. The move recommended was "baseball pitch," with the throwing hand raised next to your head, followed by "pledge of allegiance," swiveling the arm inward, the hand touching your chest. I kept uttering the phrase, but resistance in my shoulder joint during the pledge part warned me against completing it. Melissa, unaware of the magic medical chant I kept repeating while on my back, thought that I'd injured my head and was hallucinating, a sudden sports fan gone patriotic. Eventually standing up, I leaned over to relieve the dull throbbing, letting my arm dangle loosely, and it popped back in then, just as it did now. It had happened again after that, once when I jumped from a rock shelf above Shinumo Creek and the jolt of landing wrenched the bone out; once when I slipped while descending sloped shale outside of Nome; and once when I crossed Thunder River in flood and got swept off my feet—especially troubling, since you need a firm grip for self-rescue. Handicapped thus, alert to the risk, you learn to move differently, more conservatively, gingerly even, eventually, one would hope. But lifelong habits die hard.

This is no country for men past their prime, or for the lame. This is why the Park Service had me sign a liability waiver, warning against an "unusually difficult and potentially dangerous" hike.

With my clipped wing pressed to my rib cage, hand tucked into my waistband for support, I scramble back down the canyon. At the first of the water pockets, I make camp on the slickrock and fix dinner more or less one-handed. Where the geology shelters you, as it does on the Esplanade, I travel without a tent. Tonight, with cold stars piercing the night, I wish for a hole to curl up in and lick my wounds.

Days later, back on the Supai highway, stiff-shouldered but still making miles, I come upon Bean Cave, whose former lodger I've read about. A signature at eye level in the shallow niche reveals it as one of Walapai Johnnie's far-flung dens. In 1928, young John D. "Walapai Johnnie" Nelson joined the search for Glen and Bessie Hyde. He had fought in the Philippines and later worked as a pack-trip guide around these parts. Often blind drunk by noon, he was nevertheless popular with the outfitters who fired and rehired him, according to one boss, about fifty times every season. A 1954 Kodak ad shows him herding dudes past Bryce Canyon hoodoos. Smiling, he leans on his paint pony, relaxed in batwing chaps, hat tipped back rakishly. You can tell he was charming, a spinner of yarns, fully at ease, someone you'd want as a guide—a spitting image of my younger, wrangling-days self, I'd like to think, except for his raven hair. He must have had grit. He built the trail that drops precipitously through the Supai to a leafy shaded spring named after him. By the time I've panted back up from there to the Bean Cave, my water bottles are almost empty again.

The vestiges of Walapai Johnnie's tenure in the Grand Canyon transport me back to my own days of working on horseback. My alcove then was a twelve-foot, oven-like trailer near Tucson that contained a two-burner gas stove, legions of flies, and pints of sand, sifted in through the cracks. I was living my Western dream, guiding for a trail-riding outfit in the Santa Catalina Mountains. Broke, exhausted, and reeking of stables, I cut short my cowboy "career" when some nag kicked my chest and I had to pay for X-rays myself.

Like some horses, and a few dudes, some of the men with whom I worked have stayed with me ever since: "Boots," a busted-up bronc rider turned stuntman and horse handler in Hollywood; Onario Orozco, lithe and lean as a riding crop, proud as a hidalgo, and *muy macho*—a fine specimen of conquistador horsemanship (last thing I heard, the brand inspector detained him when he tried to cross a remuda into Mexico for my ex-boss, who wanted to use those horses on multi-day trips over there); "Catfish," listed thus in Big Bend's twenty-page phonebook, a rafting and horse-packing geezer (so I thought, still in my thirties), whiskered, testy, and territorial—prone, like his namesake, to "pectoral spine displays"; and lastly, Dave Alloway, a twentieth-century Daniel Boone with a droopy mustache and white felt hat, a former state park ranger who taught survival skills to the Air Force and Border Patrol, skills he'd perfected in the Chihuahuan Desert and Australia. He was the first foreigner to complete the 120-mile Pilbara Trek across the murderous Outback. Dave's motto, *It ain't over 'til you're buzzard chow*, inspired his company logo of a vulture perched on an empty water canteen. The soft-spoken Texan died of septicemia from an untreated fracture after a horse stomped his foot.

In their fierce stubbornness, their frugality, and the rough exteriors that hid ancient souls, these men resembled their mounts and the prickly landscape that nurtured both.

Before I set out on my journey's last leg—Walapai Johnnie's commute, a century-old switchback that could kill a mule—I meet three backpackers fresh from the North Rim. Perched on a boulder, legs primly crossed, I chat for a while with their young female leader. As they get up to leave, I stand and pivot, facing the group to hide my half-bare behind. After weeks of abuse from sandpaper rocks, my lone pair of shorts hangs in tatters. I'm wearing a T-shirt, boots, a crooked smile, and not much else. I must look like the hobo king of the alcove clan. I probably smell like him, or his civet cat, too.

Classroom with a View

PARKER, LOOKING A BIT like a young Al Pacino, gasps as he steps waist-deep into the "warmer" shallows of the reservoir-fed Colorado River near the Grand Canyon's Cathedral Wash. Together with trip leader and river guide Sarah, he walks a seine net on poles through backwaters muddied by the Paria River's sediment, which has dyed the normally bottle-green stream below Lees Ferry latte brown. The first sweep of this preferred habitat of juvenile fish yields one polka-dotted rainbow trout fingerling and two native speckled dace. Beginning in the 1920s, the National Park Service introduced rainbow and brown trout into Grand Canyon tributaries like Bright Angel Creek, for the pleasure of sport fishermen. After the completion of Glen Canyon Dam, the now clear and frigid waters that jet from its spillways were stocked with more trout. These trout in the river's main stem have become a threat to the canyon's native fish species—humpback chubs, flannelmouth suckers, and bluehead suckers; they compete for food and prey on the young of these rare, protected species.

As one of ten teenagers, Parker embarked on a weeklong adventure with Grand Canyon Youth (GCY), a nonprofit utilizing this concourse of light as one of the world's most exciting classrooms. The adventure, ideally, will be one of the mind. True discovery, to paraphrase the philosopher Arthur Schopenhauer, is not to see what no one has seen but to see it and think what no one has thought. The Flagstaff-based program promotes stewardship of public lands and learning through participation in all aspects of a trip. Five guides, a student coordinator, and a United States Geological Survey scientist act as mentors as well as instructors on this one. We are the only people allowed to fish endangered humpback chubs—strictly catch-and-release, though—on the run commencing at a mild agitation near Lees Ferry, the Paria Riffle.

To get a grip on the science and routines of a river journey, the youths are assigned to groups with tasks rotating daily: cook crew, dishes crew, toilet or "Groover" crew, and science crew. Every evening, the science crew sets baited and non-baited fish traps—treble hoop nets with different mesh sizes—from the beaches at camp. One type of bait, the artificial "stinky cheese" for catfish, soon gains notoriety among the students.

The different setups serve to determine the most effective method for removing nonnative fish. Past attempts by the Park Service to weed out the unwanted have largely failed. Elec-tro-shocking stuns fish, which then float to the surface where the "aliens" can be gathered, but it can also injure the declining native ones.

After running a warm-up rapid at Badger Creek, the students are busy preparing lunch sandwiches under leaden clouds that bloom in typical monsoon-season style. A rain shower's lashing briefly checks the three-digit temperature. Drifting downstream in the rafts, the guides get acquainted with the students, whose interests and personalities quickly appear. The motivations for coming here are as diverse as the GCY students' backgrounds. Matthew, tall, blond, and politically savvy, once stood on the South Rim during a geology school project and decided to hike to the river or float it some day. Joshua, part Hopi and the son of a former Grand Canyon outfitter, has wanted to visit some of the canyon's powerful places since age fourteen. "Aly," a South Korean fireplug, joined court-ordered, on probation, but also likes private river trips.

Many first-timers get hooked on river life and keep coming back for more, validating GCY's mission: to inspire curiosity about a landscape and its natural communities. The Flagstaff program director sees students as fires to be kindled rather than vessels to be filled, though we do need to keep them hydrated. Assisting the US Geological Survey and National Park Service with their research introduces them not only to methods of aquatic biology and stream ecology, but also to the ways different land-management agencies operate. Some might even pick a career among cacti, scorpions, and snakes.

Long before they launched at Lees Ferry, these teens performed community service, two hours for each day they'll spend on the river. They volunteered in Flagstaff's soup kitchen, at orphanages in Peru, or with the Arizona Desert Bighorn Sheep Society, building rainwater catchment basins. Sara, a GCY alumna with a nose stud and thumb rings, restored houses in post-Katrina New Orleans. "GCI definitely got me started on the idea of service," she enthuses self-assured as only youth can be. On this trip, she takes turns at the oars and ends up rowing Grapevine, a bouncy 8 on the Grand Canyon's 1 to 10 scale of whitewater. A pre-med student interested in working for Doctors Without Borders, Sara seeks to reconcile social and environmental activism. She is so smitten with GCY that she considers working summers at the warehouse or, one of her dreams, rowing a baggage raft. (I could tell her about the less-than-dreamy side of rowing with half a dozen pressure-cooking Groovers on a sweltering day but decide not to burst her bubble.)

Students like Sara, or Parker, or Parker's twin brother Cody, who could be surfing his home beaches near Malibu instead of spending much of his summer on a working-and-learning vacation, seem like another endangered species. Their appetite for natural science and outdoor activities should not be taken for granted. Visits to US national parks steadily increased from the 1930s until 1987. Since then, until the pandemic, backcountry use of these parks had been declining by a little more than one percent each year, possibly as the result of a more sedentary lifestyle. Youngsters in particular suffer from "nature deficit disorder," a term coined by Richard Louv, author of *Last Child in the Woods*.

Louv links the absence of nature in children's lives largely to our obsession with television, video games, iPods, and the internet. He sees rising rates of obesity, attention disorders, and depression as consequences of this break between the young and nature. Declining knowledge of our national parks eventually might lead to a society that is less concerned with conservation. The preeminent threat to places like the Grand Canyon, even more serious than extinctions, is that future generations could lose touch with them or will see them as mere playgrounds or photo backdrops.

Another danger to the canyon becomes explicit to the participants of this trip. Since 1996, Glen Canyon Dam has released three controlled peak floods to improve fish habitat by mimicking pre-dam conditions. Those inundate the river's dry side channels and depressions, forming backwaters in which juvenile chubs and other native fish hatch and hang out. The water is slightly warmer in these natural hatcheries, and they shield fry from adjacent strong currents. Experimental releases from the sediment-trapping dam also replenish eroding beaches with sand from the channel, shoring up habitat for numerous plant and animal species and archaeological sites in the river corridor. Ideally, such releases are timed to coincide with the rains that engorge tributaries like the Paria, whose sediment load they deposit throughout the main canyon. To help fine-tune the dam's discharge, Adopt-a-Beach, an ongoing project by the Park Service, enlists river runners to monitor the canyon's beaches, documenting changes through repeat photography. Replicating the angles of pictures taken after the last artificial flood in 2008, the students who scramble across baking boulders quickly understand that North Canyon's shoreline qualifies as a success. We snap a group photo on the restored beach and shove off, but only after a many-voiced, unselfconscious shout of GCY's slogan: "Yay, Science!" This may sound cornball, but their enthusiasm feels genuine. Whether it is the canyon working its magic or simply fresh air, work, and fun and considerate peers, or the easygoing adults, this attitude is what parents and teachers dream of when they lie awake at night.

Half of this trip, subjectively, is spent loading and unloading boats. It's the physically most demanding aspect of river running. Skinned knuckles are the baggage boatmen's badges of honor; the trucker's hitch is their "Bunny Ears," shoelace knot. The students form fire chains to convey the dismantled camp down to shore. I break a first sweat in the mornings, water dripping off my nose, when I strap in camp chairs, rubberized drybags with tents and the student's gear, thick inflatable sleeping pads, and the umbrella that keeps the ice in my food cooler frozen longer and my passengers from getting lobstered. Unloading in the afternoons, the metal, too hot to touch, will have to be splashed with water. Lifting the monster kitchen box while perched on round bars of the raft's aluminum-pipe frame is a two-person job. Stowing Dutch ovens, cast-iron griddles, tin pails, folding tables, propane bombs for the cooking stove, and steel toilets in various stages of fullness (and ripeness) in the front and back hatch and foot well likewise requires balance, especially in a rocky eddy. Walking on the raft's tubes, which you also do with an unwieldy hand pump when you top off air lost from leaky compartments, channels the skills of sailors carving up a slick whale. A senior guide I know slipped on a wet raft and twisted his bum knee and had to be medevac'd by chopper (and a replacement flown in). Inevitably, some item that shows up late or doesn't find space on another raft will have to be accommodated. Once, Lava's fury ripped off the stack of ten plastic buckets I'd shoddily tied to the top of my load. The river takes and the river gives, and, luckily, we retrieved most in the eddy that mills below the rapid and that built Tequila Beach, where boaters toast their successful runs.

At camp we gather each night for student presentations, which can range from knot tying, or the medicinal properties of Mormon tea, to the Rocky Mountain School artist Thomas Moran. He painted the canyon's "tremendous architecture" repeatedly, at different times of the day. Cloud shadows transfixed him, as did mists after storms, and monsoon cumuli, and virgas also—ghost rain showers, veils that never touch ground because dry air dissipates them. I'm convinced "jellyfish" designs in the Grand Canyon's rock art depict clouds with such atmospheric tendrils.

Tonight, Matthew talks about flash floods and drives home his points with a water-filled bucket and a wet-sand model of a deathtrap canyon. The sludge he unleashes stirs the memory of a sleepless night spent in White Creek, on the North Bass Trail. During a break in the monsoon thunderstorm that rolled through for hours, I mistook the roar of the swollen creek higher up for the sound of a distant jetliner.

Not everything is serious science; our itinerary leaves ample room for introspection and play, both of which foster a relaxed learning environment. One evening is spent creating light choreographies with glow sticks and long camera exposures, performing in a low-budget Cirque du Soleil. The first time I jump off my raft to cool off, floating alongside, with my heels hooked over the spare oar to keep the boat from getting away, it's like the gates at the Belmont Stakes clanging open. A contest of backflips and bombshells off the bouncy bow ensues, and I have to holler to reel them back in before the next rapid. The thought never occurred to them until they saw me plunge, apparently. Less athletic or more self-conscious students, soaking lifejackets or hats, chill by evaporation. "If you're on or by the river and you're hot, you are dumb," I always say. As an antidote to the stifling heat, our mob douses two baby-blue motor pontoon boats—Behemoths compared to our rafts—only to find that our bailing buckets are no match for the long-range squirt guns of their passengers.

We next stop at Stanton's Cave, half a mile down from South Canyon, although there is not much to see except for the jade snake of the river, from up high, framed by the ruddy curving mouth. The Park Service barred the entrance with a huge one-ton metal-slat gate to safeguard archaeological and paleontological treasure, while letting Townsend's big-eared bats that roost inside flurry in and out. The cave harbors Pleistocene and early-Holocene faunal remains of dozens of species, including condor, snow goose, Harrington's mountain goat, and Yesterday's camel, a Camelops species that winked out about 13,000 years ago, roughly when humans arrived—it is "yesterday's" only in the canyon's vast timeframe. Signs of human tenancy came in the form of split-willow figurines, braided deer and bighorn sheep effigies, some pierced by symbolic missiles, that hunters placed inside between 3,000 and 4,000 years before our visit. The cave, 140 feet above the current river level, also contained the earliest evidence of humpback chubs: bones embedded in flood-deposits as old as the figurines. I fantasize that a boater in the Wisconsin glacial period could have moored a craft and stepped right off it into the shady hollow here.

Impressive as Stanton's is, it's far from unique. There's a whole world hiding below the Grand Canyon, a warren of vaulted galleries and rooms that even the most seasoned of hikers never get to explore. Double Bopper, the canyon's longest cave, worm-holing a remote North Rim Redwall bay, was first entered only in 2008. So far, forty miles of it has been surveyed. In its passages, bats thousands of years old, mummified by the dry air, hang from walls snarled with gypsum ribbons, looking as if asleep.

Off-limits without special permits, the Colorado Plateau's humongous stone hollows have attracted scientists since the 1930s. The dung of extinct troglodytes carpets some. Another hid parts of mammoth, scraps from the meal of a scavenger that might well have been a condor ancestor. One of the Grand Canyon's most famous is Rampart Cave. Willis Evans, a Paiute foreman of a Civilian Conservation Corps (CCC) camp at Pearce Ferry, the takeout of longer river trips, discovered it in 1936. It contained the hair, bones, and fossilized feces of Shasta ground sloths, grizzly-size browsers with a stout tail and grapple-hook foreclaws. This mulch, which can be radiocarbon-dated, had accumulated to a depth of sixty inches. It showed that sloths denned in this cave for 25,000 years. Among the deposits, paleontologists also found signs of horse, marmot, lynx, desert tortoise, cougar, lizard, ringtail, mountain goat, and mountain sheep. Pack rat middens and pollen further aided in reconstructing the cave's late ice age surroundings, proving that a mix of woodland and desert plant species had colonized this region 30,000 years ago.

To prevent vandalism of the Rampart site, the Park Service had yet another steel gate installed. But locked doors entice certain characters even more, and in 1976, someone forced an entrance; somehow the remains caught on fire and a priceless record of the past was destroyed.

Roughly synchronous with Evans's discovery, the Grand Canyon ferryman Merle "Pop" Emery stumbled upon a hole filled with pay dirt of a different kind. Beneath a ceiling of live furry bodies, a crust of dark-gray matter coated the floor: bat guano, a great natural fertilizer composed of insect shell dross. A mining engineer estimated there to 100,000 tons of it; at a value of about $100 per ton, a literal shitload of money. The cave, gaping 800 feet above the river, must have looked like Aladdin's to him. After a small airstrip and a tramway to Hualapai lands on the West Rim had been constructed, mining of this chitinous ore began in earnest in the late 1950s. Hoes and rakes broke up the dry fecal matter, which a giant suction pump then vacuumed into a cable car. Alas, the hoard held only a smidgen of wealth—a mere 1,000 tons of guano. The rest was limestone rubble, and the venture, a bust.

Back at the rafts, we find evidence of current wildlife activity. Ravens hacked into a clear plastic drybag with snacks clipped to the top of one load and extracted melting candy bars. Some bags are now being made from transparent material so you can see what's where in there; but so do they. Each camp and river sightseeing stop seems to have its resident pair of marauders, who I suspect alert neighbors and stagger their efforts in Venn diagrams of voraciousness. Once, when I'd explored off the Beamer Trail, I returned to my pack to interrupt a sooty duo that had unzipped a pocket, from which they were extracting dirty socks. Another Bonnie and Clyde, faced with Ritz crackers experimenters had arranged in a row, cashed out by stacking them like poker chips instead of flying off with a single one. On an Outward Bound trip, a winged rogue snatched a whole bag of goodies a student had hoarded to binge at the end of his solo time, only to see his Ziploc become airborne. The thief started in on it on a shelf across the river as if taunting the victim, just barely beyond the reach of a good right arm and cobble. (We instructors would not have condoned such violence anyway, believing in Leave No Trace and natural consequences as a teaching tool.) It's easy to see how Raven earned his mythical reputation as a pickpocket. Occasionally, two of the canyon country's brainiest creatures engage in scavenger battles of wits that even entail teasing. "The raven watches the coyote and the coyote watches the raven," the wildlife biologist Adolph Murie observed. "If one has found a source of food he is sure to be joined sooner or later by the other."

We land at the mouth of Redwall Cavern, which gapes in the cliffs like a bandstand or giant shell. A game of Ultimate Frisbee leaves the youths sweaty, panting, and mud-daubed, and a dust cloud hovering in the air. At the back wall, I undo my sandals and wiggle my toes in cool, ankle-deep sand. The huge twilight cove muffles our voices. While we take in the view from the cavern's back, a moment of silence settles over the group. We sit quietly and listen to a riffle murmuring in the sunlight outside. "The water sweeps rapidly in this elbow of river," Powell observed, "and has cut its way under the rock, excavating a vast half-circular hall, which, if utilized for a theater, would give sitting to 50,000 people." The major misjudged the alcove's true size but surmised from the driftwood inside that at high water a raging flood must cover the floor.

Well, no more. Those were the pre-Dominy days.

Impressed with the mother rock that roofs our lunch site, Powell christened this section "Marble Canyon." The Redwall Limestone may be the most prominent feature in the canyon's lithic archive, a 500-foot gutter collecting the river's spillage.

Solution cavities riddle its flanks, dug, unlike the cavern, by rain percolating down from the plateau. A shallow sea submerged much of the continent—from a mountain range in Nevada to Appalachian foothills—during the Mississippian period, 330 to 360 million years ago. In Redwall Cavern, you can sense that lost ocean's weight. Skeletons of tiny marine organisms at the sea-floor fused into bedrock; many larger creatures became encased as fossils: nautiloids, corals, brachiopods, sponges, and crinoids. If you're anything like me, or most of the human tribe for that matter, you'll have a hard time wrapping your mind around even a number as low as one million. So envision each year that exo-skeletons from this Paleozoic broth sunk to the bottom as a single glass marble. The sum that accrued in the Redwall would fill one third of the fuselage of a jumbo jet. No, that won't work either for me, I'm afraid.

Like Powell's "Marble Canyon," the lush "Redwall" that frames it is somewhat of a misnomer. The cliffs appear to be salmon-red; but where chunks have cleaved off or the river has been scouring, the pachyderm-gray of limestone shows. The explanation is sim-ple. Minerals from the Hermit Shale washed down by rain have stained surfaces of the lower formation.

After lunch we gather around a boulder at the cavern's en-trance. Long-stemmed crinoids or "sea lilies" web its glaze, their heads lacy as fern. We stand there and marvel at time's finger-prints. Geology, for the essayist Corinna Cook, is "a lullaby in low elephant pitches," a palliative in an era of stress. Here, shot through with flashes of "Taps," it piques a sense for catastrophic realities. Nothing quite shakes your complacency like volcanic ejecta or a vanished species underfoot. Water we pour from our bottles in Nautiloid Canyon's polished grotto enhances the chambered-shell outlines of extinct squid relatives studding the limestone floor, for which that canyon was named.

There obviously is a physical dimension to learning. Laboring to the top of the Redwall at Eminence Break, Matthew pauses on the trail. "Phew! I've got even more respect now for the ancient Puebloans," he says, wiping his brow with a bandana. The fault line at Eminence Break marks a cross-canyon route to the North Rim by way of the Anasazi footbridge, whose remains we saw from the river, wedged into a chimney up high. Some students peel and sample tunas, the wine-dark fruits of the prickly pear that were an ingredient in the ancients' diet. On calm water stretches, they row rafts. One will take over the boatman's seat when his guide is washed out in a rollercoaster rapid. A few will swim rapids, voluntarily and involuntarily, learning when to breathe (in a wave trough) and when not to breathe (counter-intuitively, on a wave's crest, where the view opens up).

Creature comforts and inconvenience are equally part of this educational package. At President Harding camp, students bathe in the eddy, and Sara takes scissors to Matt's mop head—a strangely domestic scene in entropy's rubble. Just after dinner, we notice a haze near the South Rim. The light turns cadaverous, the air brisk above the dulled river. A few minutes later, a wind gust whips spray from the water, headed straight for our beach. When it hits, a gigantic dust devil ravages camp. Folding tables get toppled; ground sheets, clothing, and tarps take off on the gyrating column. Students escape the pelting into the bow of the raft I've been captaining, where, hardly sheltered but comfy, they tell worst-injury stories until the wind dies down and a gibbous moon paints Tatahatso Point ghostly white.

"Extremely violent storms of short duration, often accompanied by strong winds are not uncommon at the Grand Canyon," Emery Kolb noted laconically. Adding imagery, the brothers wrote that it could get so turbulent that "it blows gravel." Katabatic evening blasts occur when cooling, denser air flowing like water down declivities funnels into gorges. While the men on Powell's first voyage of discovery waited to eat dinner at Echo Park, wind fanned their campfire, which quickly engulfed some pine trees. It soon rushed down the canyon and hounded the crew to their boats. Barely escaping the sheeting flames, they ran a tricky rapid at dusk. I've seen a squall lift an eighteen-foot raft off a trailered stack of four, knock down the guide who'd unfastened the straps, and cartwheel it down the shore, into the ruffled flood.

We routinely pick up "micro-trash," food bits on the beaches, leaving each camp cleaner than we found it. We eat messy lunches, gut-bomb nacho salad in a tortilla cone, for example, standing shin-deep in the river. "Food attracts ants, which attract lizards, which attract snakes," I tell students. "Next thing you know, you're dealing with elephants." I once fried kung pao chicken on a shallow breakfast griddle on a commercial trip—no wok in the park that time, either. When I tried to dispose of the cooled oil, I managed to douse myself with it. By morning, the shorts I had rinsed and hung out to dry were coated solidly black, crawling with legions of ants.

With the daily setting and retrieving of nets and the smell of stinky-cheese bait wafting through camp, our conversations inevitably return to the subject of fish, especially humpback chubs. The pre-dam Colorado's seasonally varying water temperature, suspended sediment, and flow shaped this fish with the telltale submarine bulge. Biologists think that this prominent feature diverts water around the body, allowing the chubs to maintain their position in swift currents, if not in the mad race of the most adaptable. We learn from Parker's student presentation that the chub rarely thrives outside the Grand Canyon anymore; only six populations remain in the wild. The largest of these, numbering fewer than 10,000 individuals, now lives and spawns near the mouth of the Little Colorado. Each humpy is said to be worth a million dollars, the amount spent on research and their protection. Two men in a 1911 photo pose near Bright Angel Creek with a string of pale-bellied two-pounder chubs whose worth today would equal a lottery jackpot. Ben Beamer, who prospected from a stone cabin under a Tapeats Sandstone ledge overlooking his ten-acre "ranch" at the mouth of the Little Colorado, in the springtime saw hunchbacked fish "so thick that you can lean over the water's edge and pull them out by the tail two at a time."

Government scientists routinely catch and tag chubs to assess their habits and numbers. Beginning in 2009, they helicoptered young humpback chubs to Shinumo Creek, forty-five miles downstream, to establish another viable population and thereby hedge bets against the species' extinction through any localized, catastrophic event. Highway 89 crosses the Little Colorado at Cameron, and a tanker truck wreck could easily erase the colony at the confluence.

Not too surprisingly, when today's science crew pulls the fish traps at a camp near there, three humpback chubs flop in the mesh. Passing them through a hoop scanner, the students realize that two of the fish already carry micro-transmitter identity tags. Handling the chubs as they would kittens, they measure total body length and the length of the forked tail, which indicate age—but the untagged specimen does not want to be measured. In a spastic reflex, it leaps off the measuring board, jackknifing toward the river's edge in an effort to escape. A student grasps it and gently puts it in a bucket, rinsing the sand from its gills and opalescent skin. After they have finished recording the capture data, Sarah injects a chip the size of a rice grain into cartilage of the fish's belly with a sterilized syringe. The students then place the captives back in the river, where they resume their aquatic pursuits.

In the parade of days that constitutes river time, this group has reached the end of their journey. Tomorrow, before sunrise, the students will climb out of Pipe Creek, following the Bright Angel Trail to the South Rim. Another group and their coordinator will hike in to the lower Grand Canyon, for their eight-day float through the planet's past.

Shortly before the exchange, we float underneath Phantom Ranch's two suspension bridges, from which backpackers wave at us. Before we left the rim on our night hike into this canyon,

Melissa and I had admired a thirty-pound canvas folding boat, an ancestor of Klepper kayaks and packrafts, displayed at the Kolb Studio. It had belonged to the college dropout turned pioneering backcountry outfitter and river guide, Dave Rust. Rust built the first trans-canyon tourist trail, including a cable tram across the river, and before the park was established ran a tent camp with a shade ramada and Dutch-oven fare at Bright Angel Creek, the seed for Phantom Ranch. Sepia-toned photos show ladies in Stetsons, cravats, and riding skirts seated in the airy tramway's cage. Likely, passengers did not know that on its maiden voyage, loaded with camp materiel, it had sunk with a splash after a sixty-foot fall when the cable snapped. On a windy day, one caged tourist felt like "the clapper in a bell." Teddy Roosevelt, on a lion-hunting trip, enjoyed the conveyance so much that he crossed repeatedly and even took a turn on the crank that reeled it in. Rust, his bonanza notwithstanding, professed to "count whatever money I may receive from any group of travelers as nothing, absolutely nothing, less than nothing, if they do not leave these breaks loving these gorges, these painted cliffs, and these dusty deserts."

Having met their homebound peers and two GCY guides on the way down, the new batch is as excited as the previous one was. Perhaps even more, since the second half of the canyon awaits them with more and larger rapids. After a quick lunch and safety briefing near Phantom Ranch's downstream suspension bridge, they get baptized at Horn Creek Rapid, rated 7 to 9. The canyon presses in on itself here in the Granite Gorge, tortured and black. Depending on flow levels, boatmen either split the rapid's "horns"—two smoothly domed waves at the top—or bypass them on the right side.

River life is life distilled into basic commandments. It is mindfulness honed into Zen essentials:

Choose runs.

Camp.

Cook dinner.

Catch fish.

Consider beauty.

A good boatman, we say, knows when to act, when to react, and when to rest. For my favorite time of the day, after chores have been finished, I sit in a chair on the deck of my raft, lotioned up (smelling "like cookies," according to guides moored downwind from me), wrapped in a cerulean turtle sarong, a mug of merlot by my side (though not on this trip with youths; oh, the hardship). Facing the river, I watch its swirling moiré of first bronze, and then copper, both with royal blue, as cliffs briefly flare before losing their color. Best seat in the house—this is my kind of streaming! The current maintains a silvery glow long after that light has bled away. A fifth-century hermit, Sarah of the Desert, lived for sixty years on the banks of the Nile without ever looking at it, which was taken as a sign of her dedication and rapt attention to God. The poor woman sought heaven while turning her back on it. Unfailingly, as any campfire or wind in cottonwoods, the mesmeric kaleidoscope makes me pensive. This mirror flood and its mineral load are on a journey. As am I. As are all of us, all species, the entire planet. "Everything is flowing—going somewhere, animals and so-called lifeless rocks as well as water," John Muir wrote during his first summer in the Sierra. "Most of us don't look at the Grand Canyon and see it moving," the science journalist Britt Wray agrees, "but it is." Similarly, for the philosopher of extinction Thom van Dooren, "a species must be understood as something like a 'line of movement' through evolutionary time." All three cribbed the thought from Heraclitus, of the-same-river-twice fame. Only fragments from a single work by him have survived, shards of a Greek vase, but oh, what fragments they are.

People who know the Grand Canyon well agree that there are in fact two canyons: the one seen from the top, a lifeless, abstract tableau, and the one experienced intimately at the bottom. The typical rim visitor, one of six million per year, stays from five to seven hours and spends an average of seventeen minutes looking at the abyss. River runners, conversely, take it in every waking minute, 100 to 200 hours, depending on the duration of their trip. That's a lot of time to mull over the succession of eons and our insignificance pitted against them.

Later, my porch transforms into a cradle free of creepy-crawlies and sand. Bucking on the bowline, swinging through an eddy, it puts me to sleep. The current keeps slapping the underside, never resting, glugging like a happy drunk, while perfumed breezes caressing my skin take its heat away. River voices braid into my dreams. Each time I awake, the Milky Way's angle has shifted between black canyon walls, a silent, single-hand, star-belt clock, its face streaked mercury by the odd shooting star. Sleeping onboard, I am held as in an alcove, despite marked environmental differences—strange, since in the rapids a raft is not always the safest place.

I cover up with a cotton sheet toward dawn, more for privacy in the thin gray light than for warmth.

Besides plenty of fishing, we do our share of good old plain sightseeing. At Shinumo, we visit the old William Bass camp above the falls, with remnants including a washtub and vibrantly blue enamel coffeepot, before seining several dace, suckers, and fingerlings of the transplanted humpback population in the plunge pool. It feels good to rinse off the river silt in the falls' thrumming shower, though the cleansing effect is rather short-lived.

At Deer Creek, a cannot-miss stop, we tunnel upward on the trail through greenery mantling the cliff face. We grip tree roots as handholds now and then, to finally reach the upper slope's scorching switchbacks, which we follow to the portal through which these 150-foot falls roar.

The awe Deer Creek awakens in most people who land there is timeless. It's no wonder really that, like the Little Colorado River confluence, it became a hub in a landscape held sacred. Southern Paiute "songlines" web the western desert with a network of invisible capillaries, linking the Grand Canyon and the Pacific Ocean. Salt Songs, Talk Songs, and various hunting song cycles consolidate homelands to the south, at Lake Mead, with northern ones near Zion, the Hopi Mesas, and Escalante. For Larry Eddy, a Salt Song lead singer, "The songs are the glue that holds us united and makes us into one tribe."

Trails these songs codify align mythical and historical sites, as they do an embattled present and a nomadic past no less hard. They link ancient villages, hunting grounds, and sites for burial or for collecting medicinal herbs, or salt, a valued commodity once. Often sung at memorial gatherings for the deceased, and "since Ocean Woman and Coyote set the world in motion at the beginning of time," the Salt Songs perpetuate Southern Paiute ritual country. "We sing so that the spirits that dwell in those sites know that we haven't forgotten them," says Vivienne Jake, a director of the Salt Song Trail Project, which preserves this eroding lore. More specifically, the canon recounts the meanderings of two mythical sisters, a wild goose and a small shorebird. Assisted by spirit helpers, chanting along the way, the two named caves, springs, mountains, and other locations. These sites of traditional significance are *pohagani*, "houses of power." In today's recitals, the bird-ancestors' journey is not so much told as relived.

The trails headed toward sunrise do not end at the Colorado River; they merge and cross over into the spirit realm at Deer Creek Narrows, where only the dead or those with special powers formerly ventured.

From the top of the climb, for miles in both directions, we see rough talus and serried cliffs. They hem in the river, which mirrors the bellies of cumulus clouds. Our rafts lie beached near the trailhead, corpuscles the Plateau's bloodstream delivered.

Past the portal, inside the narrows, with the sky almost shut out, we follow a catwalk above the abyss. The creek tumbles several stories below us, ringing hollow, as if running through a culvert, or a cathedral. I've seen clients freeze here, struck with vertigo. "To that wall all timid ones are glued by the horror that rises from the fathomless depths into which a false step, or the slipping of rock, might drop the trembling traveler." The film-maker and photographer Burton Holmes, who launched the term "travelogue," described the South Rim's Grandview Trail thus, yet his words better fit the balancing act through these narrows. The challenge is wholly a mental one, of course. If the path were chalked out on a sidewalk, all would stroll down it with noncha-lance, hands in their pockets and whistling.

Where the ledge pinches off and guides sometimes must coax the fearful into continuing, off-white, "negative" handprints at eye level levitate on a wall on the still more exposed far side. By blowing paint through hollow reeds or spitting it onto hands pressed against stone, pilgrims left five-fingered blank patches surrounded by pigment mist. The spatter auras suggest individual absences. Perhaps they were part of an initiation. More than just tokens of derring-do, they constitute links with the past, flagging the end of life's trials and trails for those who walked here before. I can only hope that the young bucks in our group won't try to match the dare of the hand-printing Paiute youths.

As a terminus in the hallowed songscape, Deer Creek's nar-rows and falls merit special consideration. The Kaibab Paiutes re-quest that visitors show respect, that they stay out of the narrows' bottom, stick to the trails, and avoid any impact or noisiness. The falls briefly became a popular rappelling destination, but the Park Service prohibited that activity, to the chagrin of some "these-are-my-public-lands" canyoneers.

To the Nuwuvi, the Southern Paiutes, the natural and su-pernatural are one and the same and need to be cared for. No substance exemplifies this better than water. They see it as a living thing. Endowed with its own spirit, it must be approached humbly, in an act of worship, as ordained by the Creator. This is where the fortunes of the falls, river, humans, and fish intersect. The tribe realizes the importance of water's health for ours and for a harmonious world. The Southern Paiute Consortium, founded in 1993, ensures participation of the Kaibab and Shivits bands and the San Juan Paiute tribe in the management of Glen Canyon Dam. Concerns include not only ecological ripples from dam operations, such as beach erosion, but also the behavior of Grand Canyon visitors. Outreach and education therefore are a part of the consortium's mission.

Upstream of the narrows, "The Patio" flares open, an oasis flooded with sunlight. River rats and backpackers from the North Rim love its pools, rustling cottonwood shade, and smaller falls, fringed with ferns, mosses, snapdragon-like monkeyflowers, and watercress. The slickrock floor and striated, pink Tapeats Sandstone benches above the plashing and gurgling invite rumination. It does get busy at lunchtime, though.

Deer Creek's magic dwells in its whittled depths, its resonant silence and quiet insistence. To truly hear it, the elders remind us, "You have to listen with your spiritual ears." I always hike ahead of groups or linger behind on The Patio for that reason, for a few minutes alone. Liquid babbling has pulled me from reveries each time I've lounged on those banks. The stream's voice heralds people approaching when none are.

On the trail between The Patio and the primitive campground upstream, fellow GCY guide, botanist, and Park Service archaeologist Greg Woodall points out blue agaves (the source for tequila), which, native to volcanic soils of Central and Western Mexico, normally do not grow in the Grand Canyon. The ancients likely transferred seeds here and cooked amber syrup from the sap of the plants' stripped and pressed hearts. Greg passes around some of the nectar in a glass bottle—it's sweeter than sugar.

It was Greg who found George Mancuso's mangled body on the sand island at the Little Colorado confluence, where the red beast had dropped it. Life and death are thrown into stark contrast in this setting, one of the reasons why GCY's founders—

three river guides—chose it as a classroom.

Waiting for stragglers from our group, I wade into the plunge pool instead of sitting on my baking raft. The falls hit with a deafening force that makes swimming into the vortex impossible. Try as I might, I can't overcome the barrier of gusting vapor and current the pounding generates. Perhaps it is better so. In this, as in similar nooks, perspiring cliffs and saturated air created a hanging garden. Where the falls carved a cleft into the Tapeats Sandstone, runoff triggered spurts of maidenhair fern. Droplets bead the fronds, lacy tresses that radiate an impossible green. Monkeyflowers nestle in soil pockets among boulders at the foot of the falls, quivering between water and light, hummingbird favorites. Their mouths flash brilliant-scarlet, quintuplet tongues lolling around tiny yellow throats with tiny white tonsils—ahem, stamens. Cliff or alcove shade combines with abundant, year-round moisture into microhabitats not only for mammals, birds, amphibians, and insects but also for plants, many of which can only be found on the Colorado Plateau.

Near a trip's end, the staff gathers each student group for an informal review. As dusk muted the colors surrounding Cremation camp on the eve before Phantom Ranch, we'd circled up the upper-half gang at a sacred datura plant. They looked tanned and a bit disheveled. As a mood setter, we had watched one of the porcelain blossoms unfurl within minutes for its one-night stand with a sphinx moth. "Until now, I've never had an interest in geology," Hayden said. Matthew had enjoyed getting to know people from different backgrounds. "You don't have to have electronics to have fun," Matt admitted; he had lost a fishing rod in the river and otherwise taxed the guides' patience with his short attention span. Parker expressed surprise at how pristine the inner canyon had felt, despite thousands of visitors per year. Asked what they would miss most, one of them thought the sound of the river. Asked how the journey might affect their future, another thought he'd be more aware, trying to live with the earth instead of against it. Some GCY alumni veer more concretely into new directions. Spurred by their Grand Canyon experience, former students have embarked on studies in geology, fisheries biology, or environmental policy. Rennie, from our lower-half trip, now hooked on fish, wants to become a stream ecologist like her dad. Paul, whose student presentation focused on knot tying, intends to go into engineering to develop outdoor equipment for people with special needs, after traveling with that population on two GCY River Buddies trips.

Some lessons had been learned the hard way. One morning, at dawn, a gullywasher had flattened the tents of students who had pitched them close to the canyon wall, below several pour-offs. Others had bivouacked in their sleeping bags. Luckily, no debris had been sluiced from those chutes. Warming up under a kitchen tarp staff had set up with four oars, sipping hot chocolate while falls of the same hue kept on splattering, the evicted, resembling bedraggled muskrats, giddily rehashed details of the deluge. For many of them, that was a highlight.

At times, danger lurks where you least expect it, even in places you think you know well. While our charges cliff-jumped at Pumpkin Spring, squealing and hollering, I'd taken a dip in the geothermal pool; it was lukewarm, murky, slimed with algae, rimmed by a bulge of mineral flowstone striped orange and green, and, beyond my ken, brimming with unhealthy levels of arsenic. And here I was worrying about brain-eating amoebas, belly floppers, limestone lacerations...

Throughout miles of stillness and thrills, our journey below the rim loosed something inside a few of these youths, something like rockfall, the course of which, though inevitable, can never be safely predicted. But regardless of the path they would choose, regardless of whether they would defend wilderness or build careers at its expense, I daresay that none forgot days spent among red cliffs and booming rapids in the company of strangers, some of whom became friends.

The Roundabout Way to Rainbow Bridge

WHILE MELISSA FINISHES STUFFING her backpack at the end-of-the-dirt-road trailhead, I savor a half-rack of ribs bought in Page and warmed on the truck's hot dashboard as we bumped around Navajo Mountain's base this fine summer day. Seated on a gnarled juniper, I mull over my reasons for returning to this place. Apart from wanting to share it with my wife, "a certain morbid curiosity" compelled me, like Edward Abbey, "to see again, after an absence of many years, the shimmer of brassy waters under the sun, the tapestried walls of half-sunken canyons, the crooked little grottoes that wind back into the underworld of stone."

Having largely shunned Lake Powell in the past, I am ready in late midlife to face "America's Natural Playground" (in the hype of marina concessionaire Aramark), the blight that rubbed out Glen Canyon. As recent converts to packrafting, we both look forward, if guardedly, to reaching Rainbow Bridge the roundabout way.

We pass five backpackers from Colorado as we descend the trail into the canyons. They will be the only people we see until Rainbow Bridge. Navajo Mountain, Naatsis'áán, bulges with stately presence beyond the rim, snowcapped even this late. It plays a crucial role in the sacred geography of the Diné, who believe it to be the head of Earth Woman, a configuration of landmarks stretching from Utah into New Mexico. Naatsis'áán, a possible launch site of Tiyo's journey, is also the birthplace of Monster Slayer, one of the twin culture heroes that enliven Diné mythology.

On cliff palisades backing the pack trail that drops into aptly named Bald Rock Canyon, we spot a life-size petroglyph of a Navajo horse with ornate saddle and bridle. At our first camp, in the gorge's bottom, miniature cascades splash across laminate sandstone. Cottonwoods shade the spacious patio. In the distance, cream-colored sandstone scarps gouge Earth Woman's forested brow. Before sunset dabs vermilion onto her scalp and darkness drowns deep-pink walls, I explore the throat of an alcove hundreds of feet above the canyon floor. I discover ruins, a flint tool and a metate, a flat, deeply worn "mealing stone." The rounded-cobble mano with which a woman ground corn kernels on it lies next to it.

We don't bother pitching our tent, bedding down on natural flagstone instead, soon pulled under by the creek's chiming.

The devil is in the details, or rather, in redrock country, in the detours. Its opposite also resides here: Divine transcendence. Sublime mystery. Off-trail progress through this terrain is always painful and seldom straightforward—as the raven flies is not as the canyoneer walks, except on the two Phantom Ranch bridges. But it holds countless rewards, bestowing memories nested like Russian dolls that sustain you forever.

I recall my first visit to Rainbow Bridge, fifteen years ago, with my friend Morris, a one-armed retiree living in Hanksville, Utah. (He lost a limb to a farming machine decades before.) We'd started our multi-day trip from the side of Navajo Mountain, opposite to where Melissa and I parked this time. In the grid of dirt roads that score the reservation, we somehow had managed to miss the trailhead near the remains of a defunct tourist lodge. Instead of treading the well-worn pack trail to Yabut Pass, Morris and I dropped into Tsagieto Canyon, one of numerous drainages channeling into Aztec Creek. It should eventually funnel us to the bridge, we thought. According to my map, Tsagieto joins Aztec Creek, which in turn merges with Cliff Canyon, then with a connector, the slickrock fault of Redbud, and at long last, Bridge Canyon.

The verdant touch of spring then was evident throughout the canyons, as it is today. Gnarled cottonwoods had softened with pea-green, semi-translucent foliage, which unfolded tenderly toward the light. A miniature forest of seedlings had sunk taproots into the moist sand along the creek's margins. One old-timer's roots in a heart-wrenching gesture of patience and parsimoniousness embraced a fat streamside boulder.

We soon descended Forbidden Canyon, another name for Aztec Creek, which really should have been "Forbidding." Its tightening rock throat forced us to benchwalk above gaping narrows pitted with potholes too deep to wade. At exposed spots, we found crude steps hacked from the stone—footholds for mules or men. Rotting belay posts had been used to lower their packs.

Livestock could be a liability as much as a boon in this rimland. The guide of an early tourist excursion "fell over with his horse when it was impossible to keep balance... He got loose, the horse fell over backwards several times, broke its neck, slid down sheer rock and fell about fifty feet over a cliff, the sound was awful."

My calves and thighs were crosshatched from bushwhacking; a cactus spine had lodged in my little toe while another had punctured the gallon-size water jug I'd strapped to my backpack. For good measure, the palm of my hand throbbed with a cut suffered from climbing over a barbed-wire fence the previous day. Morris, under his sweat-stained baseball cap, looked only slightly better. My focus on the pain, like our benchwalking, came to an abrupt end when we found ourselves boxed in by walls and a drop thirty feet high that required a rope, which we hadn't brought.

A black, water-polished boulder close by bore chipped initials: *JW*. It marked the point where the veteran guide and Kayenta-based Indian trader John Wetherill was thwarted during an earlier attempt to find Rainbow Bridge. In 1909, with the help of a Paiute guide, meandering for weeks, he succeeded and became the first white man to behold this natural wonder. We did too, that time, though only after backtracking and picking up the trailhead near the crumbling lodge and its decaying corral.

Two days later, en route from Redbud to Cliff Canyon, we passed a rock-art panel in an alcove. The figure that stood out most to me was the white silhouette of a flute player. Commonly mistaken for Kokopelli, and sometimes shown with a humplike bulge that could be a pack, it represents the deity of the Hopi Flute Clan. The pictograph commemorates the Hopi ancestors' wanderings toward the tribe's current home on the mesas after they emerged from a mythic underworld into the fourth, the present one. The people split up on separate courses to lands the creator had chosen for them. Traveling in each of the four directions, to where land meets the sea, they measured their new world step by step, thereby claiming it. In the course of their journey, they branched and branched again, forming the clans that still organize Hopi society. Each clan treasures stories—and icons like the flute player—that are specific to these peregrinations.

Talk about reaching a destination circuitously.

The next day, Melissa and I delve deeper into this maze. On a simmering hillside, a hogan built from juniper trunks broods in the sun. Silvered with age, light beaming through substantial chinks, it holds a shepherd's effects: a kerosene lantern, a primitive stove, coffee pot and sundry containers.

We wend our way down lush and luscious Bridge Canyon for what feels like an eternity. Guiding the final approach, Wingate sandstone blinkers our vision. One last bend straightens out, and there it is. The curve of a mustang's neck. A dream's trajectory. Muscular yet weightless—the most elegant rock parabola you'll ever lay eyes upon. Despite having seen photos, nothing could have prepared us for this. The second-largest geological bridge on earth glows as if from within, powered by midday glare. Clouds flock in the blue space above, like Churro lambs gone astray.

Powell the geologist, on his maiden voyage, spoke of "rock forms that we do not understand." This is one of them, with an added, spirit dimension. The Rainbow of Stone consists of two beings, male and female, stretching across the canyon. All other rainbows stem from it. Diné worshippers plead at Nonnezoshi to be cured of bad dreams. At a nearby spring, they pray for healthy horses, cattle and sheep. Harm will come to the People should the bridge fall, a prediction says. An old Navajo man, White Horse, demonstrated the strength of their beliefs. Passing under the bridge, he would not return the same way but rather climbed around it laboriously. He'd forgotten the requisite prayer. Compare that to tourists who pioneered a route to the back of the arch from above, which involved chipped steps, bolts, and belays. In 1928, one, a magazine writer and eventual *Life* magazine photo editor, "After twenty minutes' work with a 3/8-inch cement drill…was able to make a hole in the hard sandstone dome of the buttress." He then "quickly hammered in one of the steel spikes and passed the rope through the iron ring." Some damage from backcountry engineering at the bridge has since been mended. Scars on the spirits (and spirit) remain. Six years earlier, the Bernheimer party had found "trail-making" down the Redbud Pass slit impossible. Wetherill "planned and directed the tedious hand-drilling and blasting." They named the breach "in grateful recognition of a red bud tree which furnished us with strong and tough crowbars." If you're quick to credit coarser sensibilities of those times as an excuse, remember that White Horse, John Muir, and Charles Bernheimer—a self-styled "Cliffdweller from Manhattan"—were contemporaries. (Muir admittedly had his own blind spot when it came to indigenous land tenure, promoting the expulsion of American Indians from the new national parks.)

The more things change, the more they stay insane. Some clueless sap north of Arches sank anchors excessively on three easy (5.3-rated) climbing routes, smack dab in a thousand-year-old petroglyph panel. The Fremont creators, without belay or fancy Five Ten shoes, had worked on that rock face for hours. Even sweat from your fingertips corrodes fragile rock art; never mind rubber soles, chalked-up digits, ropes, and dangling climbing hardware. The bolter in an online forum denied that he had defaced antiquities, which he referred to as "graffiti."

In 1927, at the age of twenty-two, the future Harvard ethnographer of the Navajos, Clyde Kluckhohn, saw "the multicolored arch of solid rock" on a 2,500-mile undergraduate horseback jaunt through the Southwest. "Until recently," he wrote in *To the Foot of the Rainbow*, the bridge was "easily the most inaccessible and least visited of the natural wonders of America, for the trip was long, toilsome, and dangerous... at least several weeks, and there was a considerable expense involved." He doubted that the span would ever become a tourist's paradise. Then an Indian trader from Winslow built a rough road to within Navajo Mountain's shadow, and things never again were the same.

Having made his will after buying "sufficient provisions for an army for a year," and having sought the trail for three hectic days, Kluckhohn, one companion, and a guide resigned themselves to forging their own course. There were places so tight that he could not turn around on his "ill-broken, stupid" pony Maybe So, on whose hard flanks he blunted his spurs. He had to back up, mounted, instead. They ran into a motion-picture producer, who scouted ahead of a party that included muleteers; the Colorado cattleman cum amateur archaeologist, John Wetherill; the dentist and writer of Westerns, Zane Grey; and Grey's Japanese cook, with a puppy riding in his lap. (Sunset Crater, near Flagstaff, was designated a national monument after the same producer, a huge fan of the author, apparently, wanted to blow up the cinder cone to create a landslide for a Zane Grey adaptation.) The view Kluckhohn encountered farther on was "Rock, rock, rock; thousands upon thousands of red domes ... "

They reached the bridge "prepared for the disenchantment which the real often gives to one's dreams." But the sight greeting them was "more than recompense for the hardships and dangers of the trail."

A bronze plaque at the span's foot—dragged behind a mule, on a travois—credits Nasja Begay, who led the first Anglos with "Hosteen John" (Wetherill) here in 1909. He, in fact, was Muu'puuts ("Owl"), a Southern Paiute of the San Juan tribe, which lives dispersed across the Navajo reservation. The following year, President Taft declared Rainbow Bridge a national monument, and Wetherill, whom one client had pegged as a "thoroughly high-bred and highly educated man," became its first custodian. The back pocket of Navajo Mountain remained accessible to the hardy and dedicated only. *To see the Rainbow—aloof—remote / You had to hike or you had to float,* as Vaughn Short, the Robert Service of canyons, put it. From the mid-1960s on, Glen Canyon Reservoir allowed boatloads of thrill seekers, tens of thousands in some seasons, to buzz in from Page for an effortless day trip up the narrows of Bridge Canyon. Tranquility and the bridge's physical survival became endangered when the manmade tide threatened to erode its sandstone foundations. At the last minute, a lawsuit by the Sierra Club, supported by many Diné, prevented further encroachment.

In the ramada near the floating docks, we filter drinking water from a reed-lined rill. A ranger group greets us while sneakered tourists, a few smoking, stroll up from "the lake."

Abbey visited Rainbow Bridge from the river during a Glen Canyon float trip with a one-legged buddy in 1959, the year I was born. They had enough bacon and beans for two weeks, catfish hooks, and little rubber boats made in Japan, much too small and flimsy, that came in suitcase-size cartons and which they ended up hitching side-by-side. They navigated with a Texaco road map of Utah until a rapid snatched it from them, long before they reached the quickly filling reservoir.

The two-hour trail up from the river, which Abbey hiked alone, unspooled for six "rough, rocky, primitive" miles, "a distance regarded as semiastronomical by the standard breed of mechanized tourist." The creek at the canyon's mouth had formed "a chain of emerald pools, some of them big enough to go swimming in," pools so clear that he could see "the shadows of the schools of minnows passing over the grains of sand..."

Anticipation for such hikers approaching the bridge from the

Colorado, I venture to say, built *physically* with each step, as it did for Zane Grey descending "wind-worn treacherous slopes on the way to Nonnezoshe" and for me in Bridge Canyon, or as it does when one nears the Grand Canyon's rims by boot after crossing piñon-juniper or ponderosa flats, instead of exiting a car or bus at a viewpoint. It's the frisson of delayed rewards, now unpopular, and the joy of earning them, in the outdoors, in a healthy way.

The hardest part of our trip lies ahead: crossing the historian Jared Farmer's blasted "aqua-park for the affluent" in six-foot inflatables, dodging houseboats and wakes from frat-boy-manned powerboats below the cliffs' bathtub-ring scum stain of salts, minerals, silt; we'll get approached, though, by one pleasure barque whose skipper thinks we're in trouble and asks if we need anything. When I say "Brews, brother," he hands us a six-pack of cold ones which we'll destroy at an overnight camp on an island of nothing but slickrock. Near shore, we'll glide above flooded fire rings, hearths only a few seasons old, built by a lost tribe. Before night swaddles us on a whaleback without sand or vegetation, we watch Naatsis'áán sink into Earth's penumbra. The day after, we'll hump fifty-pound packs through a subtropical tangle of tamarisk, up Cha Canyon, past ribbon falls and beaver ponds, back to the trail. We'll have to find strength in a thought Abbey recorded when he guiltily sojourned on one of the fleet's condo-behemoths a few years before his death.

"Though much has been lost, much remains," the word trickster consoled himself at roughly my age.

True enough. On calm days, the reservoir seems leaden, inert. But geologists say that hundreds of feet below, the Colorado still flows, a ghost river, restless, bound for the sea.

Confessions of a Cat Lover

THE STRUCTURE PUTT-PUTTING DOWN the Colorado River below Moab resembles a Klingon mother ship. Or perhaps the microscopic view of some weird protein: six H-shaped molecules grouped around an elliptical one. The molecules are lashed to a motor-powered support raft. Bold letters on the tubes proudly announce this traveling circus: *OUTWARD BOUND*.

This is a private trip, an "invitational" consisting solely of Utah instructors who work for this well-respected outdoor education program. These people were *not* sent by their parents. They are here because they are fearless women and men. Almost all of them have as many river miles under their bow as wrinkles on their faces. But there are a few rookies along, as well as logistics staff who keep the Moab program base stocked with boxes of hardtack (the infamous "plate armor"), dehydrated onion soup, bloat-inducing summer sausage, two different kinds of flavorless cheese, and bottles of Pepto-Bismol. Most of the figures on board recline to the stuttering of gangsta music with counter-beat coughs from a four-stroke with a mind of its own. Only one man, the program director, stands proud and alert, at the helm. Occasionally, he tilts the motor and lifts the propeller to avoid plowing sandbanks or gravel bars, which in a low-water year seem to make up the bulk of the river. The raft's repair kit holds a spare propeller, just in case; the odd mangled one decorates a wall at the warehouse.

They are on a three-day trip in November through Cataract Canyon, after a long and rewarding summer season. A mere three-day trip through this gorgeous gorge is an unforgivable sin. But that is all the time they have before they move on to more gainful unemployment, on the ski slopes of Colorado.

Their run through Cataract is a first, a piece of history in the making. They are test pilots, most of them, about to take on formidable whitewater on a craft with a reputation for being "capricious." The boaters call them "paddle cats," or sometimes "pieces of feces," or simply "cats." Muddling the waters further, indulging our hasty society's need for abbreviation, some folks refer to this canyon as "Cat," if affectionately—"I can tell my Mom I did 'Cat'"—even using the word as a stand-in for the river, as in "Cat is flowing over 40,000 CFS [cubic feet per second]." I too have been here, *done* Cat, before. The language echoes that of peak baggers and trophy hunters. ("I got my bear.") More often than not, Cat has done me—in.

Regarding lower-case cats, it needs to be seen if these can carry students safely through Class IV rapids.

What exactly does a paddle cat look like? Imagine a medieval apparatus of torture strapped to a set of inflatable tubes. Two seats resembling the rock-hard benches of workout machines ride atop two linked pontoons. They are integrated with aluminum foot guards and front bars under which the pilot may wedge his or her knees for leverage and balance. Between the tubes sags a drop hatch of very limited storage capacity. In it, watermelons, signal flares, Band-Aids, instructor manuals, driftwood for campfires, a drybag with costumes, or other essentials may be carried. Seated paddlers are easily mistaken for Easy Riders of the waves, or for monkeys straddling monstrous blue rubber bananas.

The frame of this Procrustes chair has been designed specifically for our program. No expenses were spared. Rumor has it that a miniaturized prototype was tested in the program director's bathtub, with a blow dryer operated by his girlfriend simulating strong headwinds. The laudable idea behind the design was that student pairs would have to communicate and cooperate to maneuver this...boat.

That is the theory. But it does not matter much yet, on this overcast late-autumn day. Right now, bags of peanut butter–filled pretzels are ripped, and the crew contentedly chews their cud.

Soon enough, we beach our unwieldy craft, landing near a

camp known as Tamarisk Hell. The scene that unfolds—swarm behavior: chaotic coherence—is reminiscent of the Omaha sector on D-Day. Instructors leap into the shallows. (At this time of year they make it to shore without being strafed by mosquitos.) They unload crates of food, stoves, pails, sleeping bags, gas cartouches, the boom box, and Frisbee missiles, camp chairs, Therm-A-Rests, jerry cans of drinking water, a grill, and a fire pan; they clip life jackets, uncoil ropes, and wrestle with tarps or tents. Someone in a rush in the tamarisks finds a room with a view for the "Thunderjug," a portable toilet required by Park Service regulations. One also may hear the troops refer to the receptacle coyly as "The Unit." This device evolved from a primitive ancestor. Its Ur-form was "The Groover," an army-issued steel box for grenade launchers bearing a stenciled warning: *Caution—Explosives!* Before the era of wooden toilet seats, lengthy sessions on this rocket box caused additional indentations in bare backsides—hence the name.

The evening is spent pleasantly enough, over tall tales and burritos, washed down with liberal amounts of mood-enhancing beverages.

Next morning, the time has come to face harsh realities. The mother ship is broken up, and instructor pairs launch their cats. My copilot is Heather. Heather is half my age, twice as graceful, and works three times as hard at the Moab base. Her doe-brown eyes brim with an unspoken question: you know what you're doing, right? While I ready the boat, I try hard to avoid her gaze.

Our rig immediately displays typical cat behavior: it turns on a dime, but the tracking sucks. I try my best to keep its nose pointed downstream. Unlike on an oar-powered double-tube cataraft, with a single boatman ideally in control, it is much harder to synchronize the paddle strokes of two people—especially when nobody wants to be captain. As a result, we careen down the still-mellow river like a drunken water strider.

My mind turns to Outward Bound courses on which I've worked with these craft. A favorite pastime of students on calm stretches is "flatwater polo." Two mobs of kayakers attempt to toss a water bottle between the tubes of a paddle cat, while the seated "goalies" are defending that space viciously with their paddles. (We always make them wear helmets for this.) It's a free-for-all, without rules whatsoever. Tackling, biting, splashing, ramming, unseating, flipping, and dunking opponents, slinging mud or holding them back by their stern loops—anything goes.

Some cynics maintain that this is the only use for a pee-cat.

One time on the San Juan, after fierce winds kicked the river into a frenzy and formed an invisible wall, everybody had to de-board. With throw-bag ropes meant to save swimmers in an emergency clipped to the frames, we waded the river, dragging cats downstream and to camp. Except when we stepped into holes in the river bottom, momentarily disappearing. A few kayakers harnessed their boats in front of the deadweights, pulling them like building blocks for Egyptian pyramids.

Another low-water year, that one.

Before I even get to have my first muscle spasm, the rumbling of Brown Betty, our first rapid, jolts me from my reverie. The river is flush with sediment from recent rainfalls upstream, and right now its convulsion resembles a Bloody Mary more than a girl with pigtails and bows. Those old backpacker knees hurt like hell, so I don't bother folding my six-foot frame into the contraption. I am sure I can ride this baby like a rocking chair.

Due to slight communication problems, we enter the rapid sideways. Next thing, I look up at the raft, catching Heather's expression—that age-old, *Why are you leaving me at a time like this?* Her face could use some color right now. "What do I do?" she yells over the roaring. "Try to keep the damn thing—" I swallow the rest of my answer with a pint-size gulp of sludgy Colorado. At this point, I seriously consider finishing this trip in the water, safe and snug in my life jacket. But solidarity gets the better of me, and with the help of my maiden in brilliant neoprene I remount the cat. No need to mention that I did not dress for a swim. I begin to shiver instantly, and my teeth chatter so hard I worry about breaking a filling. But this beats an outhouse at forty below.

On a previous trip, I was lucky to retrieve a half-full pint bottle of Jim Beam doing rounds in an eddy. It probably washed out of a boat flipped by one of the munching holes for which this canyon is known. In my present state, some of that Southern antifreeze would sure come in handy.

Perhaps it would even improve my aim. Sober, I miss the fun of the standing monster wave at Rapid No. 10 by overcompensating for the current pushing outward at the bend. The half-moon of fine sand directly below promises heaven: the canyon's best beach camp. Everybody else who lands looks as dry and unconcerned as the surrounding desert.

Most rapids in Cataract remain unnamed. A USGS surveyor looking for dam sites in the early 1920s numbered them, a man daunted by whitewater at the physical and ideological level. He settled on a choice site a few miles upstream from Lees Ferry, near the end of Glen Canyon. The eager engineer who, dreaming of thirteen dams across the entire drainage basin, embarked to subdue the unbound Colorado, a "river of menace & destruction," will stay anonymous here since he shares a name with a glypher friend. Let silence stifle his bloodline.

At this beach, on an Outward Bound course I worked, mayflies had erupted so thickly they furred the rafts, drybags, and tarps with grayish translucent husks we brushed off with the palms of our hands as if they were city worries. Scorched ones, falling, had added their bodies' protein to our dinner pot of stew, and the students were convinced that staff had planned the trip to coincide with the winged blizzard as an additional challenge. I had in fact never witnessed a hatch like that, which you cannot predict. It did not help that, in line with our program's aims and merchant-marine origins, we'd shipwrecked the students the night before. In this activity, we give them a scenario and five minutes to grab a limited number of what they deem to be emergency items. They then get to spend the night on the bottoms of two rafts we flip and moor in a calm eddy, a life-jacketed team, living with the consequences of choices that we instructors have hastened.

Tonight's entertainment consists of various party tricks, including pouring flames from a bottle and walking around with bottle caps in your eye sockets and belly button without dropping them. The star attraction is a bacon-grease bomb in the campfire—seething saved drippings in a can doused with river water—which leaves everybody in awe at the mushroom mini-cloud and the performer with singed eyebrows. (Don't try this on a stovetop.) A proposal to run an obstacle course with quarters pinched between butt cheeks, to be dropped into a bucket at the finish, finds only little resonance with the crowd. Most of us retire early, satisfied by an honest day's work and a steep learning curve.

On our last day, a challenging trio of big drops awaits us, growling downstream. The lump in my stomach may not entirely be the result of overdosing on a breakfast of syrup-drenched pancakes, eggs, and cowboy coffee. ("It ain't cowboy coffee if it doesn't dissolve a spoon or float a horseshoe.") T.S. Eliot never saw Cataract, to my knowledge, but here, despite upstream dams, the river still *is* "a strong brown god—sullen, untamed and intractable," as am I, before my first cup in the morning.

Rapid No.15 is merely a warmup. Early river runners on a mining expedition christened this roller coaster "Hell to Pay" in 1891. Their version of Kilroy-Was-Here, scratched on a boulder on shore, cheerfully reads: *camp #7, hell to pay, no. 1 sunk & down.* "Number One" was half of their miserable fleet of wooden tubs. A purported ledge of pure silver in the Grand Canyon that they were chasing turned out to be nothing but mica and schist, fools' dreams glittering in the sun. Charged with finding the Colorado River–Green River confluence we passed yesterday, the surveyor

Captain John N. Macomb in 1859 could not conceive "a more worthless and impracticable region," expecting "repetitions and varieties of it for hundreds of miles down the cañon of the Great Colorado..." Worthless? Impracticable? Not at all. Repetitions and varieties? Riffs on near-eternity? Yes!

There's only one stress-free way to skin this cat. Four notorious marker rocks close ahead spice up this stretch of river, lined up like a baseball diamond. Perhaps, the nature of our run is owed to the fact that I grew up playing soccer (or Fußball, with a long *u*, though we fussed about our passes and being offside too). While we are scraping first base, the old Abbot and Costello routine sloshes through my head. I don't know who or what is on first, but without the cat's foot-guard, my toes and kneecap would be. This feels more like pinball than baseball.

"Left turn."

"Not so much—I mean, *right* turn!"

"Stop!"

"Back—paddle!"

We barely miss the pitcher's mound, and a merciful current carries us clear of second base. Not exactly a home run, but we are alive.

While my brain soaks in a marinade of adrenalin, memories of a past near-disaster here rear their ugly heads. Only a few weeks before, one of the rafts on an Outward Bound course had smashed sideways into first base. The metal pin of one oarlock broke, and the oar itself bent like putty. But improvisation is a leitmotif in every river runner's life, a talent equally well applied to dressing, cooking, finances, car maintenance, and courtship, sometimes with unorthodox results. With a dexterity acquired over decades in the Great Outdoors and somebody else's penknife, I had sawed a length from bleached bones of driftwood that littered our beach. I whittled it down to the diameter of the fractured pin. I rammed it into the oarlock, thrilled by my own cunning, and then slid in a spare oar. We pushed off into the current. After a few strokes, my homemade splint shattered under the strain. Climbing back onto my seat from the bottom of the raft, I felt consoled that, at least, they didn't chain us to the benches anymore. Not easily defied by the river's verdict, we replaced the useless joint with three buff paddlers on starboard. Under the scrutiny of other outfits, our lopsided act negotiated the rest of the rapids with the grace of a crippled crab. The guides of the competition hooted and catcalled from recliners on shore, toasting our effort with cans of cold Pabst Blue Ribbon. Beneath life jackets adorned with graffiti and the company logo, our chests inflated with pride. Not only had we saved face as individual boatmen once more, but we also upheld the reputation of our fine outdoor program.

At Big Drop One, our only job is to keep her straight and not get bucked off. If I wore a hat, this is the part where I would slap my thighs with it, whooping and hollering. I feel like a centaur—half man, half rubber duck—all out of my depth.

Our run through Big Drop Two is so-so, but at least uneventful. Idyllic Little Niagara rushes by, too fast to allow us to make a mistake. The cat in front of us is less fortunate: it parks on a tabletop boulder, tubes half out of the water. The pilots shift their weight, trying to wriggle her off—in vain. Eventually the captain steps out onto the boulder. She puts some muscle to it, straining until I'm afraid her head might burst. When there is sudden movement, she almost misses the boat.

Then comes the big one of the Big Ones. Naturally, we miss the boulder gate of the entrance slot, running a pour-over this side of Mossy Rock instead. We spear almost vertically into the accompanying hole, leaning back in our seats like choreographed bull riders. In an out-of-body experience, I observe the peculiar response of the cat as it bobs back out with a corklike move. Before I have a chance to thumb my nose at Satan's Gut, we have been sluiced out at the tail of the rapid.

By now, my copilot has even stopped cursing me under

her breath. The worst lies behind us, or so we think.

A rambunctious wind starts to blow, crimping the water's surface. It shoulders the cats into a wide eddy, where they sit like decoy ducks. When I look to shore, the scenery still floats by, but in the wrong direction. The baggage boat, with its twelve-foot-long oars, manned by our junior instructor Mikey, seems to fare slightly better.

Eternities of paddle strokes and teeth gnashing later, I see the mouth of Gypsum Canyon cleave sandstone parapets on river left. The four-day hike to the highway should feel like a Club Med vacation. I am glad I announced my intention to leave our party here, *before* the trip. Let nobody blame my Momma for raising a quitter.

I soon stand on shore, trying to straighten from my Neanderthal posture. Looking at boiling clouds the color of slate, I wonder what further boating adventures I shall miss. With a sigh of relief and a strange popping from my knee, I hoist my sixty-pound pack before I wave the disappearing flotilla goodbye.

So Long, Promised Land

As the old year fades from view, I am busy again boxing things up for another move to Alaska. Sifting through detritus accumulated over the years, I try to decide what is essential, what is too heavy or bulky, what can be left behind. Stacks of discolored photos quickly distract me from my task. Lost in reveries, I shuffle these souvenirs of a love affair with the Colorado Plateau, a troubled relationship that began more than three decades ago.

I was exploring the Southwest in 1982, as a tourist. Smitten with the sublime light, the uncluttered space, dendrite canyons, and silk-and-steel rivers, I decided to live there some day. Life had other plans, but I kept gravitating toward the red rock gardens, where Moab became a basecamp of sorts. Eventually, I moved there for good, and later, to Flagstaff. Following my conviction that a perfectly sized town is one in which everything, including wilderness, lies within easy walking or biking distance, I settled in Moab on the tail end of the uranium-mining boom. I felt fortunate, as this muscular and reclusive landscape became not only my home but also my workplace. During summers, I spent more days on the Colorado and its tributaries than in town. My working outfit as a river guide consisted of sandals, sunglasses, and shorts. Peoples' faces often lit up with envy when I asked them to step into my "office," the raft. "Tell me the landscape in which you live, and I will tell you who you are," the Spanish essayist José Ortega y Gasset prompted. I say, tell me who you are, and I'll tell you the landscape in which you *should* live. It works both ways. Many whom I told said they wish they could. I wondered what stopped them and sometimes even asked.

The greater your dreams, the harsher your awakening. Too soon, I became aware that the Promised Land, like many other refuges these days, suffered from industry, greed, and encroachment.

"We were killing the last good place," in Chuck Bowden's words. The West's troubled legacy revealed itself in, among other facets, cattle grazing the canyons inside a national monument—"Escowlante." Behemoth thumper trucks sounded for oil, destroying living soil crusts and vegetation bordering Canyonlands National Park. Politicians supported proposals to extract and process oil shale along the Green River's marvelous Desolation Canyon. Nine-Mile Canyon, a veritable rock-art gallery leading to it, has lately been eyed for a spur railroad for transporting natural gas. Commerce and people in garish getups discovered my hideout, pronouncing Moab the "Mountain Biking Capital of the West." For the longest time I denied living in a resort town, even when the annual Jeep Safari forced me and many other residents to flee it for a week, to avoid traffic and the attendant party and shopping mayhem.

We had a joke in our guide repertoire, one barbed dart in a quiver of many: How can you tell when spring has sprung in the canyon country? The license plates are turning green. Coloradans had a green plate with a profile of snowy mountains, and by April at the latest, they'd grow weary of white. Abbey "did a better job of advertising [Arches] than the local Chamber of Commerce ever did, but if Ed hadn't done it, someone else would have," a fellow ranger there said. "He stimulated a whole horde of nature-lovers, real and self-styled, who would love Southeastern Utah to death, and others who would like to take it back to the Pleistocene."

Abbey's writing hadn't brought me to Moab in '82. I discovered it later, in Alaska, when a craftsman friend nicknamed "Birch Bark Bob" recommended *The Monkey Wrench Gang*. Thus are careers made and others unmade. A drop of the elixir of radical thought bloomed to color my placid existence.

In sync with rising visitor numbers, the affluent started to buy second homes in town. Property prices and taxes rose accordingly, forever placing the dream of a little shack of my own beyond reach. Millionaires lived for two weeks a year in their mansions in the red swells, while I did not own a rug to pee on. The cost of some frou-frou coffee drinks soon began to equal half the hourly wage dirtbags and river rats like me made in service industry jobs, naturally without benefits beyond sun, exercise, and fresh air. Moab had no shoe repair place—to us, they were "cobblers," remember?—no affordable health care or housing, no food co-op, noise control.... Instead it sprouted real estate offices, art and souvenir boutiques, motels and gas stations, jeep, bike, and boat rentals. Trinket stores began hawking "dirt shirts" to tourists—tees dyed orange with pigments from the slickrock that enclasps town; but you could save twenty bucks and easily fashion your own just by wearing a white one for weeks of backpacking and boating without ever washing it. More and more mountain and road bikers sheathed in Lycra rubbed sweaty shoulders with more and more hikers, climbers, jeepers, base jumpers, skydivers, kayakers, rafters, golfers, and vintage car lovers. They all rubbed my nerve endings raw. They drank dry the bars that served watered-down, 3.2 percent beer, clogged the river and canyons. The off-season many locals welcomed as a change of pace and reminder of why they had chosen this town in the first place shrank year by year, cropped at both ends by mountain unicycle festivals, paddleboard races—do they run back and forth *on* or *with* or *to* the boards?—and other bogus events. It got harder and harder to escape unwanted company in the Best of Beyond, which now resembled the Rest of Beyond. I would have preferred my domicile to be famous (if famous it must be) for record-breaking pumpkins or the nation's oldest hay barn.

Revisiting a favorite haunt in the Escalante watershed the first time in ten years, the changes appalled me. Foot trails cut through cryptobiotic soil's knobby carpets, betraying people's laziness, a need to shortcut across canyon meanders. These "desire paths," in the cultural geographer's lingo, must be replanted also to control erosion. On hillsides, the itch to hurry like runoff had entrenched ruts along fall lines rather than switchbacks. I desired to intercept their makers and spank them with prickly-pear paddles. They'd not simply trampled single tracks in that monument but whole networks, into each crusty surface. Some morons, between what one wit rightly called "the most beautiful slickrock and sandstone walls this side of Mars," had clearly misread the Bureau of Land Management's plea to leave behind nothing but footprints. Where one tread, others were likely to follow. Perhaps they were ignorant of the consequences, though they seemed pretty obvious. At popular campsites, which appeared strangely denuded even for this arid country, wooden signs directed visitors to pit toilets installed, and hopefully emptied, by poorly paid seasonal monument staff. The voices of nearby campers echoed around slickrock bends, undermining the intimacy with the land I had hoped for. Aluminum pull-tabs and charcoal from illegal campfires had replaced the arrowhead fragments, potsherds, and thousand-year-old corncobs once safe in alcove vaults. On Cedar Mesa, cameras now eyed ruins and rock art, trying to catch vandals in the act. Elsewhere, fences guarded petroglyph panels, and boardwalks channeled tour groups.

Faced with these changes, I realized for the first time that too many hikers degrade a wild place as easily and permanently as do too many cows. While it seems obvious and convenient to point fingers at off-road vehicle drivers, any sentient biped will have to admit that he or she is part of the problem. *Homo ambulans*, too, leaves nothing but traces and too often takes peace and quiet from the backcountry.

The ecological concept of "carrying capacity" denotes a landscape's ability to sustain a particular number of organisms, depending on their foraging techniques or food requirements. Without irrigation, deserts support small bands of hunters and gatherers better than they do high concentrations of sedentary agriculturalists. Throughout this canyon country, the crop now largely consists of tourists, and public lands managers still struggle to establish acceptable levels for recreational uses. Acceptable for whom, I wonder. Grand Canyon National Park in a 2006 update of its River Management Plan increased non-commercial-user days by almost one third, trying to appease private boaters at the expense of mountain lions, bighorn sheep, silence, and solitude. And private boaters are still unhappy, clamoring for more. An already overtaxed "resource" is stretched to the limits. The park's zoning system, regulating backcountry hiking permits, is still rare on the Colorado Plateau. According to this allocation, a limited and seemingly justifiable quota of overnight permits is issued per zone. When filled, hikers either have to wait for openings or else settle for a less popular destination. With high visitor numbers in the spring and fall, the National Park Service and other agencies face a conundrum: to channel use and impact into fewer areas, or to spread it evenly over the lands entrusted to their care. In short, land managers accept that there will have to be "sacrifice zones."

But even official closures of fragile places mean little in a culture lacking respect and restraint. Years ago, the author of several self-published guidebooks praised one southeastern Utah gorge as "the gem of Canyonlands." Informed by the expert, people flocked to that sandstone cleft. (If you have only a weekend, you want to make sure it counts. No time to waste on mere two-star attractions.) Soon after, the Park Service decided to close that canyon, the only one livestock had never grazed and that, as such, formed a valuable baseline for assessing impact on the park's clipped districts. Hikers still go there, now for the extra zest of tasting the forbidden fruit. Park outlets no longer carry said hiking guide, as it caused too many search-and-rescue missions.

Unfortunately, national glossies with circulation numbers as large as city populations hook affluent vacationers with paradoxical headlines like *The Ten Least Known But Most Scenic Hikes of the XXX*—insert your favorite wilderness here. One rag even includes GPS coordinates for "points of interest." Read: sensitive areas. While we gain certainty with electronic plotting devices, we are losing much. Biologists reported that, after one feature in that magazine, visitor numbers in Yellowstone's XYZ Valley multiplied, and that the resident wolf pack temporarily left its home range, which elk then clipped down to nubbins.

Even the Four Corners' Navajo reservation, which long had been spared the worst excess, perhaps due to its "Third World feel" or from a vague sense of guilt and trespassing, plus a user-unfriendly permit system, now sees tourism's side effects. A few canyons were made off-limits, except when escorted by Diné guides, after a flash flood killed eleven visitors. This was possibly to avoid costly extractions of tourists or even more expensive liability suits. About a dozen more canyons were recently closed to all outsiders. Sadly, non-Navajos hiking without permits, harassing livestock, littering, and disturbing archaeological ruins brought on these closures.

For years, I remained content to take paying customers down rivers and canyons. But I slowly realized that many, if not most of them, were only after the shiny skin, not the meat and bones, or, heaven forbid, the soul of a place. They considered wilderness a sort of outdoor gym-cum-tanning salon, a thrill ride with a picnic on the side, pretty scenery to write postcards from, or perhaps worst of all, just another checkmark on their adventure "bucket list." I've heard of people who tried to visit fifty-nine US national parks in fifty-nine days. My suggestion to them: spend fifty-nine days in one park: Grand Canyon below the rim, or Gates of the Arctic. You might truly learn something and will earn bragging rights. Or you might vanish, evaporate like a cloud.

But who the hell can afford two months in a national park? Even without the loss of income, such a vacation, not counting gas, gear, or provisions, would cost you a thousand bucks for camping rough, in the lovely dirt below the rim. It's thirteen hundred if you stay at a campground. Multiply that by four for a typical family, and you see why the underfunded still are excluded from our parks.

Certain rich Germans in the early nineteenth century felt

compelled to donate all their precious-metal jewelry to aid the government in the struggle against Napoleon. Burghers and nobles instead wore iron necklaces, tokens of patriotism. What if today's moneyed elite gave just one percent of their wealth to combat inequality and environmental destruction? What if they gave a damn?

One Moab river company did not hire me because I was too outspoken in my "environmental convictions." (They never sensed other, socio-political ones. Don't label me "Bernie Bro," though; he favors the working class over ecology.) Vacationers did not want to hear about mining or overgrazing or hydroelectric dams. They wanted rapids. They wanted fun. They wanted gourmet food, horseshoe games, solar showers, and, if possible, sleeping cots on the riverbank, or a little "canyon magic" by hooking up with a chesty blond river guide of either sex. The manager told me I would set a bad example for the younger guides and that his company was "pro growth." Later I heard that a luxury tourism conglomerate had swallowed the outfit. As if canyons and rivers were not enough, outfitters now offer theme trips with yoga, watercolor painting, writing workshops, music bands, and stargazing. Since when does wonder at the night sky need to be emceed?

The former Moabite and critic of industrial tourism Edward Abbey named the spiritual price paid by those who depend on it for their livelihood: "They must learn the automatic smile." I had a hard time with that, though it cost me some tips and the goodwill of my boss.

I reached the low point of my guiding during a Marlboro Adventure Team trip, an event for winners of a contest to promote smoking and rugged individualism in countries in which advertising for tobacco products was still legal. I prepared myself for trouble when I saw the trip leader remove the motor rig's spare outboard from its box, which he then filled with booze and coffin nails. The organizers urged us to flip boats in the rapids, to provide the cameramen on shore with footage for commercials aired in South America, home of the tobacco plant and a bastion of asphalt lungs. So we ran holes sideways deliberately. Between rapids, they asked the paddle-raft guides to tie on to a motor rig that dragged boatloads of macho, hung-over, helmeted conquistadors to the next "cool" spot, which for them, exclusively, was the water's commotion.

Worst of all, I sensed—no, I *knew*—I was part of the problem. My writing about the Four Corners' besieged landscapes seemed to make little positive difference; simply educating the public would never provide a cure. As my Coyote Gulch visit had shown, the lofty goal of enlightening backcountry users about wilderness ethics and etiquette demands optimism with regards to human nature. Defaced rock art, kivas that Boy Scouts use as bouncy castles, campfire rings like sacked-stone fortresses, torn-out Wilderness Study Area markers, fouled waterholes in even the most remote quarter, and trees sawed at national park campgrounds because they're "in the way," quickly put dampers on such enthusiasm. Once, on the South Bass Trail, I had come upon gear and underwear strewn about, a ripped tent, and backpacking-meal pouches rodents had gnawed into micro-trash. It suggested an abandoned camp of the homeless or a crime scene. Concerned with the hiker's fate, I had reported my find to the backcountry ranger only to be told that this was business as usual during spring break, when novices in over their heads ditch everything and walk out. "We'll send someone down there to clean it up," the ranger had said.

I could not rid myself of the feeling that, by publicizing this region, I ultimately contributed to its defilement and destruction.

An argument can be and has been made that public lands need to be used recreationally to ensure their continued protection and funding, to keep them from rapacious developers or corrupt politicos. On the other hand, more than three million visitors per year might easily enjoy the Grand Canyon to death. There are no easy answers to this dilemma.

Some of the boxes that will hold desert keepsakes—the Navajo sandcast silver-and-turquoise belt buckle I wore as a horseback guide and the katsina doll bought from the Hopi family that took me in—still have old addresses on them; I think half of all my belongings must be in transit or storage at any given time. When I see the labels, more bittersweet memories come rushing in. I'm reliving the anticipation and reluctance I felt each time I shipped these boxes off. Disenchanted with academic rituals at the postgraduate level, unwilling to objectify cultures, and unable to secure grant money for my PhD project, I'd dropped out of school. There were few guide openings at the time for someone with little experience, and much competition for those. The desert's siren song beckoned, seconded by opportunity. I'd been offered an outdoor instructor position in a youth program in Arizona. With my moorings already cut, I followed the current. The rest is rivers-and-canyons history.

Have I capitulated? Perhaps. But who can stem this tide? Where a younger person may have the optimism and energy, I do not. Still, always the canyon country will be my home, in the sense Thom van Dooren defined, as "a place that calls out in some way to be returned to."

I am aware that moving to Alaska is not a solution. The political climate in the Big Dipper state matches that of the Beehive one. As an itinerant, I will become part of the problem there. It can't be avoided. Now well past middle age, I feel that time is running out. To rephrase Aldo Leopold, I simply don't wish to grow very old without wild country to be old in, or at least, to look at and ponder in my dotage.

While relocating to Alaska in mid-winter seems unwise, I cannot think of a better place to start a new year, or a new chapter. Let it be cold. Let it be dark. Let summers be buggy and bears haunt the woods. And let us keep some places raw and unspoiled.

Acknowledgments

The title of this collection could also be that of a polemic about finding a publisher, or rather, one who won't sacrifice a writer's vision to the bottom line. I would like to thank the editors of the following publications, some now defunct, in which different versions of essays from this collection first appeared: *Backpacker*, *National Parks*, *Sierra*, *Northern Arizona Mountain Living*, *Sojourns*, *Red Rock Stories*, *bioStories*, *The Journal of Wild Culture*, *Cross Country Skier*, and *Inside/Outside Southwest*. Agnieszka Kaczmarek brought to my attention that Ed Abbey's "Cape Solitude" was a pseudonym, a fact which, reading his essay, I had overlooked. He made it up, sort of, perhaps to protect the place or as a stand-in for many similar spots in the Grand Canyon. GCY Executive Director Emma Wharton graciously allowed me to accompany her canyon kids as a journalist-guide and took in stride complaints about a certain someone, caught on film, rowing barefoot through Upset Rapid, behavior the public deemed "unsafe." (I would lose my flip-flops farther downstream when whitewater flooded the foot well of my raft, but that and how I replaced them is a story for a different time.) Lance Newman, Michael Ghiglieri, Jeri Ledbetter, and the late Terry Brian got me baggage-boat trips through the canyon, so I could reach the required number of five and begin guiding there. Thanks go to Todd Seliga, North Rim backcountry ranger and two-time solo thru-hiker—a worthy successor of John H. Riffey—who was ready to rescue me during my trans-canyon attempt and instead provided dinner and a place to sleep at the Toroweap ranger station. Rich Rudow and Chris Forsyth helped with transportation and other logistics that time (including a long-sleeved shirt for my sunburn and a replacement pair of hiking shoes). Pre-trek, Andrew Holycross opened his Phoenix home and pool to me, and a jug of homemade Limoncello to share. Ned Bryant circulated stats of the Grand Canyon thru-hikers.

Tom Martin of River Runners for Wilderness not only informed me of the number of people who'd finished the traverse at that time but also wrote a line in an email to me that made the heart of this topophile sing and his feet twitch: "The landscape is the map and the traveler watches distant landforms ahead become near neighbors then recede behind one." That's what happened for forty consecutive days in the Grand Canyon, over and over and over again. (It also could feel like being on a treadmill, with the scenery unchanging.) Fellow Flagstaff writer Scott Thybony shared explorations in the Painted Desert as well as information about rock-art panels with me that will remain top secret. Austin Raymond and Jerry Kien at NAU and Rex Lee Jim and Gene Vecenti of Diné College translated Navajo astronomical terms for this book. Justin Richland at UC Irvine and Dorothy Washburn at the University of Pennsylvania kindly sent me their articles about the Snowbowl controversy. Early readers Scott Slovic and Jack "Nature Abhors a Maximum" Loeffler gave valued feedback on the manuscript. Once again, Doreen Martens polished my prose to slickrock smoothness. Richard Quartaroli sat for a final, close reading—any errors left are mine.

Before I even had a publisher for this book (whom I later ditched over artistic differences), my wife Melissa Guy, a former graphic designer, humored me by turning an idea of mine into a fine mock-up cover that throughout the long process kept me energized. She wrapped everything up as an eye-catching package, guided by me, whom she calls "the art dictator."

I am extremely grateful to the writers, thinkers, and Native traditions upon which these essays built. We all stand on the shoulders of others. In canyon country, this is sometimes the only way you'll reach the next ledge. My greatest doubt, however, remains undiminished. What if, as the culture critic Naomi Klein fears, "words—written on the page or shouted in protest—change only what people and institutions say, and not what they do"?

About the Author

Michael Engelhard worked for twenty-five years as an outdoor instructor and wilderness guide in Alaska and the canyon country. In 1982, during the obligate Grand Circle Tour of the Southwest's national parks and monuments, he had fallen hard and fast for that gorgeous desert. He received a Master's degree in cultural anthropology from the University of Alaska, Fairbanks, where he also taught very briefly, and aborted a PhD—indoor classrooms, the trenches of departmental politics, and froth like "the thingness of things" just weren't his cup-a-chino. His most recent books include the Alaska essay collection *What the River Knows* and *Arctic Traverse*, the account of his thousand-mile solo Brooks Range trek from Canada's Yukon border to the Bering Strait. A fence sitter and migrant by training and inclination, he lives wherever his needs are met best, like the creatures he so admires.

www.ingramcontent.com/pod-product-compliance
Lightning Source LLC
Chambersburg PA
CBHW022049020426
42335CB00012B/610